# HRIS Development

## A Project Team Guide to Building an Effective Personnel Information System

# HRIS Development

A Project Team Guide to
Building an Effective Personnel
Information System

Alfred J. Walker

VAN NOSTRAND REINHOLD COMPANY
NEW YORK   CINCINNATI   TORONTO   LONDON   MELBOURNE

Copyright © 1982 by Van Nostrand Reinhold Company Inc.

Library of Congress Catalog Card Number: 82-2616
ISBN: 0-442-29003-9

All rights reserved. No part of this work covered by the copyright hereon may be reproduced or used in any form or by any means—graphic, electronic, or mechanical, including photocopying, recording, taping, or information storage and retrieval systems—without permission of the publisher.

Manufactured in the United States of America

Published by Van Nostrand Reinhold Company Inc.
135 West 50th Street, New York, N.Y. 10020

Van Nostrand Reinhold Publishing
1410 Birchmount Road
Scarborough, Ontario M1P 2E7, Canada

Van Nostrand Reinhold Australia Pty. Ltd.
17 Queen Street
Mitcham, Victoria 3132, Australia

Van Nostrand Reinhold Company Limited
Molly Millars Lane
Wokingham, Berkshire, England

15  14  13  12  11  10  9  8  7  6  5  4  3  2  1

**Library of Congress Cataloging in Publication Data**

Walker, Alfred J.
  HRIS development.

  Bibliography: p.
  Includes index.
  1. Information storage and retrieval systems—Personnel management.   I. Title.   II. Title: H.R.I.S. development.
HF5549.W29    025'.066583    82-2616
ISBN 0-442-29003-9         AACR2

*To Heather, Jenni, Matt and Sam*

# Preface

In order to be as useful as possible to the Project Team undertaking the very difficult job of creating a new or improved Human Resource Information System (HRIS), I have organized this book under four main parts, with core chapters in a sequence that approximates the flow of most personnel system development. The actual development process — the step-by-step guide to HRIS installation — begins with Part II's "First Steps..." and concludes with Chapter 10, the last of six chapters in Part III on "Design and Installation." The material in Part IV has been presented in such a way that the reader who wants to know about HRIS cost/benefit analysis or vendor evaluation first can begin there.

The organization of this book has also been motivated by some beliefs about "why systems go wrong" in this area. Not only has the early promise of computerized personnel systems gone largely unfulfilled, but even the HRIS installations I have seen completed over the last fifteen or so years have often been fraught with costly delays, misdirected efforts, and unrealized objectives. Other organizations, including some with huge employee populations and highly sophisticated personnel demands, have succeeded with less wasted effort.

Thus, the first introductory chapter, "The HRIS Shortfall: Past Problems and Present Mistakes," puts HRIS development in its historical perspective and underscores at the outset the most common reasons why personnel system development projects get into trouble. These "Ten Most Common Mistakes," listed here in approximate order of severity, are intended to prevent the Project Team from misjudgments in the early stages of development, errors that can seriously delay or even doom the entire HRIS project. If they are recognized early, these potential pitfalls can be avoided or neutralized through measures recommended in later chapters, as indicated in Chapter 1.

The second part of the introduction is Chapter 2, "Defining an HRIS: Basic Concepts and Modules." Here the five basic concepts involved in the definition of an HRIS — the data base, data entry, retrieval, the Human Resource Information Center, and data quality — are discussed with examples. Each of these concepts must become a functioning reality if the HRIS is to be complete. Next, HRIS modules are explained. These modules are the building blocks of the HRIS; each performs a major personnel function, such as EEO, Training, or Human Resource Utilization. Ten major modules are discussed, although system developers are cautioned against attempting to install more than three or four in the first phase of the project.

The sequential stages of HRIS development begin in Part II, "First Steps: Preparation and the Needs Analysis," which consists of Chapters 3 and 4. Chapter 3, "Getting Started: Guidelines for the Proposal to Management and Establishment of the Project Team," deals with the most important preliminary steps that should be completed before making the proposal to management to commit funds for the HRIS project — actually a commitment to undertake the next stage, the Needs Analysis. This proposal should reflect an understanding of the organization and its objectives as well as the role of personnel in the organization currently and in the future. It should also include some general description of the overall HRIS installation project, covering the stages identified here as Proposal to Management, Needs Analysis, System Specifications, System Design, System Development, Installation and Conversion, and Evaluation.

This sequence can be presented in broad strokes in the initial proposal to management, but the particular needs, schedule, and costs of the next stage (the Needs Analysis) should be explicated in some detail. Chapter 3 also recommends a number of methods for improving the chances that a proposal will be understood and accepted, such as visits to other HRIS installations, courses conducted by industry groups, vendor presentations, and other ways to generate informed interest. After a descriptive example of the kinds of information that should be in the proposal to management, guidelines on the selection of a Project Leader and Project Team are presented.

Chapter 4, "Conducting the Needs Analysis," proceeds from a general discussion of the overriding objectives that will guide the conduct of the Needs Analysis to detailed recommendations for the orderly collection and analysis of information that will determine the boundaries, interfaces, and scope of the HRIS. The ultimate purpose of this stage is to ascertain broad system configurations — which modules will be needed in the first phase of development — and to arrive at an integrated Human Resources Information Plan.

To accomplish this, various methods of collecting information about the organization are explored, focusing on user interviews. Specific procedures that will assure the accuracy and usefulness of these interviews are stressed, from adequate preliminary groundwork through interviewing technique to standardization of results. Key information that should be gathered in the Needs Analysis, including not only the needs of potential users but information on present personnel data procedures and existing systems, is pointed out in this chapter.

When this information has been analyzed appropriately, the Project Team can construct a recommended system configuration that will be the basis for work in the next stage, System Specifications.

Part III, "Design and Installation," the heart of the project and of this book, comprises six chapters explaining the tasks of the Project Team from completion of the Needs Analysis to final conversion and implementation. This part closes with a chapter on federal regulatory requirements, needs that have shaped the modern HRIS in many ways.

Chapter 5, "Specifications: Data Base Elements, Codes, and Edits," and Chapter 6, "Specifications: Output Reports, Interfaces, Tables, and Processing Routines," tell how to completely and accurately specify the user requirements determined by the Needs Analysis. These specifications will be used in the design stage; explicit guidelines are presented to minimize the ambiguity of these "instructions" and assure that the final design will be responsive to users' needs. Types of data elements, codes, edits, reports, tables, interfaces, and routines are identified and discussed, with detailed instructions for their specifications.

Because systems will vary and should be tailored to individual needs, "kinds" of data elements and other items that should be in an HRIS are urged on the Project Team rather than specific items, interfaces, and routines. The purpose here is to match an organization's personnel needs correctly and thoroughly with HRIS design through valid specifications. Thus, guidelines are presented for developing procedures — such as a standard format for data element selection, tests of data elements, different circumstances behind the reasons for different types of control codes, types of edits and their uses, kinds of reports that an HRIS may generate and their benefits and limits, and the purposes of typical kinds of tables and processing routines — and how to specify them. Checklists are provided to help the Team be inclusive in their specifications for these items, which will in many respects shape the operating characteristics of the final HRIS. The timeliness and frequency required for output reports, for example, will fundamentally influence system design.

The guidelines on interface specification in Chapter 6 include a discussion of the highly important, often controversial interface with the Payroll System. Pros and cons of the "interface or absorb" decision are explored so that the Team can make this decision based on the organization's situation.

In Chapter 7, "Design Considerations: Major Influences on HRIS Design," general principles applicable to the effective design of the data base, its file arrangement, and retrieval methodology are discussed. The point is stressed that although the design stage is primarily the responsibility of data systems members of the Project Team, "human" functions must also be considered. If the HRIS is to be readily operated, personnel users should be kept in mind when forms and procedures are designed.

An overall scheme of design work is presented that proceeds from the broadest concept to repetitive detailing of tasks and subtasks, leading to a fully described set of chores from which the personnel and data systems Team members will develop the "products" discussed in Chapter 8.

Key design considerations explained in Chapter 7 include the need for history in the HRIS, how to determine data base activity and size, output reports, the nature of modern distributed processing, and external files and interfaces. In each of these areas, guidelines are presented to improve the Project Team's understanding of options — how many bytes of storage will be needed for various functions, for example — rather than strict design prescriptions or abstract "rules" that may have no relevance to user needs.

Chapter 8, "Program Development and Conversion," describes the coding and conversion processes as they relate to the needs of computerized personnel systems. General guidelines on work allocation and scheduling are provided, followed by specific methods of developing an effective test plan and user tests, and recommended steps in the conversion plan. This chapter puts special attention on the development of strict tests for each programming module. User acceptance tests are critical in this process, and guidelines for conducting some of the more important user tests are detailed. Operating considerations, especially techniques for minimizing data base accuracy from conversion onward, are also discussed in this chapter.

Chapter 9, "The Human Resource Information Center, Privacy Issues, and Skills Inventory Guidelines," describes the purposes and procedures for implementing these important aspects of automated personnel systems. The purpose and functions of the Human Resource Information Center (HRIC) — the centralized training and control organization that serves as the day-to-day link between users and the HRIS — are listed and described. One function of the HRIC is to assure data base security and privacy, and the effective implementation of privacy policies — and what such policies should require in modern organizations — is discussed with recommendations.

Finally, this chapter presents guidelines and specific procedures for setting up a Human Resource ("Skills") Inventory as part of a Human Resource Utilization module. This inventory is a means of collecting information about skills and abilities from employees themselves and putting it in a computer format for efficient use by the organization's staffing group. Such applications can epitomize the decision-making profitability of an HRIS.

A comprehensive, up-to-date review of the record-keeping and other needs of government agencies is provided in Chapter 10, "Using the HRIS to Ensure Compliance with Federal Regulatory Requirements." All relevant laws are discussed, and possible future changes are noted.

Part IV, Chapters 11 through 13, is concerned with "Corporate Perspectives and Profitability" and includes information on how to identify and measure the costs and benefits of an HRIS, how to evaluate vendors of prepackaged personnel systems if your organization decides on this development option, and finally, "Future Trends," explaining the reasons why computerized human resource information systems are expected to be increasingly important to employers in the years ahead.

As indicated in the discussion of the proposal to management in Chapter 3, the top management of some organizations will require a fairly comprehensive cost/benefit analysis of HRIS installation before approving the expenditures needed for the initial stages of the project. Chapter 11, "HRIS Savings, Benefits, and Cost Justification," provides both general and specific guidelines on how to determine savings that will occur because of the new system, beginning with the caveat that it may be difficult to justify the HRIS with direct dollar savings alone; improved information for decision making, legal compliance, and other intangible benefits should be considered. This chapter recommends a procedure to identify direct and indirect cost savings in each of the major functional areas of personnel: Benefits, EEO, Training, etc. Typical savings that might occur in each of these user areas are provided in checklists, and other kinds of more generally applicable savings are brought out for the Team's consideration. Finally, HRIS costs are discussed, and factors that will bear on the overall justification of HRIS installation are summarized.

The important subject of vendor evaluation, should your organization take the development option of going outside for a prepackaged personnel system, is the focus of Chapter 12, "Development Choices: Prepackaged Systems and Vendor Evaluation." Although this may seem an anomalous inclusion in a book about how organizations can build an HRIS of their own, going outside for all or part of a computerized personnel system is either necessary or expedient in some situations, as discussed in this chapter. In order to properly evaluate the growing array of systems and vendors in today's marketplace, however, the organization should first establish an internal Project Team, carry out a limited version of the Needs Analysis, develop uniform criteria that reflect the organization's needs, and present vendors with a clear set of requirements for the proposed system or module. These and other steps in software evaluation are spelled out in some detail, reflecting past experience with organizations that made hasty choices that they later regretted. On the other hand, I have yet to encounter an organization that said it had spent too much time on software evaluation.

Chapter 13, "Future Trends" in HRIS applications, depicts the changing and expanding role of various human resource functions in a changing society and work force. As discussed here, the "future" use of computerized personnel systems is already here in a handful of organizations in this country, in which online systems featuring minicomputers in distributed networks are used to produce a range of outputs from regression analysis graphics to personalized letters to job applicants. Although the microprocessor revolution behind the wider availability of hardware is still going on, most of the future growth of HRIS use in America will probably not come because of technological breakthroughs or new equipment. Rather, it is my view that the information needs and analytical decision-making requirements of an increasingly sophisticated personnel environment will propel the spread and growth of these systems. More diversified benefits programs, better ways of measuring productivity, more effective utilization of employees' skills and propensities, enhanced employee involvement in the decisions that affect their careers, better ways of measuring the effectiveness of training and other increasingly costly programs, the need to reduce the costs of compliance with regulatory requirements — all of these and a host of other potential issues raised by a changing work force and a changing society point to the need for more efficient and responsive human resource information systems.

My thanks to Ly Seamans, with whom I have worked for years and who helped review the text; to Ren Nardoni, Jim Sheridan and Wade Roemke whose knowledge of the field and advice was extremely helpful; to George Buxton, Norm Harrison, Joanne Lechowicz, Jim Reese, Elliott Scott and Frank Swain who have each in their own way aided me in producing this book; and to John Monaghan who was invaluable in organizing the material and presenting it in a more understandable fashion.

ALFRED J. WALKER

# Contents

**PREFACE** vii

**PART I. INTRODUCTION**

1. **The HRIS Shortfall: Past Problems and Present Mistakes** 3
   1.1 Historical Overview of Computers in Personnel 4
   1.2 The Ten Most Common Mistakes Made in HRIS Development 8
      1.2.1 Being All Things to All People – All at Once 9
      1.2.2 No Personnel Expertise on the Project Team 9
      1.2.3 Separate Systems Are Vulnerable to Errors 10
      1.2.4 Avoid Superfluous Complexity: Resist Demand for Reports 10
      1.2.5 Insufficient or Waning Management Support 11
      1.2.6 Design by Committee 12
      1.2.7 Technical Marvels Fail if not "User-Oriented" 12
      1.2.8 Loose Project Control 13
      1.2.9 Promising Force Reductions: Savings that Don't Occur 14
      1.3.0 Building When You Can Buy 14

2. **Defining an HRIS: Basic Concepts and Modules** 16
   2.1 Basic Concepts: Essential HRIS Characteristics 17
      2.1.1 Data Base 17
      2.1.2 Data Entry 18
      2.1.3 Retrieval 19
      2.1.4 Human Resource Information Center (HRIC) 21
      2.1.5 Data Quality 22

xv

2.2 Modules of a Computerized Personnel System 24
2.2.1 Basic Personnel Module 26
2.2.2 Human Resource Utilization (HRU) Module 26
2.2.3 Benefits Administration Module 27
2.2.4 Job Evaluation Module 27
2.2.5 Position Control Module 28
2.2.6 Attendance Control 28
2.2.7 Safety Module 28
2.2.8 Employee Benefits Statement Module 29
2.2.9 Equal Employment and Affirmative Action Module 29
2.3.0 Training Module 30

## PART II. FIRST STEPS: PREPARATION AND THE NEEDS ANALYSIS

3. Getting Started: Guidelines for the Proposal to Management and Establishment of the Project Team 35
   3.1 Understanding the Organization 36
   3.2 Understanding the Project: HRIS Development Stages 38
   3.3 Generating Informed Interest and Support 41
   3.4 Making the Proposal to Management 43
   3.5 Establishing the Project Team 46

4. Conducting the Needs Analysis 51
   4.1 Objectives Will Guide Schedule Preparation 53
   4.2 Administrative Details and the Needs Analysis Schedule 54
   4.3 Methods of Collecting Information: Pros and Cons 59
      4.3.1 Interviews 59
      4.3.2 Questionnaires 61
      4.3.3 Direct Observation 61
   4.4 Preparing for the Interviews 62
   4.5 Conducting the Interviews 64
      4.5.1 Interview Objectives 65
      4.5.2 Guidelines for Interviewing 65
      4.5.3 Key Information to Gather 67
   4.6 Analyzing the Collected Information 69
   4.7 Develop Broad System Configurations 73
   4.8 Determine Best HRIS Configuration and Prepare Recommendations 76

## PART III. DESIGN AND INSTALLATION

5. Specifications: Determining Data Base Elements, Codes, and Edits 81

|       |                                                                    |     |
|-------|--------------------------------------------------------------------|-----|
| 5.1   | Determining Initial Data Base Elements                             | 82  |
| 5.1.1 | Standardized Data Base Element Specifications                      | 82  |
| 5.1.2 | Project Team Methodology for Element Selection                     | 85  |
| 5.1.3 | Perform Data Element Tests: Key Questions                          | 87  |
| 5.1.4 | Final Review with the User                                         | 88  |
| 5.2   | Determining Major Control Codes                                    | 89  |
| 5.2.1 | Employment Status Code: The Biggest Aggregate Picture              | 89  |
| 5.2.2 | Employment Type Codes                                              | 90  |
| 5.2.3 | Transaction (Input) Codes                                          | 91  |
| 5.2.4 | Standard Entry Format: Input Numbers                               | 93  |
| 5.2.5 | Screen Input Method                                                | 94  |
| 5.3   | Determining Editing Requirements                                   | 95  |

6. **Specifications: Output Reports, Interfaces, Tables, and Processing Routines** — 98
    - 6.1 Determining Output Report Specifications — 98
    - 6.2 Interfaces: Links with Payroll and Other Systems — 107
        - 6.2.1 Required Interface Specifications — 107
        - 6.2.2 Interface or Absorb? — 108
        - 6.2.3 The Payroll System Interface — 109
    - 6.3 Tables — 115
    - 6.4 Processing Routines — 117

7. **Design Considerations: Major Influences on HRIS Design** — 120
    - 7.1 Human Functions Must Be Considered — 122
    - 7.2 Designing for Historical Change — 124
    - 7.3 Determining Data Base Activity and Size — 128
        - 7.3.1 Methods of Segmentation — 129
        - 7.3.2 Active Employee Data Requirements — 130
        - 7.3.3 Tables and Reference Files — 137
        - 7.3.4 Applicant Records — 137
        - 7.3.5 Inactive Employee Records — 138
        - 7.3.6 Total Storage Requirements — 141
    - 7.4 Analysis of Reports — 141
        - 7.4.1 Categories of Reports — 141
        - 7.4.2 Design Considerations of Reports — 143
    - 7.5 Distributed Processing — 146
    - 7.6 External Files and Interfaces — 148

8. **Program Development and Conversion** — 150
    - 8.1 Program Development for Personnel: Five Guidelines — 151

|  |  |
|---|---|
| 8.2 Develop System Test Plan: User Tests Key | 153 |
| 8.3 Conversion and Implementation Plan | 156 |
|     8.3.1 Conversion Plan Considerations | 157 |
|     8.3.2 Field Trial: First Step in Implementation | 158 |
|     8.3.3 Parallel or "Quick Cut" | 159 |
|     8.3.4 Field Collection | 159 |
|     8.3.5 Treatment of Initial Errors | 159 |
| 8.4 Operating Considerations | 160 |
|     8.4.1 Privacy and Security | 160 |
|     8.4.2 Data Base Accuracy | 161 |

**9. The Human Resource Information Center, Privacy Issues, and Skills Inventory Guidelines** — **165**

|  |  |
|---|---|
| 9.1 The Human Resource Information Center (HRIC) | 166 |
|     9.1.1 Timing of HRIC Installation | 166 |
|     9.1.2 HRIC Functions | 166 |
|     9.1.3 Documentation and Training of the HRIC | 167 |
|     9.1.4 User Training | 168 |
|     9.1.5 Staffing Levels of the HRIC | 169 |
| 9.2 Privacy | 170 |
|     9.2.1 Data Base Elements Limited to "Need to Know" | 171 |
|     9.2.2 The HRIC as Watchdog | 172 |
|     9.2.3 All Data Are Private: Access Limited | 172 |
|     9.2.4 Disclosures to Outside Agencies | 173 |
| 9.3 Key Application: Skills Inventory Needs | 173 |
|     9.3.1 Need for the Human Resource Inventory | 174 |
|     9.3.2 Work Experience (Skills) Vocabulary | 175 |
|     9.3.3 Collection of the Inventory Data | 178 |
|     9.3.4 Selection Standards and Support Procedures | 179 |

**10. Using the HRIS to Ensure Compliance With Federal Regulatory Requirements – and More** — **183**

|  |  |
|---|---|
| 10.1 Wage and Hour Laws | 185 |
|     10.1.1 Fair Labor Standards Act of 1938 | 185 |
|     10.1.2 Equal Pay Act of 1963 | 187 |
| 10.2 Fair Employment Laws | 188 |
|     10.2.1 Title VII of the Civil Rights Act of 1964 | 188 |
|     10.2.2 Executive Order #11246 (1964), Revised Order #4 (1972), and #14 (1974) | 190 |
|     10.2.3 Age Discrimination in Employment Act of 1967, as amended in 1977 | 192 |

|  |  |  |
|---|---|---|
| | 10.2.4 Vocational Rehabilitation Act of 1973 (Handicapped) | 193 |
| | 10.2.5 Vietnam Era Veterans Readjustment Act of 1974 and Executive Order #11701 | 194 |
| | 10.2.6 Other Fair Employment Areas | 194 |
| 10.3 | Occupational Safety and Health Act of 1970 | 195 |
| 10.4 | Employee Retirement Income Security Act (ERISA) | 199 |
| | 10.4.1 Eligibility and Vesting Calculations | 200 |
| | 10.4.2 Pension Plan Calculations | 201 |
| | 10.4.3 Plans Covered | 201 |
| | 10.4.4 Benefit Guarantees | 202 |

## PART IV. CORPORATE PERSPECTIVES AND PROFITABILITY

**11. HRIS Savings, Benefits, and Cost Justification** — **207**

|  |  |  |
|---|---|---|
| 11.1 | General Guidelines of Cost/Benefit Analyses | 208 |
| 11.2 | Possible Savings in User Areas: Checklists | 210 |
| | 11.2.1 Benefits Administration | 211 |
| | 11.2.2 Wage and Salary Administration | 211 |
| | 11.2.3 General Personnel Administration | 212 |
| | 11.2.4 Force Planning | 212 |
| | 11.2.5 Staffing and Career Development | 213 |
| | 11.2.6 Training | 213 |
| | 11.2.7 EEO Administration | 214 |
| | 11.2.8 Medical and Safety Administration | 214 |
| | 11.2.9 Other User Areas of Personnel Savings | 214 |
| 11.3 | Savings Outside User Areas | 215 |
| | 11.3.1 Computer-Related Expenses | 215 |
| | 11.3.2 Temporary Help | 215 |
| | 11.3.3 Standardization and Uniformity | 216 |
| 11.4 | HRIS Costs | 216 |
| | 11.4.1 Development Costs of the HRIS | 217 |
| | 11.4.2 Conversion and Installation Costs | 217 |
| | 11.4.3 Ongoing Costs | 217 |
| 11.5 | Overall Justification | 217 |

**12. Development Choices: Prepackaged Systems and Vendor Evaluation** — **220**

|  |  |  |
|---|---|---|
| 12.1 | Establish an Internal Project Team | 222 |
| 12.2 | Determine the System Requirements | 223 |
| 12.3 | Alert Management: Get Their Approval | 224 |
| 12.4 | Develop the Evaluation Criteria | 225 |
| 12.5 | Develop and Request Proposal | 229 |

|  |  |  |
|---|---|---|
| 12.6 | Initial Screening of the Vendors | 230 |
| 12.7 | Presentation by Vendors | 230 |
| 12.8 | Detailed Evaluation | 231 |
| 12.9 | Narrow to Two Vendors: Go to Contract | 231 |
| 12.10 | Final Selection: Sign Contract | 231 |

**13. Future Trends: Decision Making and Analysis** — **233**

13.1 Technology Now Available for User-Oriented Systems — 239

Index — 241

# HRIS Development
## A Project Team Guide to Building an Effective Personnel Information System

# Part I
# Introduction

# 1
# The HRIS Shortfall: Past Problems and Present Mistakes

The purpose of this book is to describe clearly how an organization can develop a Human Resource Information System (HRIS) that responds to organizational needs. Its goal is to provide an organization, whether a public institution or a private company, with guidelines and step-by-step procedures for installing a computer-based personnel system that works for them — an HRIS that delivers on the early promise held out for these systems but rarely realized in fact.

The promise of mechanized personnel systems has not been overstated for the most part. If anything, HRIS promoters and planners have set their sights too low, focusing only on the record-keeping possibilities of computerized personnel systems or their ability to turn out reports required by government regulatory agencies.

Although important and even necessary in many cases, these objectives fall short of the real profit-making potential of an effective HRIS: its ability to provide managers with the tools of analysis, human resource information that helps decision makers make the right decisions about the organization's employees — its most complex and possibly most expensive resource.

Especially in the area of human resource utilization, an efficient and usable HRIS provides managers with the tools needed to analyze trends, developments, and their causes in an increasingly sophisticated personnel management environment. An effective HRIS provides the data and relationships needed promptly and at reasonable cost for analysis of Human Resource Planning models, evaluation, career pathing for members of a changing work force, and dozens of other programs designed to integrate organizational goals with individual goals — programs that barely existed in personnel departments ten years ago. Even today, because computerized personnel systems have been slow in reaching their potential, many organizations have a better inventory of their furniture than of their employees.

In this chapter, the reasons why computerized systems have not had the impact they should have had on personnel functions are summarized. As can be seen, these reasons no longer exist, and new priorities have emerged that make it even more probable that the HRIS-based "personnel office of the future" is ripe for realization in the 1980s.

Since this is a book about HRIS development — a specific guide to Project Team installation methods that will lead to an effective system — the rest of this chapter is given over to cautionary principles of HRIS development today. These principles include the most common mistakes I have seen made over the years, and I describe how you can avoid these pitfalls in creating a successful HRIS.

## 1.1. HISTORICAL OVERVIEW OF COMPUTERS IN PERSONNEL

Much has been written about the fact that the use of computers in personnel has "lagged behind" applications in other organizational functions,* especially in the private sector, where data processing was adopted early by engineering, accounting, and other functions. However, by the early 1970s data processing was more widely used for personnel work by government agencies than by Fortune 500 companies.†

The "uneven progress" of computer technology in the personnel department of the past‡ has been caused both by changing technology and the changing role of the personnel department in most organizations, each exerting somewhat different pressures at different stages of history.

---

*E.g., Lee, Sang M., and Cary D. Thorp, Jr., *Personnel Management, A Computer-Based System,* New York, Petrocelli Books, Inc., 1978, Chapter 1.

†Tomeski, E. A., and H. Lazarus, "Computerized Information Systems in Personnel — A Comparative Analysis of the State of the Art in Government and Business," *Academy of Management Journal,* March 1974.

‡Walker, Alfred J., "Arriving Soon: The Paperless Personnel Office," *Personnel Journal,* July 1980.

*Postwar Period.* The earliest automated personnel systems in America were the payroll systems of the 1940s and early 1950s, which used machines primitive by today's standards, such as tabulating and electrical accounting machinery (EAM) equipment. This equipment was sufficient for the limited objectives of personnel departments of the time, which usually were limited to the employment function. These systems kept little more useful personnel data than name, salary, location, date of birth, sex, and department code but nonetheless satisfied the requirements of personnel functions as they were perceived by most organizations in the postwar years.*

*Mid-Fifties: Hardware Explosion and Skills Systems.* With the rapid growth of the computer industry in the 1950s and early 1960s, advances in technology far outstripped the apparent needs of personnel departments for more elaborate systems. An exception was in the aerospace and other defense industries, where the first nonpayroll personnel systems, forerunners of today's Human Resource Inventory (HRI; see Chapter 9) or skills inventory applications were developed in the late 1950s.

The primary objective of defense industry skills inventory systems was to put together project teams to bid for or work on government contracts. Forms were sent to selected employees, who entered their skills, abilities, education, and other credentials, and this information was recorded on tape or cards for later analysis and searches. Critical skills were highlighted, and planning for future contracts was facilitated.

Outside the defense industry, however, personnel departments in this country took little part in the technological advances of the period. Most of the programmers at the time were engineers and scientists, and the computers were used as "number crunchers" instead of being integrated into more complex business systems. These data processing resources were being directed into nonpersonnel areas such as accounts receivable, order processing, and inventory control, since they were perceived to be more important areas of the business to mechanize.

---

*This section is essentially based on the author's lecture material over the years, summarized in Alfred J. Walker, "A Brief History of the Computer in Personnel," *Personnel Journal,* July 1980.

Since programmers were still a relatively scarce technical resource, the only organizations that could afford to have these people work on Personnel's problems were the giants: General Motors, AT&T, Mobil, General Electric, and a few others. In these companies, it was seen that the power of the computer could be used to make the work of recording basic information about employees more efficient and then to automatically generate repetitive and detailed reports previously done in a time-consuming fashion by clerks and administrative personnel. But storage costs were high, and information kept was limited by the capacity of an 80-column card or card image on tape. In the absence of stand-alone personnel systems, payroll systems were revised and updated, and personnel programmers would add selected pieces of information to the payroll tapes to extend the usefulness of existing systems to Personnel.

The result of this jerry-building of personnel systems was frequently tapes or cards packed with codes and unintelligible zone punches. In order to produce a given set of statistics — say, a weekly turnover report — a "fixed report" program was necessary, which had to be developed separately if it could not be matched to the payroll cycle. Naturally, top management wanted such reports, and the result was a proliferation of stand-alone programs and separate systems created just to produce a single set of statistics. Any data useful to management were available only through this report format.

*The High Hopes of the MIS Era.* The frequently redundant collections of data accumulated by the second-generation systems of the early 1960s were seen by clearer minds as wasteful, counterproductive, and inefficient. Increasingly, systems designers and data planning managers began asking, Why not capture the data once and make the data available to all who need them? Is not the data needed for Payroll also needed to ascertain labor distribution and product costs? Why not tie these systems together?

Growing interest in this type of Management Information Systems (MIS) thinking coincided with the introduction of the IBM/360 line and other large-scale machines. Large projects were undertaken to trace the flow of necessary information through a company and then to develop comprehensive "master plans" for information needs. Parts of these MIS plans included personnel data and payroll; the latter was given higher priority because it was generally agreed that it was more important to pay employees on time than to produce headcount reports.

For most of the 1960s, systems designers struggled to make the MIS concept work for personnel, usually with disastrous results. After more than ten years and expenditures in the millions of dollars, designers finally came to the conclusion that it was not within the power of mortal men and women to build one system to handle everything from order entry to accounts receivable, including Personnel's needs. The precepts of MIS theory never took into account the thousands of job steps, inputs for changes and other decisions, and exits and reentry points that had to be incorporated into a system and constantly updated to make it work. Projects to include personnel in an all-encompassing MIS simply got too large for most companies, and in the mid-1960s new priorities — brought on by the Johnson and Nixon administrations' legislation on EEO, benefits, and other workplace conditions — diverted attention from the effort.

Exceptions to the generally slow progress made by computers in personnel departments in the 1960s included many larger banks and insurance companies. With high white-collar and clerical labor costs, and little organized labor, these firms were seeking ways of isolating and paring administrative and turnover costs. They sensed that the computerization of personnel paper-handling costs was just as likely to save money as computerized check clearing or claims handling, and high turnover rates in these industries gave managers the added incentive to use automation to help select the right person for the right job. In the late 1960s, Manufacturer's Hanover, Bankers Trust, National Bank of Detroit, Chemical Bank, Hartford Insurance, Bank of America, and others got started.

*The 1970s: Governmental Needs and New Systems.* Spurred by the governmental reporting requirements of EEO, OSHA, ERISA, and other legislation of the 1970s, most organizations with more than a few thousand employees developed some sort of automated personnel system. At the same time, the falling costs of computer processing and storage, as well as the development by vendors of software programs and packages affordable by more companies, made personnel systems less prohibitively expensive. Time-sharing costs also came down relative to other business costs, and for the first time companies without computers found it possible to develop personnel information systems.

Today, the personnel departments of most large firms and public institutions have computer-retrieval specialists on staff who work with a bewildering and complex array of statistics, keeping track of information as disparate as affirmative action plan results and dental plan results. Not only did these jobs not exist ten years ago, in many cases the personnel plan itself did not exist.

The growing importance of personnel functions such as human resource planning and utilization — efforts to assure the best possible present and future use of human resources — is another major force behind HRIS development today.

## 1.2. THE TEN MOST COMMON MISTAKES MADE IN HRIS DEVELOPMENT

Over more than fifteen years of observation and direct involvement in the development of Human Resource Information Systems in scores of organizations of all kinds, I have developed a list of "Ten Most Common Mistakes" that recur with remarkable consistency in personnel system installation.* These errors have held up well over the years; unfortunately, the same mistakes that were being made in 1965 and 1970 are still being made today and, to one degree or another, are being made in companies large and small, regardless of geographic location or organizational purpose.

In this listing, the first four or five "mistakes" are usually the most serious. Any one of these can be severe enough to put an HRIS installation project in immediate jeopardy. If your organization is dissatisfied with its present HRIS or is having trouble with its development, chances are, you will recognize one or more of these mistakes; if you are about to begin an HRIS project, this listing should help the Project Team avoid the most common errors made by others and prevent costly repetition.

---

*This listing first appeared in *Personnel Administrator*, July 1980, as "The 10 Most Common Mistakes in Developing Computer-Based Personnel Systems, and How to Avoid Them." Reprinted from the July 1980 issue of *Personnel Administrator*, copyright 1980 by the American Society for Personnel Administration, 30 Park Drive, Berea, OH 44017, $26 per year.

### 1.2.1. Being All Things to All People — All at Once

Too often, the HRIS Project Team starts out by trying to conquer the world. The Team's impulse is to solve as many problems as soon as possible, to be all things to all people in the first phase of development.

This attitude is in part the natural result of the way HRIS installations proceed in most organizations: in the Needs Analysis stage (see Chapter 4), Team members interview many potential users of the system, listen to many complaints, and are given a lengthening list of tasks and objectives relating to EEO, job evaluation, pensions, and other areas.

In any modern, fairly robust personnel organization today, there are at least ten and possibly as many as twenty major functions that can be combined in the new HRIS. I know of one large company that identified eighteen possible functions and, in an overly ambitious start, selected nine of these to develop in the first phase. They found out, to their chagrin, that it would take eight years and $6 million to get through the first phase.

As a rule of thumb, in the first phase the Project Team should not attempt to develop more than three or four of the ten major personnel functions, or HRIS "modules," described in Chapter 2. Moreover, in setting up priorities it may be unwise to emulate the romantic heroes of the literature of our youth, who always took on the biggest bully first.

For the good of the project, you want to succeed in the first phase, establish a track record, and do what you said you would do. A large initial system simply adds complexities in design, coding, training, and installation. Taking on the most troublesome problems first may sound heroic but is often a matter of asking for early defeat. Do not risk cancelation of the project by trying to do too much too soon.

### 1.2.2. No Personnel Expertise on the Project Team

A truly amazing phenomenon is a personnel systems Project Team with no understanding of personnel. Although it would appear to be only common sense to have personnel experts on a team developing a system that will be installed, paid for, and operated by Personnel people, I have seen situations in which HRIS Project Teams had virtually no background in the business of personnel.

One large utility in the East, for example, had assembled a team of data systems staff members and new hires whose members had not even heard of ERISA or the OFCCP. Without a clear picture of EEO requirements, company benefits, the wage and salary administration process, and other areas of personnel that will be covered by the system, such a project team is likely to yield a product that the user may not recognize.

Furthermore, the Project Team should know the primary business of the organization, as discussed in Chapter 3. A Team with little or no understanding of personnel business and objectives within the organization, while not unheard of, is handicapped in developing a system responsive to Personnel's needs.

### 1.2.3. Separate Systems Are Vulnerable to Errors

From the outset, the new personnel system should be tied to the payroll system. The same input that is used to hire a new employee or change an employee's salary, job, or department should be used to simultaneously feed both the payroll and personnel systems. Thus systems must be integrated, in one of the ways explored in Chapter 6.

A personnel system isolated from the payroll cycle — and one major financial institution I know of tried this — means that users have to make all changes such as salary increases and new job titles twice. At first, people are willing to do this with some care; eventually, the personnel system becomes inaccurate and out of date and is likely to fall by its own weight.

A related fault of isolated personnel systems is that their operators often fail to use the "best source" for much employee information: the employees themselves. Using secondary sources for some information — educational data from manual records and some benefits information from enrollment cards signed at the time of employment and never updated, for example — further builds a potential for inaccuracy.

### 1.2.4. Avoid Superfluous Complexity: Resist Demand for Reports

Personnel users being interviewed by HRIS designers are invariably tempted by the cornucopian potential of data systems, the possibilities laid out as "possible output" thanks to some of the more modern features of computers.

Automatic procedures can in fact produce an almost infinite variety of complex reports and graphic output or can be made to interface with other nonpersonnel systems in the organization to produce elaborate and costly reports. But the inclination to do so should be resisted strenuously by the HRIS Project Team. Personnel work is complex enough on its own.

An example of how complexity can stall an HRIS project was provided by a large New York City bank a few years ago. The bank called in consultants to find out why their two-year-old personnel system was running late in development, and we discovered a system designed to produce a total of 143 fixed reports, including monthly detailed salary administration head counts and benefit reports. A new system was designed to produce just 12 fixed reports, with provisions for the other 131 to be generated by an easy-to-use retrieval system. The bank's personnel system was up and running within one year.

The main intent of the HRIS is to keep an accurate, complete, and up-to-date data base that can be called upon *when needed* for reports. It is not intended to be an automatic, self-perpetuating reporting system, nor a producer of mountains of complex data — a sign that the original design has gone awry. Keep the HRIS simple in design and outputs.

### 1.2.5. Insufficient or Waning Management Support

The job of selling top management on the merits of the HRIS must not be viewed as a one-time effort, something you do at the outset and then forget about unless a crisis emerges. The status, merits, and progress of the project should be communicated to upper management on a planned, regular basis through an agenda of conferences, internal publications focusing on the new HRIS, or available house organs.

This is necessary because it normally takes two or three years to put this type of system into production, from conception to installation. Clearly, the management support needed must span the same number of budget cycles as the HRIS project. This is not to say that managers are necessarily whimsical or have short attention spans; rather, one must recognize the pace and complexity of modern management. New demands are made on company resources every day, and priorities shift in organizations. Methods of gaining and holding management support are discussed in Chapter 3.

Whatever the vehicle used to remind management of the benefits of the system and its progress, a regular, controlled reporting system is vastly preferable to infrequent "crisis-atmosphere" meetings or status reviews requested by top management. Don't wait until you're asked to justify yourself.

Overindulgence in any of these first five mistakes will almost always prove fatal to the smooth development of an HRIS project. They present immediate dangers to the project's very continuation, especially when they are not recognized in advance as potential hazards.

A second group of five mistakes made in personnel systems development presents dangers that are not usually so immediately disastrous. These are avoidable problems, however, and it should be remembered that any ailment can develop into a serious illness if it is not recognized and treated early.

### 1.2.6. Design by Committee

A statement frequently heard in experienced systems development circles and backed by a growing body of empirical evidence is: If a design can't be carried in one person's head, it won't work.

This, of course, refers to the overall design of a system or process, the conceptual structure rather than all the details, but it makes an absolutely valid point about the importance of "thinking small" in systems development. The design team should be relatively small in number rather than a large committee that spawns subcommittees, because additional people in the earliest stages slow a project down rather than speed it up.

### 1.2.7. Technical Marvels Fail If Not "User-Oriented"

The phrase "user-oriented system" has become trite in recent years, yet systems are being installed today that are not geared to the needs of users. Although great strides have been made in making systems more "human" — especially in high-level retrieval language and in word processing — some systems remain unnecessarily alien to Personnel users through the excessive use of codes, input screens, masks, and other methods and processes that are too technical.

The best HRIS installations are those which best assist personnel departments in their functions of hiring, placement, and rendering other personnel services. Any part of a system that impedes progress toward personnel goals will offset some of the benefits the system is designed to deliver.

Thus, the technical people designing and programming the system, as stressed in Chapters 7 and 8, must not work alone. Personnel users must be involved from the start to assure that the system is responsive to personnel needs and highly integrated into the work flow.

A good way to accomplish a "better fit" of a new system to users' needs is to run a thirty-to-sixty-day trial before the system is delivered in its final form. Designers and programmers should be involved in assessing the pilot run so that changes can be made before the system is frozen.

### 1.2.8. Loose Project Control

In HRIS development, as elsewhere, there's no substitute for good management. And in installing a new system, good management is active rather than passive; a good full-time Project Manager, whose recommended qualifications are covered in Chapter 3, is one who conducts regular meetings and project "walk-throughs" and is involved in every step of system development outlined in this book.

Despite their sometimes otherworldly expertise, systems people are human beings. Like most workers, they are interested in what the boss (the Project Manager) is interested in. If the boss is not interested in the project's excellence, chances are they won't be either. Thus for any sizable project, a Project Manager with effective managerial skills is essential.

The Project Manager should be from the personnel organization, have a working knowledge of computer-based applications, and have corporate standing. He or she must be able to make broad trade-offs, get to top management when necessary, and be able to keep the project moving.

Project control techniques, such as the Project Evaluation and Review Technique (PERT), and computer schedules may be helpful. But the methodology of managing systems development is secondary to the manager's skills and persistence in achieving effective results.

### 1.2.9. Promising Force Reductions: Savings That Don't Occur

One way for a Project Team to lose its credibility with top management early is to promise important reductions in force when the system is installed. There is a tendency to oversell this point — at the expense of other real savings of the type suggested in Chapter 11 — by predicting people savings in the personnel department itself or in departments where there is extensive personnel record keeping.

For one reason or another, computer-based personnel systems rarely, if ever, cause clerical or management job displacement. The system is more rightly viewed as an information-provider than a people reducer, inasmuch as the savings realized tend to be too small to account for whole people. Also, other factors may intervene.

At a major paper products company headquarters in New York, for example, the firm identified nine people out of a group of thirty-six in its benefits organization that could be let go once a new system was in place. All thirty-six of these workers had been involved in the hand-calculating of insurance claims (not paying, but just processing claims) and calculating pensions. During the system development period, however, the company reorganized its benefits department into two sections, and functions were reallocated and new duties added. The people savings never occurred, and this had to be explained to top management. A point to remember is that if people have to be cut, you may be among them if others cannot be found.

### 1.2.10. Building When You Can Buy

More and more, as the number and quality of prepackaged personnel systems available grows, companies should be looking at the alternatives to building their own systems, for reasons discussed in Chapter 12. It makes little sense to build a system from scratch, just for the pride of entrepreneurship, if a system is available that will save the organization both time and money.

Today's prepackaged personnel systems come in a wide variety of capabilities. Once the Project Team has developed a rigorous set of specifications, sound business practice calls for a review of systems on the market before making the decision to build it within the organization.

**CONCLUSION**

As can be seen from a review of the history of applications of computers in personnel functions, the use of data processing in this area has come in fits and starts over the years and has been delayed in many cases by ill-conceived efforts to make personnel functions fit equipment and data systems structures rather than proceeding the other way around. Federal regulatory requirements focused attention on the need for improved record keeping and ways to produce needed government reports, however. Today the expanding role of human resource management and more versatile systems have set the stage for final realization of the profit-making potential of Human Resource Information Systems.

Although the time is ripe for installing a new or more effective HRIS, organizations that set out to do so often make misjudgments in the early stages of development that seriously delay or even doom the HRIS project. My experience with scores of HRIS development projects over the years has shown that some of the same mistakes that were being made in 1965 and 1970 are being made today. Some of these mistakes are more serious than others, and the ten most common seen today are discussed in order of severity in this chapter. If they are recognized early, these potential pitfalls can be avoided or dealt with by the specific measures proposed in subsequent chapters.

# 2
# Defining an HRIS: Basic Concepts and Modules

The modern Human Resource Information System may be defined as a computer-based method for collecting, storing, maintaining, retrieving, and validating certain data needed by an organization about its employees, applicants, and former employees. The basic concepts inherent in this definition as well as summary descriptions of the personnel modules used to make it work are covered in this chapter.

The HRIS has also been called a Computerized Personnel System, Personnel Data System, Employee Data System, Employee Information System, and scores of other titles, some selected to reflect the system's main purpose in an organization, and some apparently chosen because they produce a catchy acronym. Names are unimportant, of course, since no two systems are exactly alike.

Also, it is worth noting that the definition specifies "*certain* data needed by an organization," not *all* data that may be available. Benefits information alone — if it included all medical and dental claims, pension, profit sharing, insurance, sickness, and accident information throughout each employee's history — could conceivably overburden even the most elaborate mechanized system. And benefits are just one area of employee information.

In addition to employee information, the HRIS will contain much organizational and job-related data, in types and amounts determined by the modules that are needed.

## 2.1. BASIC CONCEPTS: ESSENTIAL HRIS CHARACTERISTICS

At least five basic concepts are involved in the definition of an HRIS: the data base (2.1.1), data entry (2.1.2), retrieval (2.1.3), the Human Resource Information Center (2.1.4), and data quality (2.1.5). If an HRIS is built with one or more of these parts missing, a serious deficiency will result that will prevent the system from achieving its objective. Within each of these key areas, as discussed in greater detail in later chapters, the Project Team will develop the parameters and methodologies that will characterize the organization's particular system.

### 2.1.1. Data Base

The HRIS must have a data base of both employee and organizational data from which to produce needed reports, audits, and analyses. In terms of size, the optimum data base will be extensive enough to accomplish all the objectives of the personnel system yet not so large that it becomes unwieldy and unnecessarily expensive.

As a starting point, the data base must include essential items needed internally by the organization or for governmental reporting requirements. Whether included in the data base proper or in associated tables or interfaced systems, the data needed to produce necessary reports and other outputs must be reachable through the system. Data that are not part of the data base, or capable of being created from the data base are simply not part of the system.

The creation of the data base may be the most important step in the system-building process. In order to complete the total data base process successfully, a complete understanding of the entire HRIS is essential.

An input method must be devised for every element; editing and processing steps must be developed; and outlines and fixed reports must be laid out that will display the element. In a data management system environment, additional specifications will be needed regarding the expected usage of each element. Data usage factors that should be planned for include the expected number of times each element will be updated and changed, how many times the user may ask for the element in an ad hoc inquiry mode, the history required for each element, and the type of security needed.

The only way to be able to answer these questions satisfactorily is to be as familiar as possible with personnel department operations. The more knowledgeable you are about the expected usage of the system, the better chance you have of developing a well-designed data base, one that keeps all the "need to know" information with little or no superfluous, unnecessary, and expensively acquired data.

### 2.1.2. Data Entry

The second key ingredient of a viable HRIS is an efficient, accurate data entry method. If the information necessary to produce the required reports cannot be delivered to the data base in a timely and relatively error-free manner, the system will not perform as intended.

In the overall design of the HRIS, each data base element must have an origination point. Each element must be examined for its most efficient originating point, and an appropriate data entry subsystem must be designed to handle it. Once the system is operating, each data base element should have an "item owner" — a person or job function with a stake in maintaining the accuracy of that data element — who understands its purpose and importance. No item should be an orphan.

Some data base elements will come from company headquarters, such as Job Title or Department Name. These elements, which a number of employees share in common, can be stored on internal tables and will have an input method that is different from the method for data entered from the organizations or by employees themselves. Other data elements, such as expected retirement date, dates of eligibility for vacations or benefits, and similar items based on set formulas, can be calculated at the time of data entry. (Also, data can exist in a separate computerized system, and the designer must allow for an exchange of data called an "interface.")

For data that must come from the employee directly, a computer-produced document that displays vital data and also can be used to record any changes — called a "turnaround" document — may be the best method. This document can be used as the primary input vehicle. After the necessary approvals, clerical persons can key the changes to the data base directly from it. The HRIS can then produce a new document during the next maintenance and update cycle for every employee who had a change. In this way, the new document is sent back to the originator for verification. The turnaround document serves as both an input and an auditing tool. These types of data entry forms are known as "turnaround documents" because a complete cycle of loop is made in their use.

There will have to be input methods devised for the nonemployee elements as well. Depending on the scope of the system and the particular items, many input forms may have to be created to ensure that the data base can be kept accurate, timely, and complete. If an item cannot be kept current, or if in the final analysis it costs more to do so than the item is worth, the designer must examine closely the justification for including that item in the system.

Data entry systems have made remarkable strides over the past several years; with the same amount of clerical time that was once devoted to key punching and key verifying alone, the functions of entering, editing against codes and ranges, field justification, data conversion, and more can be accomplished — all without access to the HRIS. Of course, if one has access to the HRIS in an online, interactive mode, the entire update to the data base can be performed directly. But even without online access, the data entry operator can sit at a terminal and look at the results on the screen. After the operator is satisfied with how the data has been edited against the presupplied parameters, the operator releases the data into the system for later update in a batch mode.

The process of data capture has been moving away from large computers and toward the intelligent terminal in the data entry field, with the result that it is now quite cost-effective to perform as many edit and entry functions as possible in remote locations and in the larger departments where the higher concentrations of employees work and where edit failures can be resolved more quickly. This results in more efficient use of people-time and computer resources. The data entry process has to be well thought out, however, in order for the HRIS to function correctly.

**2.1.3. Retrieval**

The third key ingredient to a well-designed HRIS is rapid retrieval of needed information, in a cost-effective manner, by the user. The underlying philosophy is to provide users with the freedom to do whatever they wish with the data in whatever way they want to do it.

The data resident in the data base should be capable of being extracted and presented in an almost infinite number of formats. Producing standard fixed reports, sorting, selecting records, summarizing fields, computing new elements, and outputting data files should all be within the power of the user in the Personnel Department, with a minimum of training and without data processing assistance.

Sophisticated retrieval systems that can accomplish these tasks have been utilized extensively in the personnel environment over the past several years. It remains difficult, however, for most personnel administrators to predict exactly which analyses and reports they will need in the future. Also, many requests for information about employees come from a high level within the organization, are of an urgent nature, and thus require a short response time. Thus, it is essential to have the ability to create a new report and produce it in a manner of minutes.

Today's systems allow the user to ask a question of the data and retrieve the answer either via terminal or in a batch mode in a pseudo-English language style. A dictionary contains the description of where the element is in the data base and some specifications of the element in order for the system to properly display, sort, and protect the data from misuse.

Thereafter, following the system's simple rules, the user converses with the retrieval package, using a limited but powerful vocabulary. The system compares existing records with parameter-driven requests, selects those that meet the user's criteria, and displays the data in the manner the user desires. These retrievals can be stored in the computer for later use as well, should the user require them.

By using these high-level retrieval methods, most designers can free themselves from developing too many routine reports during the system development process. Many more hours of design and coding can be saved by allowing the Personnel Department to produce its own analyses and reports. Even fairly complex statistical reports using graphics and other similar features can be produced by users after only a few hours of training in these retrieval systems.

The dollar saving in this approach is also high. A normal COBOL program may take as long as a month or more for the programmers to write. They must meet with the user to develop specifications, design and write the program, test it, and inevitably debug it; then they must run the program and finally document it. This will cost anywhere from $1,500 to $5,000, whereas an ad hoc retrieval request may only cost $50 to $100 or less to produce the same output. These rapid-access systems have saved companies millions of dollars and years of delay in getting Personnel the data it needs.

In designing an HRIS, it should be a primary objective to have as few fixed reports as possible programmed into the system. In my experience, it is better to have fewer reports, and instead, rely on the retrieval systems to be there to handle the bulk of the reporting load. Other than vital control reports, the HRIS should be limited to the very few reports that are beyond the technical capability of the retrieval systems or are otherwise better handled via detailed coding.

This approach also is helpful in coping with the changing nature of personnel and the changing social climate that affects the American workplace. For the most part, the questions and problems with which we are dealing today will not be the same ones with which we will have to cope five years from now. Therefore, we want to try to minimize our investment in systems or programs that are limited to solving only today's problems. Personnel people will also applaud efforts to keep their system as flexible as possible, since they realize that their information requirements will change, in ways suggested in Chapter 13 of this book.

### 2.1.4. Human Resource Information Center (HRIC)

A fourth essential procedure is to formally designate a person or group of people as responsible for the day-to-day operation of the HRIS. This Human Resource Information Center (HRIC), discussed in greater detail in Chapter 9, is vital for the success of the system in several respects. First, the HRIC must ensure that the input to the system is being received and that changes to the data base are subsequently being processed.

Second, the edit checks and up-date logic that are in the system will act as a screen against erroneous entries, but these edit failures must be resolved and resubmitted if necessary by either the originating organization or by the HRIC. In either case, the HRIC must take the initiative and see that the data base is accurate and up to date.

Another aspect of the HRIC job responsibility is to act as the coordinator for all accesses and retrievals from the HRIS. The HRIC will perform all the retrievals directly or will grant certain users access to selected parts of the system, consistent with their job responsibilities.

The HRIC will also schedule the entire update and processing of the system on a regular basis. There must be someone available to oversee the job setup and program schedule from the user organization as well as the data processing organization. Questions about file retention and report distribution will inevitably arise, and the user group must have someone who fully understands the ramifications and options involved in the day-to-day operation of a computer-based information system.

Another function the HRIC will perform is that of system administration from the standpoint of privacy. Privacy concerns include not only the physical security of the data files themselves but the review of the data elements to ensure that they are truly needed and that there are no unwarranted disclosures. Employees must be able to see and copy the data the organization has about them, and if it is incorrect or incomplete, to offer changes.

From an operational standpoint, the HRIC will be charged with assuring the privacy of the use of the information once it is printed and released to a user in the organization. Although the HRIC cannot be held responsible for another department's actions, the center should see to it that the design, operation, and use of the data conform as much as possible to the fair information principles and overall privacy guidelines discussed in Chapter 9.

**2.1.5. Data Quality**

The fifth essential procedure is assuring the quality of the system parts. This principle covers the related areas of accuracy, timeliness, throughput, and availability.

Each of the data elements must have an accuracy objective that the system is designed to meet. For some elements, such as salary, date of birth, race, and sex, the accuracy level should be extremely high, and the system should be designed to accomplish that level.

The primary determinant in selecting the items that must have a high level of accuracy is to assess the penalty you will pay if the data are less than completely accurate. For salary administration purposes, such as merit reviews and payroll, one expects the salary field to be as close to 100 percent accurate as possible. The same goes for pension administration and for some EEO administration.

For other data elements there can be some tolerance for less-than-perfect accuracy. The same penalties will usually not occur if a graduate degree is miscoded or if a specific training course is omitted. One could argue that under a given set of circumstances, the level of accuracy in the latter cases is just as important. The point is that the designers must recognize that each and every data element should be assigned an accuracy level objective and that the balance of the system should be altered to meet these objectives. This may involve adoption of very strict editing procedures that otherwise may not have been employed, more widespread use of the computer-produced turnaround documents discussed above, or whatever means, within economic constraints, that you determine must be employed to reach the desired level of accuracy.

In some companies, there is a growing use of sampling techniques to determine precisely how accurate the data on a data base are. Samples are taken, in sufficient quantities to produce valid results, of the data element in question at various stages in the data stream. Error rates are computed to determine how inaccurate the data are. Appropriate measures such as increased training, new instruction manuals, better data entry techniques, or new edits can then be employed to reach the desired objective.

Quality assurance principles also extend to helping the users solve their problems of timeliness. A given report may have accurate data but may not correspond to the time period as the user needs. If a monthly premium is due for a certain insurance, end-of-month cutoffs should be observed as closely as possible.

Many systems are tied to payroll cycles that for the most part are not geared to end-of-month dates. The same problem may exist with Affirmative Action and EEO reports. If data are not posted in a timely manner, accuracy levels may simply be unacceptable, and a new entry method will have to be devised.

System availability must also be examined, and appropriate steps must be taken to ensure that the users can access the system when they need to. The largest reason for system nonavailability is usually computer downtime. However, with more reliable equipment being developed and deployed, the downtime of the central processing units is decreasing. Online systems are now generally up and available to the user for reports and analyses without interruption. In terms of total system availability, though, all parts of the system must be measured for user access. The data entry, edit, maintenance, and reporting modules are all components; if any one of them is not available, the user may suffer.

In the same way, throughput must be traced from point of data origination to receipt on a report by the end user. Examination of the entire system's cycle must be conducted to ensure that the system can deliver information on an end-to-end basis in a fashion that responds to the users' needs.

These quality assurance activities will in all likelihood become more important with time, as pressures for more precise data increase. Privacy legislation, rising salary and benefit plan costs, and a lower threshold for inaccurate data imply that unless the principles of accuracy and timeliness are adhered to closely, it may not be worth building a system in the first place.

## 2.2. MODULES OF A COMPUTERIZED PERSONNEL SYSTEM

The modern computerized personnel system is made up of a series of connected modules. Like the rooms of a house constructed in the wilderness, these modules can be built one or two at a time and added to as the need arises. Even a single "room," say the Basic Personnel Module, provides a rudimentary HRIS, although most organizations today would consider a two- or three-module system, including modules for career development and ERISA needs, as essential for minimum livability.

The point is that no sensible frontiersman would attempt to build an eighteen-room mansion before the winter sets in or the weeks before a rumored Indian attack. As mentioned in Chapter 1, one of the most common mistakes of HRIS development is to attempt to build too large a system in the first phase. In personnel work today there are at least ten distinct major functions that could require separate modules, as described later in this section, but the installation of ten or more modules would result in a very robust system and is usually not required in any but the largest organizations. A recommended installation, at least in the first phase, would consist of the Basic Personnel Module and two or three support modules, depending on the staff available to run the HRIS and the funds available for development. This relatively modest approach not only assists the Team in gaining the necessary approval and funding of the project but allows the Team to concentrate on the more important pieces of the system first, leaving less critical work until later.

In an HRIS context, a "module" is an umbrella term covering a group of related personnel activities. The specific components and parameters of modules may vary with organizations, but the ten modules discussed in this section meet the following definitional criteria:

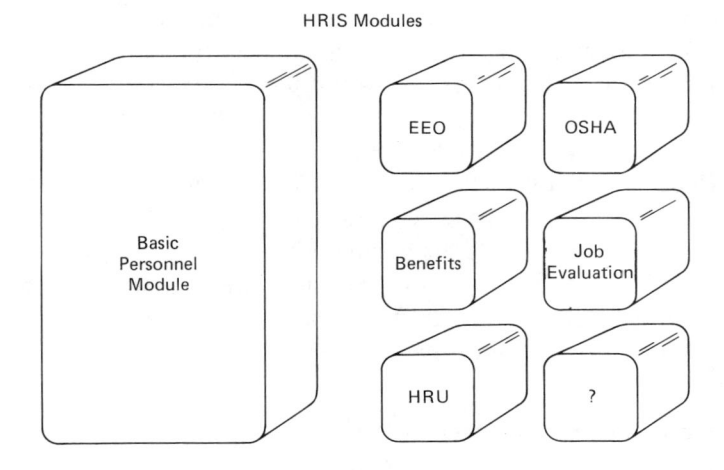

HRIS Modules

*Module Criteria*

1. The purpose of the module is directed to one specific function of personnel.
2. The module has its own input forms or screens.
3. There are some internal transformations that happen to the data, which the users in that personnel function must describe to the Project Team.
4. There are some reports or analyses that are particular to that user.
5. There may be some data elements that are unique to that user.

The following is a brief description of some of the more common modules that are being installed in computerized personnel systems today. Knowledge of these modules will improve the Project Team's understanding of the possible components of an HRIS.

### 2.2.1. Basic Personnel Module

The Basic Module provides the Central Data Base support and file organizer to which other modules and applications can be added. This module would keep such basic employee information as file control number, name, date of birth, service date, race, sex, salary, department code, job code, location code, and such classification codes as are necessary to determine employees' class and status.

Standard organizational data that apply to many employees, such as job titles, department and location, and salary grades, can be kept in this module in tabular form. An employee profile is usually provided in this module to display information about employees to the employees themselves as well as serving as a turnaround input document. Head-count statistics, turnover analyses, salary administration, and personnel record-keeping activities are supported by this module.

The Basic Module would also bring with it the HRIC methodology and generalized retrieval system. As the system grows, the retrieval system would work on the additional data elements as well, and the HRIC would control all modules.

### 2.2.2. Human Resource Utilization (HRU) Module

The Human Resource Utilization (HRU) module, called in some organizations a "Career Development" or "Skills Inventory" module, acts as the recorder for employee work experience and developmental activities. The employee uses a set of standard codes, for the most part unique to the organization, to select those work experiences, skills, educational attainments, professional credentials, and other activities which best describe the individual employee's background and capabilities. A career profile can be designed to act as a display/turnaround document in this area as well.

These experience codes are then used as job-matching selectors in a candidate search when a job opening occurs. This module assists management in promotion and placement activities, assessing departmental strengths and deficiencies, special assignments, and career planning. Future assignments or developmental experiences that are needed can also be factored into the module. The development of procedures for implementing a Human Resource Inventory of this kind is discussed in Chapter 9.

### 2.2.3. Benefits Administration Module

There is a growing need for more accurate employee record keeping in the entire benefits field, often impelled by the needs of the Employee Retirement Income Security Act (ERISA). Entry dates and eligibility dates can be stored along with elected plan status codes for each insurance and optional plan that an employee may sign for. In addition, compensation amounts and service dates can be tracked to provide the data for required reports of the Pension Benefit Guaranty Corporation, IRS, and the Department of Labor. Turnaround and display documents can be utilized here, as in the other modules, as a tremendous labor-saving device. Benefit claims information may be added to the module to provide almost total automation of some aspects of the employee benefit record-keeping operation. A more complete description of ERISA requirements is provided in Chapter 10.

### 2.2.4. Job Evaluation Module

Because of increased pressure from the federal government in the area of equal pay, a properly designed method of evaluating all positions is usually needed to ensure compliance with the labor laws. These evaluation tools require that each job in the organization be analyzed and classified according to preset criteria, such as the amount of decision making required on that job, the accountability the incumbent has for his or her actions, and the level of education or training a worker needs to qualify for the job. All these factors can be stored in the Job Evaluation Module to help record the jobs and to analyze incumbents for equality by race, sex, or other attributes.

The population can also be scrutinized by department or location to see which jobs are being filled at what level of employee. This is useful in monitoring abuses in the overall administration of the wage and salary program, such as when managers try to upgrade jobs in order to attract a better class of employee, even though the job requirements do not call for the higher classification.

### 2.2.5. Position Control Module

Somewhat similar to the Job Evaluation Module in intent, the Position Control Module enables management to track and monitor all authorized jobs in the company. A unique number is assigned to each position, and a history of the incumbents can be kept, along with the level of the job, its location and organization, and its salary grade. This information can be vital in discrimination cases in which equal pay and other treatment is at issue.

Each open job requisition can also be tracked and properly classified to inhibit the hiring and slotting of new jobs without Personnel's approval. Audit reports can be generated automatically, showing the status of any job for review purposes.

### 2.2.6. Attendance Control

Absenteeism is a chronic problem in some American industries, with millions of dollars being lost because of reduced productivity, replacement hiring, and related costs. Control of absenteeism is basically a nonautomated function consisting of several strong management practices. As a general rule, a small percentage of employees are responsible for a majority of absenteeism, however, and a computerized system can keep track of the records of employees to document attendance, spot good employees whose records are deteriorating, and highlight poor records for management attention.

Information on date of absence, day of week the absence occurred, and length of absence is retained. Also, the reason for the absence, when ascertainable, and whether the employee was paid for the absence is stored in this module.

### 2.2.7. Safety Module

The Safety Module is the application that will keep all employee injury and accident information. Under the requirements of the Federal Occupational Safety and Health Act (OSHA), emloyers with more than eleven employees must keep and maintain records of all injuries and illnesses, medical conditions, and toxic exposures. This information must be kept for specific time periods according to OSHA rules, which are outlined in some detail in Chapter 10.

Workmen's Compensation forms can sometimes be used as input forms. Output reports from this module can be used for examination by Department of Labor representatives. Data such as the nature of injury or illness, part of body injured, and date the injury occurred are also extremely useful in examining and controlling the company's safety program. In addition, the toxic substance and hazard exposures can be monitored through this module, and employees can be placed under appropriate medical surveillance.

### 2.2.8. Employee Benefits Statement Module

Most companies with a sizable investment in an employee benefits program send their employees a personalized summary of the benefits on an annual basis. These statements are produced by ascertaining an employee's current coverage under the benefit program and then projecting to that employee's retirement date the value of pension, profit sharing, savings plans, or whatever combination applies. Social Security benefits are factored in, along with any unusual benefits such as stock options.

The result is a one- or two-page report in an easy-to-read format containing the benefit coverages that the employee enjoys, shown as of today and projected to retirement. The data elements to generate this report can be kept in the Benefit Statement Module, along with tabular data for each plan and for the Social Security program payment schedule.

### 2.2.9. Equal Employment and Affirmative Action Module

One of the most important and necessary aspects of personnel record keeping is in the EEO and Affirmative Action areas. Federal requirements under Title VII of the Civil Rights Act of 1964, Executive Order 11246 (nondiscrimination in federal contracts), Revised Orders 4 and 14, and the Equal Pay Act 1963 form the basis for much of the record-keeping and reporting requirements discussed in greater detail in Chapter 10. However, there is a bewildering array of other laws and regulations — at the federal, state, and local levels — that need to be examined closely for applicability to each situation.

Basically, the EEO/AA Module will record the goals and timetables that the organization has established to correct any deficiencies in the work force. This module will then keep track of progress toward those goals by organizational unit and job group. This record will enable management to perform in-house compliance reviews and determine the company's good-faith efforts toward making EEO and Affirmative Action programs work. The module can track the utilization of women and minorities and help analyze recruitment and hiring plans; staffing, transfer, and promotional programs; and terminations. Also, the module can generate management reports in the pay practices and related compensation areas to detect possible patterns of discriminatory practice.

The EEO/AA Module can also be extended into the areas of age discrimination, handicapped, and veterans' discrimination should the company decide to monitor these areas with the HRIS.

One benefit of an EEO/AA Module is that it can keep a record of all personnel transactions if it is designed to do so at the outset of the project. Such a catalogue of chronological events may prove well worth the cost when the company must analyze situations that occurred several years earlier. Complaints of alleged discriminatory practices in pay treatment and/or promotions can be very difficult to refute without pay records or other personnel records on all similarly situated people who were in the same location or department at that time. The EEO/AA Module can keep such records against future eventualities, and this feature is usually an integral part of the module.

### 2.2.10. Training Module

For organizations that spend considerable time and money on training programs for employees, a training module can be very useful or even essential. Information such as course attended, date taken, grade, and cost are some of the items that can be recorded. These data are extremely useful in an organization's attempt to ascertain the overall cost versus effectiveness of training. Also, the data are required for EEO compliance in some instances.

Possible duplication of training programs can be uncovered with this module, along with the ability to capture and display training for consideration in employee development and career pathing. For companies venturing into new product areas and new ventures, these data can also help track which employees have attended the prescribed training courses.

**CONCLUSION**

This chapter explored the basic concepts involved in the definition of an HRIS — "a computer-based method for collecting, storing, maintaining, retrieving, and validating certain data needed by an organization about its employees, applicants, and former employees" — and discussed the features of the most common modules built to perform major human resource functions.

The basic concepts that must be realized in order to create a working HRIS are the construction of a data base, methods of data entry and retrieval, the Human Resource Information Center, and provisions for data quality. An HRIS with one of these key areas missing or deficient will not achieve its objectives, and the choices made by the organization for realizing each of these related concepts in the system will determine the nature and capabilities of the individual HRIS.

Ten major functions of personnel work are identified as suitable for HRIS modules or building blocks, although it is strongly recommended that developers in the first phase attempt to build no more than a Basic Personnel Module and two or three support modules from this list. In any case, only the largest organizations with the most robust personnel departments would want to install all these modules separately.

There can be some variance or overlap in the modules, depending on how the organization views personnel functions. For instance, the training information can easily be incorporated into the Human Resource Utilization Module if the organization elects to do so. Or the salary administration function may be so complex that a company must construct a separate module for it.

A virtually endless array of combinations and variations is possible and acceptable in the final HRIS, and decisions on the size and number of modules will be made by the design team, based on the organization's needs and resources.

# Part II
# First Steps: Preparation and the Needs Analysis

# 3
# Getting Started: Guidelines for the Proposal to Management and Establishment of the Project Team

The first objective in the development of an HRIS is to gain the support of top management to conduct a Needs Analysis of the organization's personnel problems and requirements. This chapter deals with some of the most important preliminary considerations that should be attended to before making a formal presentation to gain that support. It covers the elements of the Management Proposal and presents guidelines for structuring a Project Team that will coordinate and manage the installation of a successful HRIS.

In most of the several dozen HRIS installations with which I have been involved from the start, management's initial reactions to the idea basically boil down to this: "Why should we install it?" and "If we don't, what will happen?" The answers sought are usually in dollars and cents and call for the kind of cost/benefit analyses described in Chapter 11.

Specific cost savings and profits attributable to new or revamped computerized personnel systems, as important as they may be, should not be the only factors reflected in the proposal to management to proceed to the next stage. The HRIS proposal is not likely to make sense to organizational decision makers unless it also reflects a basic understanding of the organization itself, presents in a logical manner the components and sequence of the overall project, and specifically addresses what is to be done in the Needs Analysis.

## 3.1. UNDERSTANDING THE ORGANIZATION

Obviously, the proposed HRIS should match the organization in size and configuration. Getting started effectively requires that the Project Team also understand how the company operates and how Personnel supports management, and this is not always readily discernible. It entails knowing what business a company is really in and its management structure and also knowing the identification of key operating divisions, personnel information flow, the place of personnel in the organization, and a view of potential growth areas in the organization and personnel functions in the future.

The structure of a company has obvious implications for the HRIS configuration. Whether a company is highly centralized or decentralized will have a direct bearing on the system's structure. A centralized organization is likely to require that all input come directly to a headquarters location for processing and approval; decentralized companies may favor field input groups or satellite information centers. Or a company may be moving toward greater autonomy for field managers and may wish a decentralized HRIS to reflect this. To suggest an HRIS that contradicts organizational structure or runs counter to current policy direction will doom the project to failure at the outset.

Less obviously, the place of the Human Resources or Personnel department in the organization — its posture and strength — will affect the initial Team proposal. If the personnel department is strong in the company, there is a good chance that the project may be approved without an exhaustive fact-finding study or without a detailed cost/benefit analysis. In the absence of a strong personnel executive, however, the Project Team takes an unnecessary risk if it does not provide a well-documented business case during the proposal stage.

Regardless of the strength of Personnel, the chief executive officer (CEO) will expect the Project Team to make a strong case for the system, and in this regard the leading question invariably centers on economics. The question the CEO will ask is, "How much money are we suggesting should be spent on this project?"

The answer to that question will essentially determine the amount of time and effort the Project Team can spend on the preparatory stages of the systems development process: for a $5,000 system, not much analysis may be required; for a $500,000 purchase, the CEO expects quite a bit; and for a three-year, multimillion-dollar project, preparatory analysis must be appropriately extensive.

An important related issue that is often overlooked by most system developers is the current profitability of the company. If money has been scarce over the past year or two and the future looks no better, it is important that the Team know that the selling of the HRIS may be more difficult than it would be in better times.

Another general factor to be considered is the relationship the organization has with its employees. If the company has little or no history of caring about its employees or investing in their development — as is sometimes the case in labor-intensive industries, where workers are little more than "warm bodies" — the Project Team will either have to buck this trend or base its case solely on the cost-saving aspects of the HRIS project. On the other hand, if employee relations are important, the Team should miss no opportunity to stress the help the system can give the personnel organization in serving employee interests, especially in such areas as career development, career pathing, and overall human resource accounting.

Internal labor force trends should also be considered in order to see whether the work force is growing or shrinking and in what subgroups this movement is taking place. Because the HRIS can be used to analyze turnover rates or identify employees for job placement or training, there may be some hidden justification for HRIS installation that would be overlooked without this analysis. In a no-growth or shrinking company, for example, the precise identification of potentially surplus workers is essential to planning for layoff (or nonlayoff) programs.

In the initial process of developing a concise statement of HRIS benefits to an organization, a wide range of organization-specific factors other than dollars and cents should be considered. Each company differs. For some, the paramount benefits may be increased productivity and improvements in personnel administration; for others, the main goal may be improved morale resulting from better job placement or more effective force planning and better-informed decision making.

Because it is vital that the Project Team know how the HRIS will function to help management, the Team must understand how the organization functions and the place Personnel will have in that organization — what it has been as well as what top management may want it to become in the future.

A corollary guideline that is related to understanding the dynamics of the organization before making an initial HRIS development proposal is that you should know who in the company is the ultimate decision maker who will approve or reject the project. Knowing this, the Project Team can concentrate efforts on the kinds of questions this person is likely to ask. If the key individual is the Comptroller, questions are likely to be more financially oriented than if the person is from Marketing or Production. Particularly in the early meetings and presentation, the team should be especially well prepared for its most influential listeners.

## 3.2. UNDERSTANDING THE PROJECT: HRIS DEVELOPMENT STAGES

Before proceeding to the issues involved in generating management support for the proposed HRIS (Section 3.3), how to make a proposal to management (3.4), and how to establish an effective Project Team (3.5), an overall view of what is entailed in HRIS development is presented here. It is important that the total project be understood — at least in outline — by those involved in the proposal phase of the project.

Developing a computer-based personnel system or HRIS is no easy task. It requires a mixture of conceptual and mechanical activities, some for computers to perform and some for people. These activities range from the development of edit criteria, retrieval programs, and data entry routines to clerical and policy aspects of privacy and security management.

Over the past ten or fifteen years, however, the author has played a part in the evolution of a discipline that now enables the system developer to proceed in an orderly fashion. The approach outlined here and developed in detail in subsequent chapters has greatly reduced mistakes and misunderstandings that occurred when personnel systems were built mainly by trial and error.

To develop an effective HRIS, work should be divided into seven stages: Proposal to Management, Needs Analysis, System Specifications, System Design, System Development, Installation and Conversion, and Evaluation.

The stages will vary in length and activity makeup according to the project at hand. Also, if policy is to purchase a system from a vendor, certain stages can be reduced in terms of time and money.

However, each stage must be finished and finished in order. If a given stage is missed or not done in order, the HRIS will not function, or at least will not function to its full potential, and will ultimately be considered to have failed.

Each of these stages will develop a deliverable product that management can review and use to make a decision about whether to continue the HRIS developmental process.

1. *Proposal to Management.* The proposal stage is concerned with the broad problem or problems facing the organization and is directed toward a decision to investigate further. A concept may have taken shape, and therefore overall system parameters and a rough cost/benefit analysis may possibly be required. Policy issues are usually discussed, and impacts are stated broadly. This stage ends with a suggestion to management that an analysis of needs should be conducted.
2. *Needs Analysis.* This stage is directed to transforming the broad problem statement outlined in the proposal stage into objectives and user specifications. The primary goals of this stage are to find the true problems and develop methods and strategies that respond to those needs. The Needs Analysis will cover costs and benefits, alternatives in development, system inputs and outputs from a broad perspective, a description of the data flow and major interfaces, types of data elements, security measures, and performance specifications. Trade-offs are discussed along with development options, and management can then determine on the basis of this information whether to proceed with development or change or discontinue the project.
3. *System Specifications.* This stage defines the exact content of the system from the standpoint of the user. The basic functions of the system are described in as much detail as necessary to determine the processing routines. The final products of the system are outlined, as are all required inputs. All required manual functions are also specified. The accuracy levels and time frames that the system must meet are laid out by the users. All control,

privacy, and security measures must also be determined. The user states what he or she wants in this stage, and objectives are translated into output reports and analyses. This is the stage where the users lay out in as precise a manner as they can exactly what the HRIS will do and how it will operate.

4. *System Design.* In the design stage, the entire system is detailed with enough specificity that all functions can be examined and all programs outlined. It is in this stage that the system's designers determine how the HRIS will meet the objectives stated in the Specifications stage. Computer programs are designed, and the exact software and hardware configurations are determined. Also, delineation between human and machine functions is made, and appropriate user documentation and training programs are identified and course material developed.

5. *System Development.* The computer programs are coded in this stage. The human functions are also developed in the form of position specifications or job write-ups. All parts of the system are fully tested with data supplied by the user. Training programs are developed, and trials are performed with dummy test situations as well as live data.

6. *Installation and Conversion.* After successful testing in a laboratory environment, the HRIS is installed in the user organization and tested again before the trial run, using dummy data. The HRIS is then trialed, using live data, while the manual or other current system is being similarly run in a parallel mode, until the new system is thoroughly tested. Records are created, reports are run, and people are trained. Adjustments are made; and when it is practical, the old system is discontinued.

7. *Evaluation.* The performance of the new HRIS is measured against the system objectives that were developed in the earlier stages. The system's run costs, report accuracy and timeliness, and other operational characteristics are evaluated and reported back to management. If necessary, alterations and modifications can be made at this time to adjust the performance of the system.

Regardless of the project's time frame, all the above stages must be conducted. They may be shortened to weeks or even days in some instances, but it is vital to go through the stages in a sequential fashion.

Some overlap is acceptable, as are refinements in outputs and inputs as one proceeds. Milestones should be developed in the project life cycle to see that each stage is conducted in a thorough manner.

## 3.3. GENERATING INFORMED INTEREST AND SUPPORT

To help assure that your proposal to management will receive the knowledgeable attention it deserves, several methods of generating interest in HRIS concepts and an improved understanding of potential benefits can be pursued by the Project Team in advance of the proposal. These educational efforts will not only improve the initial proposal's chances of approval by top management, they should help to widen support for the system in its early stages, when the Team will be asking for a great deal of time and resources "on faith."

The trick here is to find out whether the top personnel officials understand the benefits an HRIS can provide sufficiently to justify a deeper look into the suitability of such a system. Should the Team be unsure, some planning for exposure is in order, and this can be accomplished in several ways.

*Company Visits.* If visits can be arranged with other companies or organizations that have personnel systems in operation, this can be the most effective means of demonstrating the benefits of an HRIS. Top officers can see exactly how the system is used and hear of its benefits from their counterparts. Arranging such visits to organizations that have demonstrably effective personnel systems should not be hard, since these companies are likely to be somewhat proud of their systems and willing to show them off to outsiders.

On the negative side, company visits usually provide a presentation that is less professional than you might wish. Systems supervisors are not necessarily polished speakers, for example. Also, there is a tendency among those already involved in HRIS operations to want to talk about file design, access times, and other technicalities of operation, when all you and your people want to hear about is potential applications.

Another problem is that the internal group may be preoccupied with the problems in their system and be brutally frank about bugs that remain to be worked out. Some of this is inevitable, but if it is adequately balanced by information on the overall benefits, it can reinforce rather than detract from this approach to management education.

Despite the drawbacks, my experience is that visits to organizations with personnel systems in operation are the best way to generate informed support of the HRIS at this stage, which may be crucial to getting the project off the ground. Management will realize that they are getting an honest presentation from an unbiased source.

*HRIS Courses.* Another effective way of generating interest in an HRIS is a training course in which the principles and concepts of personnel information systems are explained. Industry groups such as the American Management Associations (AMA) conduct such seminars and conferences, in which the basics are presented and guest lecturers cover selected topics in greater depth. A case study by a company that has had an HRIS installed is presented in the AMA course, and the stress is inevitably on the benefits of the system.

Although a great deal of general information is delivered in such courses, a drawback is that they usually take three or four days, and top management people will not devote that much time to such an activity. Usually they send a subordinate. The attendee comes back from the course with the recommendation that an HRIS be installed, but the top manager has still not seen or heard a presentation from anyone outside the organization. The impact of a third party is missing, and a disinterested outsider extolling the benefits of an HRIS (as in a visit to another company) can be very persuasive.

*Vendor Presentations.* A third method of spurring interest is to arrange for management to attend a presentation by a vendor in the business of marketing and installing personnel information systems. Most consulting firms and software suppliers in this field are able to present their products in the most favorable light and can modify the presentation to suit a potential client.

Such presentations are a way for top management to get a brief (usually an hour or so), professionally delivered pep talk from a knowledgeable source. Questions about what systems cost and how long they take to install will be raised and answered on the spot. Marketing material will be distributed and may be analyzed while the vendor is present.

The most obvious drawback here is that only the positive aspects of an HRIS are heard, and usually only one vendor's approach and wares can be heard at one time. It is often on the strength of a vendor's proposal that the HRIS project is sold, however; often it is sold and the vendor is selected at this stage. Thus, vendor selection becomes all-important. There is an effective method for vendor selection, to which Chapter 12 is devoted, but this requires application of a set discipline in the screening of a number of vendors, with any final selection delayed until after the requirements are known. For purposes of general education and to elicit wider interest among top managers, however, a single vendor's presentation may be useful. It is certainly the easiest method to arrange.

There are, of course, other ways to generate the informed interest of personnel heads and other top managers in the prospective HRIS; trade publication articles, attendance at conventions, or even conversations over lunch can be effective. The objective is to ensure that an HRIS proposal made to management will be received with interest and acted upon favorably. Whether this requires further educational efforts on your part or whether that education should be in the form of a four-day seminar or a recent reprint from *Personnel Journal* is up to the Team to decide.

## 3.4. MAKING THE PROPOSAL TO MANAGEMENT

The penultimate leg in the process of getting started, before the establishment of a permanent Project Team that will coordinate the Needs Analysis, is the proposal to management to gain approval to continue further. This proposal should be presented to either the CEO or Senior Personnel Officer, depending on the size and structure of the organization. It may be made orally or in writing. The form of the presentation is left to the Project Team to decide as long as the key points outlined in the sample below are covered.

As a rule, it is important to avoid asking for a commitment and approval for the entire HRIS project at this time. Rather, the proposal should be limited to the next phase of the installation cycle, the Needs Analysis. This limited approach is better for two basic reasons: It protects the company from committing sizable resources without sufficient analysis, and it protects you personally if you are wrong. And as a practical matter, management at this stage is far more likely to approve a three-month study at a cost of $15,000 than a twenty-four-month project costing $800,000.

From your perspective, it is important to remember just where you are in the development cycle. No real analysis or fact finding has yet been done that would substantiate user needs and problems. Therefore, what type of personnel system can be proposed to management? None, in reality. All one can do at this stage is propose that management permit the Team to begin the Needs Analysis, investigate various developmental alternatives, pinpoint expected costs, and outline potential benefits.

In this last regard, it is crucial that one does not oversell or promise too much at this stage. My experience is that personnel people at this stage are often overly enthusiastic and bill the system as the answer to all manpower problems and personnel difficulties. Historically and as far as we can see ahead, it's not.

An HRIS will not tell an organization whom to hire, whom to fire, or whom to promote. It is more accurately regarded as an information pool of data about people. It is a tool to help the organization manage its human resources more effectively — nothing more. Used correctly, the system will help people do their jobs more efficiently, but care should be taken to avoid suggesting that it actually performs functions such as managerial selection or staffing. The key idea here is to propose a system for improved decision-support data.

The proposal to management should be limited to issues involved in the investigation of data and information and not attempt to offer solutions to specific personnel problems. The ingredients of the proposal, shown in the sample below, should cover (1) what you want to accomplish, (2) why you want to do it, (3) who will do it, (4) when it will be done, and (5) how much it will cost.

*Proposal Ingredients: Sample.* This is a proposal to management to conduct the next stage of HRIS development, the Needs Analysis.

The Needs Analysis is an analysis of the information and reporting needs of the organization with respect to personnel data.

1. *What the Needs Analysis will accomplish*
    - Determination of an integrated data plan for the organization, laying out which specific steps can and should be taken to consolidate and improve personnel data processing.
    - Determination of what information is needed to meet current and projected internal and governmental reporting requirements.
    - The costs versus the benefits of automating the employee information stream and installing an HRIS.
    - The adequacy of the current organizational structure in Personnel and Payroll to meet information demands.
    - Which specific areas of personnel need to be automated now and which can wait — objectives of the system and how an HRIS will help achieve them.
    - How the suggested HRIS would interface with the current payroll system and other current systems.
    - What other companies of similar size and structure have done in this area.
2. *Why you want to conduct a Needs Analysis*
    - To ensure compliance with current and projected government reporting requirements (EEO/AA, ERISA, OSHA, and other areas including state and local requirements), which have outstripped the capacities of manual record keeping in many organizations in recent years.
    - To meet growing organizational needs for employee information in salary administration, human resources planning, career placement, benefits, and other areas of increasing concern.
    - To use technology to reduce costs, in view of the fact that although clerical costs have continued to increase in recent years, computer-related costs have held constant or dropped.
    - To help identify priorities, or those areas of personnel which need the most help first.
    - To suggest the best method of organizing and structuring the entire personnel information-gathering and reporting system — a long-range view of the personnel data function.

3. *Who will conduct the Needs Analysis*
   - An HRIS Project Team will be established under the direction of (name of Project Leader) of the Personnel Department. Representatives of the Payroll and Information Systems Departments will participate as Project Team members.
   - (Optional, according to applicability) Name of outside vendor or consultant who will assist in this project, with specific HRIS "credits" in other companies or brief resume of HRIS installation experience.
4. *When the Needs Analysis will be conducted*
   - The Needs Analysis will be completed within 90 to 120 days of the establishment of the Project Team, and the Team should be in place by (exact date).
5. *How much the Needs Analysis will cost*
   - Total approximate costs of the Needs Analysis will be ($__), made up of salary expenses of ($__) and expected consultant fees of ($__).

As can be seen, the proposal to management identifies any outside consultants and vendors that may be used so that there will be no surprises later.

In addition to the above ingredients, the proposal may elaborate on any potentially sensitive areas that may be pursued in the Needs Analysis, such as the relation of the new system to Payroll, or executive compensation functions.

After the approval of your proposal to management, work may begin on the final stage preparatory to conducting the Needs Analysis: the selection of the Project Team.

## 3.5. ESTABLISHING THE PROJECT TEAM

Before the Needs Analysis, the main emphasis has been to understand the general contours of the organization and its personnel needs and to convey to key decision makers generally what automated personnel systems are all about. The purpose has been simply to persuade management to proceed to the next stage.

Once that decision has been made, some semblance of permanent organization must take shape, and responsibilities must be assigned for the conduct of the Needs Analysis and, it is hoped, to carry the project through to final completion. Up to now, most of the preparatory activities in the "getting started" phase have involved the kind of work that can be performed part-time and have not always required people skilled in the personnel systems field. Now, however, user requirements must be spelled out specifically, and problems to be dealt with and user needs must be documented in a formal fashion that will permit analysis.

This type of work will require the establishment of a Project Team — a group of several specialists committed to full participation in the Needs Analysis under the direction of a Project Leader.

The Project Team will be required to conduct the analysis of the organization, document their findings, and make broad recommendations to management. The qualities of the Project Leader must be somewhat special in HRIS development. As in any group, the leader's guidance and direction are important to success, but the HRIS Project Leader must also be able to make vital trade-offs and important decisions about the project as work progresses.

*Project Leader Attributes.* As a rule, the HRIS Project Leader should be from the Personnel Department. The system is being designed for and paid for by the Human Resources Department, and therefore the leadership role in its installation should be assumed by the "client" entity in the organization — Personnel.

Furthermore, the most essential attribute that an HRIS Project Leader can have is intimate knowledge and understanding of the personnel activities in the organization. This knowledge of personnel is required to properly analyze the various jobs being performed, to trace the information flow, to examine the utilization of reports and records in the personnel environment, and to knowledgeably assess the required changes. Without this knowledge, accurate evaluation of human resources priorities and needs may be a chancy business, and the risks increase of developing a system that will not address the true needs of the organization.

It is not necessary that the Project Leader understand each detail of all personnel routines and tasks; an encyclopedic grasp of these specifics is rare in any case. The Project Leader should, however, possess working knowledge of how the various human resources groups work; how they fit into the overall management scheme; how information such as new hire dates, salary changes, and so on flow within the company; and an appreciation of what the most pressing problems are that the new HRIS is expected to correct.

Another essential quality of the Project Leader is an ability to identify with and understand the problems of top management. Without this attribute at the top of the Project Team, work can become bogged down in such relatively minor matters as solving routine clerical problems at the expense of larger objectives. The Project Leader must be able to take management's perspective and focus attention on the fact that this will be a system that helps managers solve personnel administration problems, not just a clerical support system.

Although it may be too much to ask that the Project Leader have a comprehensive grasp of the latest in data processing technology, the project will be greatly facilitated if he or she has a sound understanding of the principles of data processing, specifically systems design and data base administration. This technical knowledge is especially helpful when situations arise in which the data system organization's view of such technical matters as file and data base structure seem to conflict with the wishes of the users. Although EDP technology is changing so rapidly that it is difficult to keep abreast of the options open to systems designers, the Project Leader should be well enough informed to "keep everyone honest" in discussions of technical options and be able to challenge the data systems organization if they express an inability to comply with personnel needs in system design.

Finally, it is vital that the Project Leader understand the overall HRIS development process, as outlined earlier in this chapter (Section 3.2, "Understanding the Project: HRIS Development Stages"). Knowledge of the stages through which a system must evolve and the requirements for completing each stage are absolutely essential to effective project control and management. Without this, the Project Leader cannot make manpower assignments, plan for work activities, set milestones, or otherwise plan and schedule the project. The Leader must also recognize the need to produce quality specifications for the system developers so that the product will reflect the users' requirements. This deep understanding of the emphasis for precise definitions is a rare but needed quality. These project management skills will become increasingly important as the HRIS project moves toward conversion and installation.

*Project Team Composition.* The composition of the Project Team that will carry out the Needs Analysis and later stages is a subject that deserves far more attention than it usually gets. The individuals in this Team will in many ways determine the characteristics and properties of the final HRIS. The fate of your system is in their hands. Care should be taken to select the best available individuals from the various areas that must be represented on the Team.

In addition to people from the Personnel Department, including, we will assume, the Project Leader, the Team must have representatives from the Data Systems Organization or its equivalent. The Data Systems people will have to develop the technical aspects of the HRIS and run it on their computers or purchase computer time outside.

Also, it is usually advisable to have the Payroll Group on the Team as well as any other key staff members who are involved in systems development or auditing. In addition, key personnel users (EEO or compensation) may wish to participate actively if they are to be major beneficiaries of the HRIS.

Representatives from a field office or branch location of the organization may also be helpful in assuring that proper consideration is given to the problems and needs of all parts of the organization.

The most important overall objective in selecting a Project Team is to keep the Team balanced between technical and personnel disciplines. If there is a weakness in either personnel skills or data processing expertise, the Needs Analysis will almost certainly be deficient in key areas and therefore should not be undertaken.

In other words, the final establishment of the Project Team should be postponed until the right mix of skilled people with the proper background has been found and assigned to the project. Otherwise, the Needs Analysis may point the way to less-than-adequate solutions or to solving entirely wrong problems and therefore doom the project from the start.

**CONCLUSION**

Before making the initial proposal to management to install a new or improved HRIS — actually a proposal to commit the funds and resources needed to accomplish the Needs Analysis — a number of general factors should be considered. Top management may require the kind of cost/benefit analysis outlined in Chapter 11, but in any case the proposal must reflect a basic understanding of the organization and its purpose and the role of Personnel now and in the future and should present in a logical manner the overall sequence of stages of the total project, with some detail about what is to be done in the Needs Analysis.

This chapter presents guidelines for improving the understanding needed to make an effective proposal, methods of improving the climate of management opinion about automated personnel systems generally, and the kinds of information that should be included in the proposal. When approval has been obtained to proceed to the Needs Analysis stage, a Project Leader with certain qualifications can be selected and a Project Team established that will carry the HRIS through to completion.

# 4
# Conducting the Needs Analysis

When the steps discussed in Chapter 3 have been accomplished successfully, you are ready to proceed with the Needs Analysis. The chief results of the preparatory steps are that management's approval has been obtained, the Project Leader has been named, and the Project Team is established.

In the Needs Analysis, the Project Team will be determining the needs and problems of potential HRIS users in the organization and deciding which personnel functions will or will not be included in this phase of system development. The ultimate objective of the Needs Analysis is to identify the boundaries, interfaces, and scope of the system being proposed, determine which application modules will be needed, and arrive at an integrated Human Resources Information Plan.

The essential elements of an effective Needs Analysis are shown below. Because each project is unique, one or two items on the Needs Analysis Stages list may not apply to your project, but usually each is necessary. They are listed here in more or less consecutive order, although many can be performed at the same time, as discussed later in this chapter.

A word about interviews: Much attention is given here to the procedural aspects of user interviews — how to prepare Team members, what to cover, how to elicit answers, and the organization of results — apparently mechanical matters that "everybody knows." My experience has shown otherwise; interviewing technique is crucial. That technique includes adequate preparation so that the interviewer knows specifically what to ask and what materials to gather, decisions about whom to interview and in what setting, and an overall set of documentation procedures that will assure the consistency, quality, and relevance of the final results. It is virtually impossible to perform the analysis needed to recommend the best possible HRIS configuration from interview results that are incomplete or uneven. When the interviewing process has been done right, on the other hand, the Team will arrive at an overall approach and a set of recommendations without too much dissension, and the Needs Analysis Report will practically "write itself."

This checklist covers the overall steps that must be completed in the Need Analysis, in approximately this order:

### Needs Analysis Stages

1. Preparing for the Needs Analysis activities
2. Developing the objectives of the analysis
3. Functionalizing the areas of personnel
4. Preparing an overall schedule
5. Developing interviewing techniques and collection materials
6. Visiting other HRIS installations and outside information sources
7. Holding user interviews and obtaining user needs
8. Getting samples of reports, forms, and user instructions
9. Examining current systems operations and data flow
10. Analyzing the collected information
11. Deriving several methods of solving user problems and satisfying user needs
12. Identifying other considerations, such as auditing control, privacy, and security requirements
13. Developing any cost justification and benefit ratios
14. Selecting the best alternative in terms of user requirements, impact, and economics
15. Developing the conceptual framework and overall systems configuration, including the data processing environment necessary to support the recommended approach
16. Meeting with top management to discuss findings and conclusions
17. Issuing the Needs Analysis Report.

## 4.1. OBJECTIVES WILL GUIDE SCHEDULE PREPARATION

The first task of the Project Leader in undertaking the Needs Analysis is to organize and schedule the Team's resources and time for this stage. It is axiomatic that organization of work should be based on the objectives of that work, rather than on arbitrary constraints or preconceived concepts or procedural routines, so that the guidelines presented here are general and flexible rather than specific and ironclad.

It makes no difference, for example, whether the Team's work is scheduled according to the precepts of the Critical Path Method (CPM), Project Evaluation and Review Technique (PERT), bar charts, or some other methodology. The underlying logic of CPM and PERT planning and scheduling is important: tasks or activities need to be isolated and put in the proper order or necessary sequence. But the preceding question in planning the Needs Analysis for HRIS installation is, What are the objectives?

All work must be directed toward the satisfaction of Needs Analysis objectives, and in a sense these objectives represent a "moving target." They will change as the Project Team moves into the information-gathering stages of the Needs Analysis and as priorities are defined more clearly by users. Also, the rule that a new HRIS should not be asked to "do everything at once, be all things to all people" should be borne in mind here. This is crucial to another prerequisite of scheduling, the functionalizing of personnel activities, and assignment of priorities among the tasks that the HRIS modules will be built to perform.

Because each HRIS installation is unique, the objectives of the Needs Analysis may include only some of the reasons listed below or may encompass all of these and others specific to your organization's needs. And even though the objectives may change or shift in relative importance as the Needs Analysis proceeds, some sort of statement of purpose based on these possible objectives should be formulated as early as possible for scheduling purposes.

*Possible Needs Analysis Objectives*

- To develop an overall Human Resources Information Plan.
- To assess how well the current personnel system is functioning.

## 54  II/FIRST STEPS: PREPARATION AND THE NEEDS ANALYSIS

- To determine particular personnel information problems, identify user needs, and develop objectives for the HRIS.
- To make more precise estimates of the costs of developing and installing a computerized personnel system.
- To identify the potential benefits of the proposed HRIS and quantify them where possible.
- To examine the impact of HRIS installation on existing systems used by the organization, especially personnel systems and the payroll system.
- To develop a conceptual outline of what the HRIS will look like, how it will work, and how many modules will be needed.
- To identify the major inputs, outputs, processes, and types of data elements required.
- To examine alternative developmental options and recommend the best approach for this HRIS.
- To document the Needs Analysis findings of the Project Team in such a way that the findings can be reviewed by management and also serve as useful information during the System Specification stage.

There may be other objectives as well, but this set should be sufficient to enable the Project Leader to begin the work of connecting the tasks of the Needs Analysis to objectives. For example, the objective "Identify user needs" will be met by interviewing users and eliciting their problems and needs; the objective "Identify potential benefits" will also be partly accomplished through user questioning, along with an analysis of the current personnel operation compared with the proposed system.

### 4.2. ADMINISTRATIVE DETAILS AND THE NEEDS ANALYSIS SCHEDULE

Because the Project Team will operate in a task force environment, actually functioning as a separate department for a period of time, all the activities and needs normally associated with a department — from funding to manpower planning — must be considered by the Project Leader. Central to this stage is knowing what activities must take place and when they should occur so that manpower can be assigned and specific tasks can be assigned to each team member; this is essentially what goes into the Needs Analysis schedule. This Project Team will become the management and project control device over the HRIS, and proper attention to the structure of the HRIS is crucial.

Not to be overlooked at this stage are the administrative details that must be attended to if the Team is to function smoothly: data base or personnel training may be necessary for certain team members, statistical or data processing help may be needed along the way, and clerical support must be planned for. Depending on the organization and the scope of the project, various kinds of logistical assistance may be needed by the "separate department" that is the Project Team, and this requires some sort of working schedule.

Most important, however, the schedule must be directly related to the objectives of the Needs Analysis. These objectives will dictate the actual tasks that have to be performed by identifying the size, scope, and boundaries of the system.

*Functionalizing Personnel Activities.* To establish which activities will be necessary in the Needs Analysis and schedule accordingly, a preliminary "scoping down" of system objectives may be necessary. This may seem a bit presumptuous at this stage — involving as it does decisions about which of the personnel functions shown in Figure 4A are more important than others — but it must be done to devise a workable Needs Analysis schedule based only on the installation of an HRIS that can be implemented and will be funded by management.

- Labor Relations
- Group Insurance
- Pension Administration
- Profit Sharing
- Job Evaluation
- Salary Administration
- Safety
- Medical
- Employment
- Staffing
- Management Development
- Training
- Human Resources Planning
- EEO and Affirmative Action
- Relocation
- Attendance Control
- Assessment and Testing
- Tuition Refund
- Information and Data
- Career Planning

**Figure 4A. Functional Areas of Personnel Example (Not Prioritized)**

Remember, to computerize all personnel record-keeping tasks at once is impossible. Decisions must be made about which functions of personnel will and will not be included in the HRIS. One reason why the Project Leader should have a personnel background is that decisions will have to be made during the Needs Analysis and later about the relative importance of different areas of personnel and the priorities of different users, which determine the modules needed to get the system under way.

In functionalizing personnel activities, the Project Team should endeavor to list all the personnel functions that are currently being performed and "prioritize" them from an information impact standpoint. If this ranking from most important to least important is not possible, at least the functions can be grouped into three or four categories, ranging perhaps from "very important" to "not very important."

The point is that the functions must be reduced to a level at which the work involved can be assigned to modules that will handle the functions. For example, the Wage and Salary Administration function may be too broad and vaguely defined an activity at this point to specify in HRIS requirements. Its priority, therefore, should probably be lowered.

Usually, however, Wage and Salary Administration is made up of two or three separable functions: Union Wage Agreements, Clerical Salary Administration, and Management Salary Administration, for example. Each subfunction can be defined as having its own set of inputs, rules and procedures, and reports or outputs. At this more clearly defined level, the Team can evaluate the needs and problems of each function and determine its priority. An example is shown in Figure 4B.

Obviously, the list that the Team draws up at this stage is a starter list, created to get a rough outline of Needs Analysis work such as the numbers of interviews and fact-finding missions required. It is to

- Group Insurance
- Plan Enrollment and Deductions
- Premium Calculation
- Beneficiary Designations
- Claims Verification

**Figure 4B. Subfunctions (Example)**

be hoped that the Team will find upon completion of this preliminary listing that there are some functions that should not be included in the HRIS right now.

Also, the ranking process may reveal that there are too many areas with the highest priority, and further information may have to be gathered to help with the necessary scoping down of the HRIS.

As a result of this work on personnel functions, the Team should have a good picture of where to concentrate its efforts, at least at the outset. The priorities may change during the interviews, but for now a schedule can be drawn up to begin the actual Needs Analysis.

*Preparing the Schedule.* Once the tasks of the Needs Analysis have been identified and a time frame allotted to each, the schedule for this stage of the project can be drafted. This schedule can be analyzed in light of available manpower and adjusted accordingly.

The first effort should be to lay out a workable schedule for the entire Needs Analysis stage, a generalized scheme such as Figure 4C:

| Activity (Hours) | 1 | 2 | 3 | 4 | 5 | 6 | 7 | 8 | 9 | 10 |
|---|---|---|---|---|---|---|---|---|---|---|
| Project Control (60) | ─────────────────────────────────── |
| Team Member Training (63) | ── |
| Objective Setting (56) | ── |
| Functionalizing Personnel (28) | ─ |
| Developing Material (21) | ── |
| Visits to Outside Companies (84) | ─ ─ ─ |
| Interviewing Users (105) | ───── |
| Obtain Reports and Forms (105) | ───── |
| Examine Existing Systems (140) | ───── |
| Analyze Information (210) | ─────── |
| Develop Options (105) | ───── |
| Determine Other Considerations (20) | ──── |
| Cost Benefits/Justifications (105) | ───── |
| Present to Management (56) | ─── |
| Write Report (227) | ── |

Total Hours (1385) = 80% Utilization
Assumptions 4-Person Project Team 35-Hour Week = 1,680 Available Hours

Figure 4C. Ajax Co. Needs Analysis Overall Schedule HRIS Projects (Shown in weeks from go-ahead)

Subschedules can then be drawn for each activity, or even each team member if desired, and key decision points can be shown.

Although each person has a different method of scheduling work, I generally start by matching up the work that must be performed with the time allotted, beginning with the desired completion date and working backward. Each task is estimated in terms of elapsed time and total time, and lines are drawn with beginning dates and ending dates shown for each distinct activity. Some work cannot be started until other tasks have been finished, and these dependencies are noted. Several activities can be going on concurrently, though, and this allows the project to move rapidly.

The only limitation with concurrent activities is that you may not have available a sufficient work force to conduct several tasks at once. Usually, though, people can work on more than one activity at a time, and the Team members should be encouraged to do so. In this way, better use can be made of their time, especially if they are temporarily held up on their primary tasks. Normally, there is never enough time to do all the work that may be required, and some trade-offs must be made.

There are few if any immutable laws to obey in this area except to endeavor to meet the final deadline if possible. This may require planning for contingencies. For example, the schedule may have to be adjusted to get to see all the required people. Also, the schedule will be dependent on the amount of help the Project Team receives. If it is staffed at four people rather than three, more can be achieved. In this regard it is wise to get exact commitments of Project Team members on their time availability and dates due back to their departments full-time.

It is also advisable to state all time in terms of elapsed-time quantities (i.e., days or weeks) rather than dates. In this way, once the go-ahead has been received, the dates can be added later. Also, not showing calendar dates gives you a bit more protection from management's indecision. For instance, you could show a schedule starting in January and ending in March. The January date is when you expect approval from management to begin. Management may not give their approval to begin the Needs Analysis until February, but they will still be thinking of March as the completion date. A safer way is to show it as a sixty- or ninety-day activity from the go-ahead, omitting any reference to calendar dates until the project is under way.

## 4.3. METHODS OF COLLECTING INFORMATION: PROS AND CONS

Some common ways of collecting user ideas and opinions and finding out how data flows include interviews, questionnaires, and direct observation. In conducting the Needs Analysis, all three methods have been used successfully, depending on circumstances and the type of information to be collected.

### 4.3.1. Interviews

The interview technique can be a useful method for gathering certain types of information. The two primary methods of conducting interviews are in person (face to face) and over the telephone.

Both methods have their strong and weak points, and each should be examined for suitability. In general, telephone interviews should be limited to a smaller number of questions. Longer interviews should be conducted face to face. The situations should be examined before you select a method. In all cases, the interviewers should be trained and the results recorded.

One overall factor to consider is that interviews in a Needs Analysis are usually classified into two major categories: management interviews and clerical interviews.

In the management interview, the questioner is free to direct the interview to obtain the information in the manner he or she sees fit. The questioner will choose the wording and order that seems most appropriate in the context of each interview. In addition, the Team member can ask questions relating to problems in the organization without having to worry about departing from a formal list of questions that must be asked in a preset order. The managers are asked to elaborate on situations that could be changed and comment on how they believe they could use the new HRIS. Examples of reports and analyses they might desire are noted, and the conversation should be steered toward asking for examples of the kinds of information managers need and problems they may be having with data.

The more itemized clerical interview will concentrate on the information-handling aspects of the job and will be more structured in terms of format and conduct. The interviewer will examine the various inputs, job steps, and volumes of data handled, with only minor emphasis placed on possible uses and analyses. It may be helpful to elicit comments on how the information flow could be improved, but more of the interview will be spent on standardizing the responses for later analysis of the information gathered.

*Personal Interviews.* The major advantages of the personal interview can be summarized as follows:

- They yield a very high response rate.
- Information tends to be more accurate, since unclear or ambiguous answers can be clarified.
- Respondents can react to visual material.
- Sensitive questions can be handled more effectively; observations of reactions are possible.
- The language used can be adapted to the level or education of the person being interviewed.

The major limitations of the personal interview are as follows:

- The costs and time associated with the personal interview are extremely high, especially over a large geographical area and/or user population.
- Interviewers may inject their personal biases into the report.
- Unless interviewers are properly trained, responses may be inaccurate and incomplete.

*Telephone Interviews.* The telephone interview generally forces shorter and simpler coverage. The major advantages of the telephone interview are as follows:

- It is the quickest method of collecting information.
- The refusal rate is usually low.
- The approach and questions are easy to standardize and easy to train for.
- The cost is low.

However, the limitations of telephone interviews are sometimes prohibitive. For example:

- Detailed questions are very difficult to ask.
- Opinions and attitudes are less likely to be given freely.

- Respondents have little orientation time.
- Visual material cannot be presented unless it is predistributed.
- Elaboration of responses is difficult; in-depth answers are hard to record.
- Misinformation is hard to check in short periods.

#### 4.3.2. Questionnaires

The self-administered questionnaire is widely used in surveys, but it has limited value in a Needs Analysis. It may have some application in eliciting opinions as to the level of service with respect to reports and records that the users now receive. This can assist the Project Team in the design of the system.

Some of the advantages of the Self-Administered Questionnaire are as follows:

- Low costs cover many users in a wide geographical area.
- Questions can be standardized.
- Respondents can reply at their own convenience.
- Sometimes it is easier to locate users by mail than by telephone.

Some disadvantages of the Self-Administered Questionnaire are as follows:

- The person who completes the questionnaire may not be the person to whom it is directed.
- Returns are low relative to interviews.
- Interpretations of questions vary among respondents.
- Questions must be simple.
- If the questionnaire is not completed correctly, it is very difficult to get corrections or more data.

#### 4.3.3. Direct Observation

Relevant information for some HRIS functions may be obtained by observing past or present behavior. Observational methods make it possible to record behavior as it occurs, and this can be extremely helpful. For example, observers may record the number of errors in recording salary or job changes rather than having to rely on the memories of clerks questioned later.

For a number of obvious reasons, behavior observation cannot be used effectively to obtain information about opinions, motivations, or level of knowledge. The information tends to be about "what" is happening rather than when or why it is happening. Except during design, tests, and trials of the project, when user instructions on input or retrieval are at issue, the direct observation method will not give the Team a complete understanding of why there are problems and what the needs are. The interview method is best for that.

Because of the suitability of the face-to-face interview technique to the Needs Analysis process, it is strongly recommended that this be used as the primary collection method.

## 4.4. PREPARING FOR THE INTERVIEWS

The key to the interview process is consistency. Each interviewer must use the same procedures to assure that the results of Needs Analysis interviews not only satisfy objectives but can be assimilated in the end. This means that each Team member conducting interviews must know what to look for, where to look, and what documents to review as well as know and follow prearranged interview procedures.

This section provides an overall checklist of preparatory activities that should be covered before interviews begin. Several of these areas, in particular the design of the interview form and the framing of specific questions, have extremely important impacts on the overall quality of the Needs Analysis and its later usability. They will be covered in greater detail in Section 4.5.

In general, these are the areas of preparation that should be covered before interviewing begins:

1. *Training.* All Team members should be trained in interviewing techniques such as those discussed in Section 4.5, regardless of their past experience as interviewers. As will be seen, the requirements of effective HRIS Needs Analysis information gathering are somewhat more scientific than most journalistic interviewing. In addition, be sure that the interviewers understand at least the broad outline of HRIS development stages, as discussed in Chapter 3, as well as organizational structure or any other factor important to meeting objectives at this stage.

2. *Team Member Schedules.* Each Team member should have a list of names of the people he or she will interview, when and where the interviews will take place, and the names of any others who will be sitting in.
3. *Interview Form.* A standardized form for listing each question and recording the interview is necessary. In this way each respondent is asked the same questions, phrased the same way, and the form can be used as a checklist to ensure that all questions have been asked. The interview form can also serve as a recording device to hold certain responses.
4. *Computer Analysis.* In certain situations, a computer program will be necessary to analyze the current record-keeping procedures. This is especially true for large employers who have many forms and records and wish to investigate how much duplication is taking place and what it costs. A program will be necessary to record each document that is used in the personnel process, where it was discovered, how many times it is used in a year, and what the costs are of handling it. This program can then list the annual costs and point up any redundancy or duplication that is taking place. It may show that an employee's records are being stored in many places in the organization and what this is costing the organization. Later analysis will show whether all these records are necessary.
5. *Interview Questions.* Any key questions that will be asked during the interviews will have to be phrased in the most beneficial, positive manner, as recommended in Section 4.5. These may range from organizational questions about the placement and staffing of the HRIS to questions on user problems or prospective uses of online facilities. To get information on the type and cost of the HRIS, most questions should concentrate on the needs, possible cost savings, responsiveness of the system, and alternatives available to the user if this area is not fully mechanized.
6. *Selecting the Interviewees.* All employees who are instrumental in generating, processing, or using personnel data should be interviewed. Clearly, this includes key personnel officers and managers as well as clerical and administrative personnel.

In addition, the heavy users of personnel data, such as executives in large departments and Accounting and Finance, should get a chance to talk to the Team. Managers of the Payroll Group, the Data Processing Organization, and managers of any other systems that will link up with the HRIS should certainly be interviewed.

Branch locations and representative field offices should also be visited to see how personnel data are stored and utilized.

7. *User Meeting.* A formal meeting for all those to be interviewed should be scheduled at each location where interviews will be held in order to set the proper climate for the fact-finding mission. The concepts of an HRIS should be explained along with a clear message that the interviews and observations are not a "time and motion study," nor will people lose their jobs as a result of the installation of an HRIS. It should be brought out that the intent is to do things in a more efficient manner. Some transfers and cost savings may result, but no one will be laid off. The purpose of the interview and materials you will be asking for should be reviewed. A member of senior management should open and/or close the meeting to publicly show endorsement of the Needs Analysis.

8. *Interview Schedules.* Each interviewee should be contacted, and a suitable time and place should be arranged for the interview. This should be followed up in writing, providing the name and title of the Team member who will be conducting the interview. A reminder can also be made of the materials that the respondent should have prepared for the interviews and the Team's analysis.

## 4.5. CONDUCTING THE INTERVIEWS

The primary purpose of the interview is to give the Project Team information on the design of the HRIS, and most of the meeting will be directed toward this end. However, a secondary reason for holding a face-to-face meeting is to brief the user on the concepts of an HRIS and to elicit possible ways an HRIS can help his or her function. Therefore, there is some benefit in allowing a bit of low-key marketing and concept-expansion to take place during the interview.

This section contains three parts: 4.5.1, "Interview Objectives," which defines the purpose of the Needs Analysis interview process;

4.5.2, "Guidelines for Interviewing," an outline of recommended procedures; and 4.5.3, "Key Information to Gather," which describes the essential kinds of information required to carry out the HRIS Needs Analysis.

#### 4.5.1. Interview Objectives

1. Elicit and record any user needs or problems that may exist in the function being examined.
2. List any solutions to these needs in specific and measurable terms.
3. Record any benefits that may accrue from the installation of an HRIS in this function.
4. Document all personnel data inputs, outputs, and processes that take place on the data in the organization and/or function.
5. Determine the impact the installation of an HRIS would have on the operation in terms of people.
6. Document the present overall flow of data to determine who does what and when they do it.
7. Determine who needs what data and when in the new HRIS environment.
8. Get ideas on how to improve the performance of the function.
9. Allow the interviewer to present a brief, low-key marketing presentation about the HRIS.
10. Gather samples of all forms, records, and reports now being utilized.
11. Obtain a copy of each personnel plan text, law, regulation, and corporate personnel practice.

#### 4.5.2. Guidelines for Interviewing

The following are some brief procedural guidelines that may assist the Team in conducting the Needs Analysis interviews.

A. *Site Selection*
   1. First choice in the respondent's office.
   2. Second choice is a neutral site, e.g., a conference room.

B. *Introduction*
   1. Introduce yourself.
   2. Explain the purpose of the study.
   3. Explain why the interviewee was chosen.
   4. Explain how the interview will be conducted.
   5. Assure the interviewee that answers will be held in confidence if he or she so wishes.
   6. Tell the interviewee that follow-up sessions may be necessary.
C. *Asking Questions*
   1. Formulate major questions ahead of time.
   2. Ask additional or clarifying questions when necessary.
   3. Use a conversational delivery.
   4. Use transition statements when changing topics.
D. *Getting Adequate Answers*
   1. Use probe technique (nondirective interviewing).
      a. Repeat the question.
      b. Ask neutral questions (e.g., "What do you have in mind?" "Why is that?" "In what ways?")
   2. Reassure the respondent of his or her ability to answer.
   3. Encourage the respondent to talk.
      a. Use brief assenting comments (e.g., "I see." "That's interesting.")
      b. Pause expectantly.
E. *Recording the Interview*
   1. Record the interviewee's answer in full and in his or her own words.
   2. Avoid summarizing or paraphrasing the answers.
   3. All interviewer's comments should be clearly marked.
   4. Cross-referencing should be used to call attention to remarks that pertain to earlier questions.
   5. Do not use electronic recording devices unless the interviewee clearly has no objection.
F. *Closing the Interview*
   1. Answer any questions respondent may have.
   2. Ask the respondent if there is anything else he or she wishes to add.
   3. Thank the respondent for cooperating and explain that some follow-up may be necessary.

### 4.5.3. Key Information to Gather

The following are the major kinds of information needed for most HRIS installations at this stage, with some guidelines on how to obtain it during the Needs Analysis interview. The answers to your questions in some of these areas will fundamentally shape the final HRIS, especially in the areas of information flow needs, present problems, and interfaces with other systems.

1. *Background Data on Respondent*
   | | |
   |---|---|
   | Name | Functional area |
   | Department | Title |
   | Length of service with company | Number of subordinates |
   | | Location of work |

2. *Personnel Information Kept Now by Function*
   | | |
   |---|---|
   | Employee group type | Reports and outputs |
   | Data elements | Reasons for keeping data |
   | Source | Volumes and frequencies |
   | Processes | |

   The interviewer should be sure to get actual copies of all input forms; the processes, formulas, and transformations that the group has; samples of all personnel records; and copies of all output reports produced by each function. The reasons for producing the reports should be probed until they are understood. The timing and urgency for each output should be explored, along with a statement of what the consequences are for missing a due date.

   If a computer program is to be run to analyze redundancy and duplication of effort, those forms need to be prepared by the respondent and collected by the interviewer. They can be prepared in advance of the interview to save time.

3. *Flow of Major Employee Events in the Organization*
   During the interviews it is important to be able to trace the current practice of changing the major employee data elements and events such as:
   | | |
   |---|---|
   | Salary | Regular/temporary status |
   | Job title | Termination |
   | Department code | New hire procedures |

4. *List of Problems by Function*
   Each problem should be identified by the interviewer. Care should be taken to list only real problems, not the mere symptoms of problems. The respondent should be asked if he or she knows how widespread the problem is and if he or she has any suggested solutions. Typical problems include:

   | | |
   |---|---|
   | Late reports | Inefficient use of administrative resource |
   | Inaccuracies in data | |
   | Time-consuming information search | Missing information |
   | | Expensive record keeping |
   | Duplicate data | Lack of analysis capability |
   | | Inconsistent administration |

   These are problems that an HRIS can usually help solve. The interviewers may have to assess where the problem originates, since it may not start in this function at all. For example, it may be that salary information or job information is inaccurate when it arrives in the Salary Administration area. This in turn will lead to incorrect reports and analyses and perhaps even result in employees being paid improperly. The problem, though, may actually be caused by poor clerical procedures in the field locations from which the flow originates.

   There will also be a class of problems that the HRIS cannot directly alleviate, and these must be noted as early as possible, lest a false impression remain with respect to the system's capabilities. Poor benefit plan design or inadequate pay policies usually are not problems that a personnel system can solve directly. True, the system will let you know the unpleasant facts more quickly, but more often than not personnel managers know them already. An HRIS will not change policies.

5. *Extent of Personnel Plan Stability by Function*
   It is extremely difficult to build an HRIS when the very personnel plans that are being automated are changing. The designers must build in routines and processes for a plan that will be different in the future. The result is that the HRIS module will be modified and selected parts will be discarded, all at considerable cost and user dissatisfaction.

The interviewer should ascertain whether the function has achieved a degree of stability that warrants computerization. If the plan will undergo significant changes and shifts in the future, perhaps it should not be included in the HRIS at this time.

6. *Respondent's Thoughts on HRIS Design and Data*
   Each respondent should be quizzed on his or her thoughts in such key design areas as:

   | | |
   |---|---|
   | Privacy and security | Information needed: Data |
   | Use of turnaround documents | Elements not now gathered |
   | User-oriented retrieval | Timing of data elements |
   | Human resources information center (HRIC) and data administration | Priority of functions that need to be computerized |
   | | Overall data plan |
   | Payroll interface | Impact on organization |

7. *Examples of Cost Saving and Justification*
   Finally, the interviewer should be sure to ask users directly whether they envision any examples of improvements or cost savings that have not come up previously. All possible avenues of HRIS justification should be explored in the interviews. Users may know of important examples that they would not put forward unless directly asked.

## 4.6. ANALYZING THE COLLECTED INFORMATION

The Project Team should now be in a position to analyze the information collected during the interviews and make decisions about the scope and boundaries of the HRIS. The system will probably have to be installed in phases, with only two or three modules representing the major personnel functions installed in the first phase. But at this stage the Project Team should be able to develop an overall view of the objectives and needs that the HRIS will ultimately cover.

At the same time the Team is categorizing and evaluating the needs and problems revealed by the Needs Analysis interviews, they will be making estimates of benefits and savings projected under the new HRIS. In many cases these are two sides of the same coin.

Before the Team develops broad system configurations, however, the information assembled during the Needs Analysis to date must be organized for analysis. To do this, the Project Leader needs to first make some assignments and arrangements, such as these:

- Determine who will work on which aspect of the analysis, e.g., by function, such as Benefits, EEO, or Salary Administration.
- Decide who will be responsible for the categorization of information.
- Determine how the costs versus benefits will be analyzed.
- Arrange for meetings with management at appropriate intervals to assess the impact of the findings.

In the process of analyzing and organizing the information at hand, three separable but overlapping kinds of activities should be taking place: *Needs Identification,* which requires a ranking of needs, problems, and objectives; *Solution Methods,* to match the organization's needs; and *Current Systems Review,* a continuing process that at this stage tells the Project Team what should and should not be replaced by the HRIS, trade-offs, and constraints.

*Needs Identification.* The Team should list all the needs and objectives uncovered in the interviews and attempt to "prioritize" them according to urgency or criticality. This obviously requires that the Team make some judgment decisions and assumes that the Team by now has some feel for the capabilities of the system as well as objectives. Despite any misgivings the Team may have about its ability to rank needs in perfect priority order at this point, this ranking is necessary. Then the Team is in a position to eliminate from the bottom of the list those problems which they feel should not be solved by the HRIS or should be put off to a later phase. As indicated earlier, the more problems eliminated from the list, the smaller the first phase of the project will be, and the easier to manage.

Both a first-phase list of needs and an overall ranking of the problems and objectives to be met by the final HRIS should be completed. The Team should know the outermost boundaries of the system to be ultimately installed, on the basis of information gathered in the Needs Analysis from users.

This checklist may be useful in ascertaining that all needs have been identified:

- How many problems have been solved?
- Have we satisfied any indirect needs, such as "keeping up with the Joneses?"
- Have we complied with all legal requirements?
- Will the quality of data be improved?
- Will Personnel Department performance be enhanced?
- Will we reduce or at least contain some costs?
- Have we provided for future growth and expansion?
- Have we an overall plan and are we working that plan?
- Have we considered the desires of upper management?

When the problems that cannot be wholly or even partially solved by the HRIS have been discarded, the remaining needs and objectives will define the system as ultimately envisioned by the Team. The next step, which obviously overlaps somewhat with Needs Identification, is to determine specific HRIS solutions relevant to the organization's problems.

*Solution Methods.* The solutions to users' problems and needs naturally vary with application situations. It cannot be stressed too strongly that HRIS solutions should match the specific needs of individual organizations and their personnel requirements. In matching needs and solutions, relevance is essential.

Also, the Current Systems Review discussed below will show the degree or extent to which one needs to go to build a specific solution into the HRIS. Sometimes a simple change in procedures is called for; other times a drastic revision must be undertaken.

Because of the importance of developing specific solutions to specific needs, the best that can be offered here is a comprehensive checklist of some of the areas where the Team might look for solutions:

- *Reports and Analyses.* Needed corporate or government reports will be provided by the HRIS where they are not available now or are deficient.
- *Organizational Shifts.* Functions can be shifted and regrouped to provide more efficient and responsible solutions to some problems.
- *Increased Accuracy of Data.* With better controls and audits, the quality of data will improve.

- *Training.* Users may not be sufficiently trained in data entry or retrieval, and the new HRIS can prevent this from being a problem.
- *Improved Timeliness of Data.* If it now takes an undue amount of time to receive and process data, the new system can improve the overall throughput. (Try to quantify by how much.)
- *Increased Security and Privacy.* Both technical and administrative controls can be built into the HRIS to improve the security and privacy of data.
- *New Data Elements.* Data that do not exist today will be in the new HRIS. Information that is not collected at present will be available for reports.
- *New Procedures.* Within limits, new ways of handling certain personnel functions can be introduced, or present methods can be streamlined, under the new HRIS.

Broadly speaking, the entire gamut of personnel activity capabilities offered by an effective HRIS offers solutions to various information-related problems. The choice of which of these tools to stress will depend on circumstances.

***Current Systems Review.*** Concurrent with the interviews, the Project Team should be assembling information on all existing computerized personnel and payroll systems. These systems, if any exist, should now be examined on the basis of inputs and outputs to determine whether the new HRIS can replace them wholly or in part.

The payroll system especially should be reviewed, since there are data elements in common that will be shared by the systems. Chapter 6 explores this important relationship in greater depth.

Each existing system that can be replaced represents potential savings in the areas of processing, storage, and annual maintenance expense. There are trade-offs, however. If a separate module or routine would have to be built into the HRIS to duplicate the existing report or system, the costs of the new and old methods would have to be compared and a decision made by the Team as to whether to replace that routine.

Constraints that will limit the Team in developing the HRIS should also be recognized and dealt with. One such constraint would be an edict to leave the payroll system untouched. Others are the more familiar budget limits, limited resources with which to build the system, or an early target date for installation. In whatever form, constraints represent "givens" that will materially affect the design and operation of the system, and they should be recognized and evaluated in the Needs Analysis stage.

Finally, information gathered from visits to other organizations' HRIS installations should be reviewed before the Team begins to shape the HRIS configuration best suited to the organization. The most useful information will in all likelihood be from a visit to the most similar organization with the most comparable problems. At a minimum, such visits can make the Team aware of some of the pitfalls on the road to installation and conversion.

## 4.7. DEVELOP BROAD SYSTEM CONFIGURATIONS

The next step for the Project Team is to develop a number of broad configurations for the new HRIS. One of these will later be selected by the Team and recommended to management; but to assure their comparability and value as "top choices," certain factors should be considered with great care.

These different configurations represent the best thoughts of the Project Team at this time; each should be a reasonable alternative worthy of consideration. Also, it is wise to remember that doing nothing is always an alternative to management, and this alternative should be addressed along with the others.

The various configurations, each in effect a different conceptual view of the HRIS, should then be compared with the existing system, and the differences should be measured. These differences represent the processes that would be changed under each configuration, and they should be closely examined for acceptability. Each new input and major output should be listed and discussed.

Overall, the Team should ensure that a sufficient number of problems and needs are addressed within each configuration to make that alternative viable. Too few problems solved means that the scope is not wide enough, and you may not be able to justify the cost and time of building the HRIS.

As noted earlier, however, too ambitious an undertaking will yield a project too large to develop or install in a reasonable time. Because of the nature of personnel functions and their diversity and number, this mistake is more common. A delicate balance will have to be sought by the Project Team so that each configuration solves enough problems and satisfies enough needs yet is not too large to build.

Should the Project Team have any difficulty suggesting alternative configurations, the following questions may help:

- Can current methods be changed to eliminate any steps?
- Can the current methods be operated at a lower cost?
- Can an existing computerized system be used within the HRIS concept?
- Would a change in manual procedures or additional training help the current system?
- Would a different method of data entry be appropriate?
- Would application of generalized retrieval techniques on an existing system be of assistance?
- Does the distributed processing concept lend itself to this application?

Once they are broadly shaped, the alternate configurations should be discussed with the Project Team until all advantages and disadvantages have been examined thoroughly. Quantitative analysis helps greatly in this process, as do techniques such as decision tables. Each configuration deemed worthy of serious consideration should be analyzed in terms of

- Problems solved and objectives met
- Development and operating costs
- Impact on the company

as well as taking into account any constraints or trade-offs based on existing conditions that must be considered.

For instance, a full load in the existing Data Processing System would preclude an in-house-run system. This constraint should be identified since it has a bearing on the design. Examples of what might be included in broad system configurations at this point are shown in Figures 4D and 4E.

## CONDUCTING THE NEEDS ANALYSIS   75

Develop and install a system with the following components:

Basic HRIS Module to support such functions as
- Employee record keeping
- Statistical head count and turnover
- Force control
- Internal directory

EEO Compliance Module to support such functions as:
- Availability determination
- Work force analysis
- EEO-1 report preparation
- Tracking and monitoring reports

Establish a centralized HRIC to oversee the operation from corporate headquarters.

Figure 4D. Broad Configuration, Example 1.

Develop and install a system with the following components:

Basic HRIS Module to support such functions as
- Employee record keeping
- Force control
- EEO-1
- Work force analysis

Training Control Module to support such functions as
- Course scheduling
- Student enrollment
- Chargeback
- Employee record keeping

Salary Administration Module to support such functions as
- Salary Survey participation
- Equal pay monitoring
- Rate review planning and control

Establish regional HRIS input/retrieval units and regional data bases with an oversight and master HRIC unit at Headquarters. The Headquarters data base will be a corporate resource only, with update supplied from the regional data bases. The Headquarters HRIC will be responsible for overall policy, procedures, and standards for all operations.

Figure 4E. Broad Configuration, Example 2.

The first configuration highlights the EEO function, since there is really only one user area being satisfied, and establishes centralized control.

In the second configuration, the EEO function is downplayed somewhat and not developed as a full module. The Training and Salary

Administration areas, however, are given full-module treatment. Control is established at Headquarters, but autonomy of operation is allowed.

### 4.8. DETERMINE BEST HRIS CONFIGURATION AND PREPARE RECOMMENDATIONS

When the Team has weighed the advantages and disadvantages of each alternative, it is time to select the best one. It may be that the best configuration is a combination of several; the best features of each may be assimilated in an optimum alternative.

Among the most important criteria for determining the best configuration are these:

1. Number of user problems and needs satisfied
2. Developmental cost
3. Annual operational cost
4. Available and qualified human resources
5. Annual savings and payback ratio
6. Development time
7. Organizational restrictions
8. Chance of success

Other factors, unique to your situation, will influence the shape and direction of the HRIS project. The organization's cash-flow situation as you begin, the past record of success the data organization has had with systems, the urgency of particular personnel problems, and other issues will affect your decision on the shape of the HRIS, and this should be recognized by the Project Team. In any design, a practical means is best.

*Needs Analysis Recommendation.* The breadth and style of the final Needs Analysis Report will vary from organization to organization, depending on internal documentation standards. As a rule, the Team should take the time to itemize and set down as many particulars as they can about the recommended system. Once the project is approved, the Needs Analysis Report will become the basis for the system specifications.

The Needs Analysis Report should contain at least the following:

- Statement of the overall project and the underlying need for an HRIS.
- List of specific user needs and problems.
- Description of current system operations.
- Alternative solutions to these problems.
- The suggested HRIS configuration.
- HRIS description and overall flow, including inputs, types of data elements, and suggested outputs at a broad level.
- Developmental time and cost estimate.
- Organizational changes that may be necessary.
- Any constraints or other factors such as privacy and security recommendations of the Team.
- A list of the Team members and their activities.
- Other impacts on the users or organization.

This report can then be submitted to management for its consideration and the approval that will permit the HRIS Project Team to move into the specifications stage.

**CONCLUSION**

The purpose of the Needs Analysis is to determine the scope of the HRIS: its boundaries, interfaces, and application modules. To do this, the Project Team will first have to identify the objectives of the Needs Analysis for the proposed system, which may range from the development of an overall Human Resources Information Plan to the specific identification of inputs, outputs, processes, and types of data elements that will be required. These objectives vary among different organizations and represent a "moving target" insofar as they change as the Team learns more about organizational needs and user requirements.

The most successful means of obtaining information for the Needs Analysis is through user interviews. These must be prepared adequately in advance, conducted according to certain standards, assimilated in usable formats, and analyzed accurately. Guidelines for sound interviewing procedures are stressed in this chapter.

At the same time, the Team will be gathering information on all existing systems, especially any computerized payroll system, that the HRIS will interface with or replace. When this information and the results of user interviews and other studies have been analyzed, the Team can develop broad system configurations for the proposed HRIS. Several alternatives should be constructed, with an optimum choice identified (and the reasons given why it is considered best) for management's consideration. The Needs Analysis Report recommendations will form the basis for the work of the next stage, System Specifications.

# Part III
# Design and Installation

# 5
# Specifications: Determining Data Base Elements, Codes, and Edits

When the Needs Analysis has been completed — and only when this critical analysis of problems and needs has been done exhaustively — the Project Team can begin to develop system specifications. These specifications are the bridge between the HRIS user requirements, as learned from the Needs Analysis, and the design stage of HRIS development. Like the specifications a builder might give an architect, they specify end results without telling how to get there, although in the Project Team approach to HRIS development there will be continuing interaction among disciplines primarily responsible for different stages. Properly managed and executed, the Project Team method of HRIS development more nearly resembles a flowing river than a set of navigational locks. Its stages form a continuum instead of a series of discrete events. Checkpoints are needed to evaluate the system as it is being developed, but the flow should continue.

System specifications outline what the system should do. This includes not only what data to include but the form in which it should be available. In the chapters that follow, no attempt is made to dictate to differently situated organizations in different computer environments exactly which data elements to include in the HRIS, how to store and process data, or the exact formats of reports and other output. Rather, the purpose here is to provide "how to" advice on preparing guidelines that will direct the specifications effort so that the user requirements determined by the Needs Analysis will be specified completely and accurately for HRIS design.

## 82   III/DESIGN AND INSTALLATION

This chapter deals with the Project Team approach to determining which data elements to include in the HRIS (5.1), major control codes (5.2), and editing requirements (5.3). In Chapter 6, specifications for output reports, tables, processing routines, and HRIS interfaces will be covered.

Perhaps the first step in the specifications stage is to review the Needs Analysis and update it for any changes that may have been made since it was performed. Have there been any significant organizational or regulatory changes that would have an impact on its results? Again, the specifications stage of HRIS development begins the specific definition of what the final system will look like. Work should not begin on this definition until the essential questions of scope, objectives, and priorities have been answered and set forth in the Needs Analysis. When this stage has gained management's approval, the details of system specification can begin.

### 5.1. DETERMINING INITIAL DATA ELEMENTS

Much information has been developed in recent years about the technical aspects of data element storage and maintenance, in works on data base design, data base management systems, and similarly specialized areas. For most organizations installing or revamping an HRIS, however, the questions that turn out to be critical to later success occur in an earlier stage: the initial selection of the data base elements that will be resident in the HRIS, which will essentially determine the individual characteristics of the personnel information system.

Because no two personnel systems will require exactly the same data elements, the selection of these elements is more a matter of principles than prescriptions. An overall approach to the process is needed, however, that will satisfy the quantitative needs of the data systems organization and at the same time assure the accomplishment of personnel objectives. As discussed in this section, this approach should include a standardized format for data element specifications, a Project Team methodology for selecting data elements, tests of individual elements, and final reviews with HRIS users.

#### 5.1.1. Standardized Data Base Element Specifications

Before examining the critical question of how to determine whether specific elements should be included in the HRIS data base, a standardized format should be set up to properly identify and explain each element that will be considered. This is primarily a job for the Data Systems members of the Project Team, but a look at the kinds of information needed for each element shows the extent to which personnel people need to become involved in this process. The following items of information should be gathered for each element:

*Specs for Data Element Recording Form.*

1. Unique name of the Data Element
2. The precise definition of the element
3. The maximum field length of the element (size)
4. Type of element (numeric, alphabetic)
5. Editing rules and coding structures
6. Source of the element, showing both user area and input form
7. Key reports that the element is needed for and expected usage
8. Who is responsible for keeping the element accurate, i.e., the item owner
9. Approximate number of changes (occurrences) per year
10. Relationship of this element to any others, i.e., whether it computes another field
11. History and retention requirements
12. Calculation rules of how to compute the item
13. Any unique timing or turnaround constraints
14. Whether the element is to be passed to any subsystem or other file (as in an interface)
15. Any privacy or security requirements

Because computer environments differ for different systems, the exact nature and extent of the above specification for each data element — as well as the form used to standardize the information — is the proper responsibility of the Data Systems members of the team. An added advantage of having a data element recording form such as that shown in Figure 5A is that the Project Team will have in one place a list of all data elements and all information pertaining to each.

**84** III/DESIGN AND INSTALLATION

| 1. Data Element Name | 3. Field Length | 4. Type | 6. Source | 8. Item Owner | 7. Reports Where Used | 13. Timing Constraints |
|---|---|---|---|---|---|---|
| 2. Definition ||||| 5. Edits and Codes ||
| 10. Relationships ||||| 11. History ||
| 9. Changes per Year ||||| 12. Calculations ||
| 14. Interfaces ||||| 15. Security/Privacy ||

Figure 5A. HRIS Data Element Recording Form.

### 5.1.2. Project Team Methodology for Element Selection

Although the job of determining which data elements to include in the HRIS is not an exact science, the approach recommended here, which focuses on user meetings, should help ensure that the correct elements have been identified. There is no way of knowing the optimum number of elements to include, although the intuitive judgment of Project Team members may suggest that there are too many or too few.

The first step in determining data elements is for the Project Team to review the scope of the HRIS and firm up their understanding of the applications and functions that will be covered. This review of the various functions will clarify their boundaries and reestablish whether they should be part of the system. This should not be a time-consuming process, and the result should be a list of personnel applications that will have data elements supporting them. The most important determinant in data element selection, however, will be whether a piece of data is needed to produce a specific output. Data elements are needed to print reports, calculate other items, and be available for online interrogations. Elements needed only in certain reports or outputs — such as averages, totals, or other calculated fields — are not necessarily data base elements, since they usually are needed only at the time the specific report is printed, and can be calculated then. Reports or desired outputs are the key to element selection.

Therefore, the Needs Analysis interviews for the included functions should be reviewed, and a search should be made for any mention of a report, an input, or a piece of required data. As each piece of information is found, a Data Element Recording Form should be completed as fully as possible. When this process has been completed, the Team is ready to go into more detail.

A meeting with the specific users is the best way of eliciting the information needed to review functions. The Team members must review the functions with the most knowledgeable person until they have a firm understanding of each process. As a recording device to assist the Team in this area, the "Input, Process, Output" (I/P/O) technique may help. This technique will both help the Team understand the flow of data and help the users describe their activity so that the Team can decide whether there are enough data elements to support this function. Inputs for each function are listed, as are the processes that are applied in those inputs in order to create the desired outputs. The final inputs are then shown, as in the example shown as Figure 5B. The inputs described will then have to be a part of the HRIS in order to supply the elements.

These I/P/O's can be described in various levels of detail in order to gain the desired level of specificity. In this state of the system's development, the Team does not have to design an input form or the procedure necessary to fill it out, but the Team members must be confident that they have a way of receiving the data element and creating the desired output in the manner and time frame desired by the user.

During these user meetings, it is also very helpful for the Team to review firsthand the personnel plans, procedures, and legal requirements in which the HRIS may be involved. If there will be EEO reports, ERISA reports, and other reports produced by the HRIS, the

|   | Input | Process | Output |
|---|---|---|---|
| Stage 1 | – Employee demographic data<br>– Salary plan data<br>– Appraisal data | Produce Salary planning charts | Salary planning charts by organization |
| Stage 2 | – Employee demographic data<br>– Employee name<br>– Department code<br>– Current salary and date<br>– Salary grade<br>– Appraisal code<br>– Salary plan allowable percents by appraisal code | Multiply employee salary by allowable percents according to appraisal | Planning sheets by name by department in high-to-low order by salary grade |

**Figure 5B. I/P/O Example.**

Team should become as familiar as possible with the exact reporting requirements in these areas. Copies of the statutes and personnel plans should be reviewed by the Team, and any questions, unclear areas, or ambiguous instructions should be discussed with the user. In some functions — benefits, for one — there may also be administrative rulings that help define the plans. The Team should have access to these rulings and any other material that will help them. Benefit plan texts, salary plans, job evaluation procedures, and legal requirements should be analyzed for data elements, needed reports, or timing requirements. This is too important a task not to complete as carefully as possible.

The Team should review all these plan texts, documents, and procedures to get a "first cut" at the data elements. The inputs should be compared with each data element to ensure that there is a source for each. If there is no source for an "item," it is clear that one must be found, or the element will have no way of being supplied to the HRIS. The reports and analyses that the users said they wanted in the Needs Analysis should be examined to ascertain whether the elements can produce them.

This "first cut" must also be matched against any legal or statutory requirements that are known to the users or the Team and that the Team has determined will be produced by the HRIS.

Necessary interfaces and subsystems must also be examined to ensure that they can be accommodated with the data elements.

When the Team members are satisfied that they have the "first cut" to a point where they are comfortable with it, they should once again meet with the users and let the users supply the editing rules, processing routines, history requirements, and relationships. In most cases this is easier said than done, since the users will feel that this is primarily a Team function. In defense of this approach, however, the Team does not necessarily have the background in the user area, nor can its members be expected to learn everything overnight. A compromise must be struck here, with the Team and the user developing these areas jointly.

### 5.1.3. Perform Data Element Tests: Key Questions

Before the data element list can be finalized, each element should be subjected to at least the following questions:

- *Need.* Is the data element truly needed for a valid business, legal, or regulatory requirement?
- *Currency.* Can the data element be supplied to the HRIS in a timely manner or will it always be "out of date" and not useful?
- *Mechanization.* Must this element be included in a data base or is manual collection preferable?
- *Universality.* Can the item be collected for all required employees or will it be missing for some locations or groups?
- *Collectability.* Can the user really support the need for, and enforce the collection of the element?
- *Efficiency.* Does the cost of collection, maintenance, and storage of the element outweigh the benefits of collecting it?

If the users and the Team cannot make satisfactory answers to these questions for certain elements, those elements should be earmarked for possible exclusion from the Data Base.

### 5.1.4. Final Review with the User

Before the data elements have been made final, there should be several further steps in the review process to assure that the Team arrives at a satisfactory set of elements.

1. *Walk-Through.* With or without the use of the I/P/O's, every function should be "walked through" with the users. This technique of reviewing each function can uncover omissions or inaccuracies in the data base.
2. *Legislation Review.* All known legal and statutory requirements should be compared with the data element list to ensure completeness.
3. *Key Reports.* The major corporate reports or documents, such as turnaround documents and top management reports, should be reviewed to see that they can be provided.
4. *Interfaces.* All systems that will interface the HRIS, especially the payroll system, should be examined to ensure that the proper communications can be accomplished. This must be done for data entering the HRIS as well as for the data elements that the HRIS will be providing.

If the elements have passed these reviews, they can be considered final at this stage. There may still be some aspects of the elements that have not yet been provided, such as the edits or relationships, but for practical purposes the list of elements should be essentially complete.

Because the entire development process is one of more and more detail, there will be changes to the elements as time goes on. This should be recognized and planned for by the Team. Tools such as Data Base Management systems and data dictionaries can facilitate the impact of change to a list of elements. If the Team does not plan to utilize such a system, an alternative could be to have a list of the elements along with key descriptors and a summary of the capsulized information contained on it. In this way, if an element or a report is added or dropped, the relationship of the element to the report is noted and can be examined by the Team.

## 5.2. DETERMINING MAJOR CONTROL CODES

The development of accurate and effective control codes that will in effect organize HRIS data and assure smooth processing is a basic requirement for sound specifications. Four fundamental types of control codes are discussed in this section, covering the specification of codes for employee status, employment type, and transactions as well as a standard format for entry of information into the HRIS.

### 5.2.1. Employment Status Code: The Biggest Aggregate Picture

Based on how the user organization views its employee body, these are groupings of employees, ex-employees, and nonemployees (applicants, for example) that must be tracked and reported on. These status groupings are at the highest level of aggregation of employee data, but care should be taken to make sure that they are sufficiently detailed and mutually exclusive. An employee should appear in only one group. Some possible groupings of employee status are shown in Figure 5C.

These codes will be used as selectors in almost every report or analysis that is produced, such as whether to report an employee in EEO statistics or whether benefits deductions should be made from pay. In the specifications stage, the Project Team must either provide

## 90   III/DESIGN AND INSTALLATION

| Employee Status | Associated Code |
|---|---|
| Active | 00 |
| Retired | 10 |
| Resigned With Vested Benefits | 20 |
| Discharged With Vested Benefits | 21 |
| Resigned, No Vested Benefits | 30 |
| Discharged, No Vested Benefits | 31 |
| On Leave of Absence | 40 |
| Laid Off | 50 |
| Deceased With Surviving Spouse | 60 |
| Deceased, No Surviving Spouse | 61 |
| Applicant | 70 |

Figure 5C. Employment Status Codes.

the rules for calculating this code or specify it as user-supplied. These rules will also be part of the specifications.

Retention of records within the HRIS will also be based on the group to which the employee belongs. It may be that your users wish to keep all active and on-leave records in the same file and continue to post changes to them. Furthermore, records of inactive employees without vesting rights may fall into a category from which they could be moved to a subordinate file after a period of time. The logic for this separation activity depends on a sufficiently delineated code that easily permits the HRIS to categorize the employee population in the proper groups.

### 5.2.2. Employment Type Codes

Another apsect of the specifications that must be addressed early is the type of employment that an employee may have with the company. Is the employee a regular employee or a temporary? There may be other situations as well that will affect the proper determination of benefits, salary administration, and other personnel plans. A possible coding scheme for these codes is shown in Figure 5D.

| Employee Type | Associated Code |
|---|---|
| Regular | 1 |
| Temporary | 2 |
| Limited-Term | 3 |
| Occasional or Casual | 4 |

Figure 5D. Employment Type Codes

### 5.2.3 Transaction (Input) Codes

Since data processing technology has not yet progressed to the point where data entry equipment can easily and inexpensively read a longhand or oral English-language description of an instruction and then take appropriate action based on that instruction, a substitute must be found. In an HRIS, that substitute in known as a transaction code, or, to some, an input code.

This code must be supplied by the user as shorthand for an instruction to the HRIS. The codes normally describe various kinds of events that might happen to an employee (new hire, salary change, etc.) and what action the HRIS should take as a consequence (print a new turnaround document, calculate a new payroll deduction, etc.).

Coding the transactions and determining the appropriate actions to take are extremely important specifications, and these items must be gone over thoroughly with each user to ensure that they are correct.

Knowledge of personnel practices is vital in constructing this code, since such practices change from company to company. In laying out the logic and specifications, you may encounter a situation in which an employee is hired, dies, and then goes on a leave of absence. Does this sound farfetched? Not to the computer. To a computer-based system, these are all valid transactions. The invalidity lies in the sequence and timing of the transactions, and this is where knowledge of the personnel department enters the picture and where we begin to see the differences in systems between companies.

One way to develop the necessary transaction codes is to set up a decision table of allowable events and then work your way through the various combinations. If the team encounters situations or events that cannot be handled by the employment type or status codings, the codings should be revised.

## 92   III/DESIGN AND INSTALLATION

In designing these codes, it is important to allow for movement of employees into and out of the employee groups. This is the big difference between this code and other codes on an employee's record.

Some examples of transaction codes are listed in Figure 5E. The codes in whatever system you develop must drive to the employment status groups. The third digit can be reserved for the employment type code and can serve both as an input to this field and a double check. You will notice that these transaction codes match the employee groups used in our examples (i.e., X can be 1, 2, 3, or 4).

Figure 5F illustrates a decision table of the type that depict the editing logic and allowable transactions in the employment type, transaction codes, and employment status groupings.

| Transaction Description | Transaction Code | Resulting Employment Status |
|---|---|---|
| New hire | 10X | Active |
| Recall from layoff | 11X | Active |
| Rehire | 12X | Active |
| Reinstatement from leave of absence | 13X | Active |
| To layoff | 20X | Inactive |
| To leave of absence | 30X | Inactive |
| Resignation with vested benefits | 40X | Inactive |
| Resignation without vested benefits | 41X | Inactive |
| Discharge with vested benefits | 50X | Inactive |
| Discharge without vested benefits | 51X | Inactive |
| Deceased with surviving spouse | 60X | Inactive |
| Deceased without surviving spouse | 61X | Inactive |

Figure 5E. Transaction Codes.

| Incoming Transaction | Current HRIS Data Base Status Code | Is Transaction Allowable? |
|---|---|---|
| New hire (10X) | 70 | Yes |
| New hire (10X) | 00–61 | No |
| Recall from layoff (11X) | 50 | Yes |
| Recall from layoff (11X) | 00–40; 60–70 | No |
| To leave of absence (30X) | 00 | Yes |
| To leave of absence (30X) | 10–70 | No |

Figure 5F. Decision Logic Example

### 5.2.4. Traditional Entry Format: Input Numbers

There are two basic methods of entering data into an HRIS. The first is in a more traditional, batch oriented system. The second, explained below in 5.2.5, is normally used in an on-line environment. In the traditional method, the entry into the HRIS of each individual element of information on an employee should be made in a standard format. The most common format divides the 80-column input in this way:

**Traditional Entry Format**

| Data | Columns |
| --- | --- |
| Social security number (file control) | 1-9 |
| Effective date | 10-15 |
| Input number | 16-18 |
| Data | 19-75 |
| Input control number | 76-80 |

Any entries not conforming to this standard format would be rejected, since HRIS programs must be established to accept the incoming data in a prescribed manner.

The input numbers are controlling codes in the HRIS, and the most important one will have the transaction code as a piece of data. This three-digit code (assigned by the Project Team) will describe to the system what action to take on each piece of entered data, what edits to perform on it, what history to keep on it, and so forth. Every data element will have the corresponding input number it is entered with, and some may have more than one. They are most commonly broken into two groups: regular input numbers and special input numbers used to override the system.

Regular input numbers will be the standard method of entering data into the HRIS. These numbers will be permanently displayed in any turnaround documents and user instructions in the field, and these are the only numbers known to anyone outside the Human Resource Information Center (HRIC). The entry of a regular input number will cause the system to act in a "normal" manner. Editing on the data, derivations, calculations, etc., will occur as specified by the user.

Overrides or special input numbers should be established for *all* data elements in the HRIS as well. (Many data elements are calculated or derived and will not have regular input numbers.) These numbers should be tightly controlled by the HRIC and used only when absolutely necessary. Entry of these special numbers will bypass all edits and change a data field without causing any normal processing; no calculations, history generation, derivations, or printing of turnaround documents will occur. Any item in an employee's record must be capable of being corrected and adjusted should normal update and correction vehicles fail. The special input numbers provide this override capability.

Most data elements in an HRIS will have an effective date associated with them, and that date will be entered on the input transaction, columns 10 to 15 in the *Traditional Entry Format* example shown above. The incoming data will be sorted, usually by employee and within employee groups and by input number. Should there be two or more transactions for the same element, the oldest (lowest date) will be processed first. In this way the effective date is serving two purposes: incoming transaction processing, and as a piece of intelligent data, since many personnel requests require the use of dates (time since last increase, time in job, etc.).

The input control number is usually the document number from which the data were taken. Each source document from which data are entered into the HRIS should be numbered in such a way that an effective audit trail is provided. This numbering sequence can be applied by the HRIC or by the field user if remote input devices or screens are used. The input control number should be printed on the list of rejected transactions so that the supplier of the data may reenter corrected data.

### 5.2.5. Screen Input Method

In an on-line environment it is preferable to enter or change data directly into the HRIS via a data terminal. This method utilizes programs to access the employee's record and then presents the user with a set of data elements which can be changed if incorrect or a mask into which data can be entered if blank.

**Sample Screen**

AJAX: HRIS INPUT SCREEN-1

Employee Name: [          ]       Hire Date: [          ]
Home Address: [                                         ]
Birth Date: [          ]  Race: [       ]  Sex: [       ]

The cursor will direct the user to enter the data in the correct sequence and edits would control mistakes or incorrect entries. This method is usually more expensive to operate than the traditional method since it implies on-line updating of every element or at least every screen's worth of data. The traditional method batches all changes and processes them at the same time, usually less expensive than invoking the edit program for each change. The good features of the screen method — immediacy of feedback to the user in supplying the change — must be balanced against the increased cost. The Project Team then must decide which method is best since it will affect the design drastically if a screen entry method is adopted.

## 5.3. Determining Editing Requirements

To the extent possible, each data element should have its edit requirements specified by the user in the system specification stage. Edit requirements not only keep the HRIS accurate but can be specified to assure that edits are made at the source of information rather than down the line after an incorrect entry has been rejected and not replaced with accurate input.

For example, if a user inputs an erroneous code for an employee grouping, the system should display an error message that not only rejects the entry but tells the user how to get it right. In this case, a listing of allowable employment status codes might be provided. It is not enough to reject transactions at the HRIS level. The data base is still incomplete until the rejected transaction is reentered. Thus, error messages should be displayed to the user with as much helpful information as possible so that the user can resolve the discrepancy "at the source" and reenter the needed information promptly.

The types of data element edits specified for an HRIS will vary with the scope of the system, but personnel information generally lends itself to the following kinds of edits:

*Type and Size Edits.* In the most elementary checks, the HRIS will check to see whether the field of data is numeric or uses alphabetic characters or whether the data element is the right size, say, three characters in length.

*Content Check.* The HRIS program will validate the incoming transaction against an allowable code, set; e.g., in the sex field for the code "M" or the code "F." Other codes are errors.

*Range Validation.* This edit will accept any value that falls within a certain range. Salary increases for weekly employees, for example, would have to be between $10 and $50, or days of the month between 1 and 31. This check is especially useful if there are many inclusively acceptable codes within a low to high span of numbers.

*Table Checks.* Tabular checks are particularly useful where there are sets of codes to validate against and where these codes change frequently, making program changes difficult. Lists of job numbers, salary grades, schools, and training courses all make for suitable table edits.

*Associative or Relational Edits.* The associative edit, which usually requires the presence of other data elements, is the most complex and expensive type of edit but also the most effective. This edit compares data elements. Salary information can be checked to see whether the employee is actually at a certain level: Certain jobs can exist only in certain departments or locations; "Return from leave of absence" can occur only if the employee is currently on leave of absence.

This type of editing can be quite complex. For instance, if a transaction code for a promotion is supplied, the HRIS will check to see whether a new job title or salary grade has been supplied, along with a salary increase, since both are needed for a promotion to take place. The HRIS will have to edit employee status to ensure that the employee is active as well as check the new salary grade against the old, check the new salary against the old, and check effective dates.

*Warning Messages.* While not strictly an edit, and grouped separately in the HRIS because they do not represent rejected entries, warning messages can provide needed information to users at the point of entry. When the HRIS encounters a situation in which an incoming transaction meets all edit criteria but exceeds some user-supplied level, a message is generated that informs the user of this. Warning messages can also be used to notify the user that a sufficient period of time has elapsed to place a new employee in a benefit program or when a service anniversary is imminent.

Editing is one of the most complex areas of specifications, but it represents time well spent by the Project Team. If the data base becomes riddled with errors, users will lose confidence in the system and gravitate to other methods, thereby eroding the basic objective of the HRIS project.

**CONCLUSION**

In this first of two chapters on HRIS specifications, guidelines are presented for the selection and development of data base elements, codes, and edits. No attempt is made to dictate which data elements or other items that require specifications should be included in the system. Only the organization's user needs and constraints, as determined by the Needs Analysis and the continuing work of the Team with individual users, can identify the exact items that will be part of the HRIS.

Instead, guidelines are presented for effective procedures, such as a standardized format for data element selection, tests of data elements, the reasons for having different types of control codes, and procedures for assuring that edits are specified for each data element in the system.

# 6
# Specifications: Output Reports, Interfaces, Tables, and Processing Routines

Chapter 5 stressed the specific content of data base elements, codes, and edits. When these have been properly defined, the Project Team can move forward in the Specifications Stage to begin work on Output Reports (6.2), Tables (6.3), and Processing Routines (6.4).

The data elements must be developed first, of course, but in practice the Project Team will be sharpening the specifications for all aspects of the HRIS throughout the Specifications Stage covered in these two chapters. Final specifications will be developed by a process in which the system requirements revealed by the Needs Analysis are translated into specific information needed by the design team.

As in Chapter 5, general guidelines and procedures applicable to HRIS development are presented for each of the areas that must be specified. Certain kinds of information will be required in the specs for output reports, interfaces, tables, and internal processing routines. These kinds of information are explicitly listed.

The examples shown of actual reports, etc., are no more than examples, however. Your HRIS should reflect your own organization.

### 6.1. DETERMINING OUTPUT REPORT SPECIFICATIONS

The nature of output reports specified will to a large degree determine the operating characteristics of the final HRIS. If, for example, the users require access to the system on a real-time basis, with the latest data available whenever requested, the HRIS will have to be built in an entirely different fashion from what it would be if reports were needed only on a weekly or monthly basis.

While this may seem elementary, questions about the format, timeliness, and frequency of output reports may require some hard choices in this stage. In meetings with users, the Project Team must focus on reporting requirements to ensure that users are not asking for more than they actually need in the way of timeliness and frequency. Be sure that the users understand the significance of their report requests. If a report is not needed every day, it should not be so specified, because such constraints will determine the final system design and the cost of development, maintenance, and operation.

If a weekly or ad hoc (variable-format) report on a periodic basis can solve the user's problem or meet objectives as well as a daily report, the Team should generally opt for the more modest approach. When users understand the impact of their requests, they do not as a rule make inordinate demands for reports and analyses; but the Team should establish an atmosphere of restraint rather than letting users specify any and all possible reports in an unchecked environment. Otherwise, the HRIS may turn out to be far too elaborate and costly to build, install, and operate. Besides, report needs do change.

Before we proceed to a listing of report specification items and a discussion of the kinds of actual reports that can be turned out by an HRIS, these general guidelines are recommended to help the Team work with users to keep the HRIS from getting out of hand in the report specification stage:

**Report Specification Guidelines**

- Keep the number of fixed, recurring reports to a minimum. The cost-reduction objective of the HRIS can be defeated by producing too much paper.
- Try to direct all requests for reports to a centralized Human Resource Information Center (HRIC) so that this organization can determine the most effective and efficient way of handling each request.
- Limit the distribution of all reports to those who absolutely must have them.

- Limit the data displayed on reports to those elements which are essential.
- "Pilot test" the report with the user by providing a hand-generated version or a sample produced from a small population for user review.
- Keep the report readable by interpreting codes where possible on the report.
- Generate reports on an "exception" basis rather than in a way that forces users to pick out the exception from a much longer list.

*Report Specifications.* Certain information must be included in the specifications for each report, as shown in the Ajax Corporation Report Specifications: Sample (Figure 6A; page 101). These specifications should include the following:

1. Output name
2. Purpose of the output
3. Destination of the report
4. Population covered
5. Data content, including elements and calculated fields
6. Format of the report (fixed or variable)
7. Volume, or number needed per year or per cycle
8. Frequency required
9. Accuracy requirements
10. Privacy and security considerations.

More information may be included in the specifications for each report — e.g., whether its medium will be paper or computer terminal display, its timing during the year, and selection criteria — but these are the essential specifications.

*Categories of Reports.* The major classes of reports that the HRIS will produce should be specified in the System Specifications stage. In the discussion that follows, these reports are treated as categories rather than specific reports, which will vary according to your needs. The specific reports range from basic control reports needed to ensure that the system is working correctly to highly sophisticated analyses required by certain users, but all fall into one or more of these categories:

SPECIFICATIONS 101

| Name of Report | Purpose | Destination | Media | Format | Frequency | Timing | Accuracy Required | Volume | Security | Population Included | Selection Criteria | Scope of Report |  |
|---|---|---|---|---|---|---|---|---|---|---|---|---|---|
| | | | | | | | | | | | | Information Content | |
| Listing of college graduates | Provide individual information on college graduates | College relations administrator, human resource utilization | Paper | Variable | Semiannual: end of March and end of September reported period | 20th workday after | 98.5% | 25 pages per 1,000 grads | Private – college relations administrator, human resources utilization | All active employees | College graduates only | Social Security number Job code Current employment date Age Name Sex Department code Job title name Education level Degree information • Major/minor subjects | |

Figure 6A. Ajax Corporation Report Specifications: Sample.

1. *Operating Control Reports*
2. *Turnaround Documents and Profiles*
3. *Periodic Standard Reports*
4. *On-Call Reports*
5. *Ad Hoc Reports*
6. *Online Terminal Outputs.*

1. **Operating Control Reports.** This class of reports encompasses the built-in edit and balancing reports necessary for the correct functioning of the system. These output reports are not at the user's discretion. They are usually determined and utilized by the HRIC, although users' involvement in the error listings is common. Some examples of Operating Control Reports are:

- Error listings and diagnostics
- Warning messages
- Data base statistics before update cycle
- Data base statistics after update cycle
- Numbers of transactions modified, inserted, or deleted
- Base pay controls
- Registers
- Backup and recovery reports.

In addition, provision should be made to identify and report which reporting units, subsidiaries, or departments have provided information and which have not.

Also, the number of errors detected for each data element is invaluable to the Human Resource Information Center for control purposes. Each subsystem and module should be capable of being edited and updated on a stand-alone basis, and information as to when these subsystems have been processed is vital to effective HRIS control. For instance, each time the HRIS tables are processed, sufficient reporting information must be generated to permit the HRIC to decide whether the accuracy of the data base is sufficient to continue with the HRIS update or whether the tables must be corrected before work can continue.

2. **Turnaround Documents and Profiles.** One of the most visible type of reports of the HRIS will be the turnaround documents. These

multipart, multipurpose forms may be handled by every employee in the company. The Team should spend sufficient time laying out these forms to ensure that they are simple to use and are not confusing and that the grouping of the data on the forms does not lead to a high number of input errors. Some turnaround documents are:

- Basic Employee Record
- Career Development Profile
- Benefits Status From
- Safety and Accident Record.

3. *Periodic Standard Reports.* These reports are the detailed user reports that are frequently envisioned when users are asked about computer based systems and what reports they desire. The class is produced on a regularly scheduled basis, and the format is fixed. Some examples are:

- Departmental Force Analysis (monthly)
- Weekly or monthly Personnel Activity Reports
- Weekly or monthly Salary Administration Reports
- Year-to-Date Salary Statistics
- Daily Activity Report
- Weekly Labor Distribution
- Monthly Premium Billing Report
- EEO-1 Report.

4. *On-Call or "Canned" Reports.* These are reports whose format can be predefined, although frequency or population is undetermined. Also known as prepackaged or "canned" reports, these are reports developed in advance by system users and the HRIC that can be run with virtually no additional programming. The user simply requests the current information in the predefined format on the population the user needs or is authorized to access, and the canned report is produced on that population, using the most current data base for managerial analysis and decision making.

Large organizations may have dozens of these readily obtainable reports in the HRIS library for periodic or occasional managerial analysis. Examples of on-call reports include:

- List of promotable employees
- Turnover reports
- Employee list by salary grade for a specific department
- Hires by employment source.

5. *Ad Hoc Reports.* There are many requests for information that can be produced in a batch mode (usually within twenty-four to forty-eight hours) but cannot be predefined. They can be reports that use data from various files, sometimes involving considerable programming, or fairly simplistic requests for employee data. The HRIS must be able to handle as many of these requests as possible, and it is desirable to have the HRIC or the users themselves generate them. The more flexible the data base design and the more powerful the generalized retrieval system, the more the Project Team will be able to rely on this ad hoc capability and not have to spec out dozens of reports.

There is an almost infinite list of these ad hoc reports that can be generated. The importance of a highly flexible, user-oriented, generalized retrieval system cannot be overemphasized, since without such a system the retrieval capability of the entire HRIS will be severely limited, which will result in the difference between a successful system and a failure. The following is a checklist of some of the evaluation criteria that can be used in judging the relative merits of commercially available ad hoc retrieval packages. Some of these criteria are highly subjective, and many are technical, but they should be examined closely.

For one thing, with the growth of information systems over the past five years or so, it is often the case that a company already has purchased a retrieval system for another application. In such cases, the existing system should be seriously considered for HRIS use rather than having the organization purchase a second system with the same features.

*Evaluation Criteria for Ad Hoc Packages*

A. *Hardware Compatibility*
   This is a very obvious and basic consideration, but it is one of the most crucial. Some report generation systems are not

portable between hardware vendors; and if you compute faulty plans to change the equipment or alter it substantially, you may not be able to run the retrieval package on the new computer.

B. *Resource Utilization*
Of almost equal importance to the compatibility criteria is the efficiency with which the package operates on the computer. If the package uses a large amount of the main memory, it will be allocated a lower priority than other jobs and therefore will give the users slower turnaround. There is a wide range of utilization among systems that on the surface appear identical, and the system must be benchmarked properly to ascertain how efficiently it will operate.

C. *User Orientation and Simplicity*
This is a very subjective area to evaluate. A skilled programmer may have one view of how simple a system is to operate, while a personnel manager may have another. The success of the ad hoc system, though, will depend on Personnel's ability to use it and use it easily. Therefore, users should have a large stake in evaluating this area. Some of the features they should examine are:
- Does the system use high-level English language, where few instructions are necessary to generate a report?
- Are field names stored internally?
- Can a nontechnical user be conversant with the system within two or three days?
- Is the response time short (for online application)?
- Will the system produce address labels, perform sorts, take totals and averages, store column headings automatically, and give page breaks and center data on a page?
- Is computational capability provided?
- Can more than one print line per employee be generated?

D. *Additional Features*
Each system will have its unique strengths and faults, and it will be difficult to judge the relative merits of these features. There can be a great many, but some of the more important are:

- Statistical packages provided with the system
- Data Base Management System interface to systems such as IMS, TOTAL, ADABAS, etc.
- Multifile Capability
- Online Interactive add-on
- Catalog capability
- Multiple reports at a single time
- Graphics features

Ad hoc reports are by nature the "individualizing" reports of any HRIS. They are the reports that users want for reasons of their own, and they give the system its distinctive characteristics as a personnel system responsive to the organization's user needs. In this sense, ad hoc reports have the "beauty part" to play in developing your tailor-made HRIS. They are totally user-oriented in purpose and may represent the chief reason for installing an HRIS.

One caution should be underscored, however. Some training in HRIS formats and procedures will be necessary for most users before they begin developing their own ad hoc reports. Uncontrolled access to ad hoc reports — with scores of untrained users devising inconsistent, illogical, or unneeded routines — simply will not work. Most users will need a week or so of training before being authorized to develop their own ad hoc reports.

6. *Online Terminal Outputs.* As the users of personnel information gain experience with computer retrieval systems, they will realize that a certain percentage of requests call for outputs that are relatively short and concise. In this area the online capability, as differentiated from applications that are initiated online but executed in batch mode, can be very useful to the Personnel Department. Analyses of salaries, searches for selected candidates, individual employee profiles, and comparisons of levels of males versus females are all examples of online inquiries. Situations that require fast responses with limited printed material as output are the best applications.

In certain personnel work, notably in the areas of planning, benefits, and compensation, which lend themselves to numeric or quantitative analysis, online presentation features are not only attractive to look at but extremely useful to managers. Material such as age distributions, merit program percentages, and the like are particularly appropriate to pictorial or graphic presentation. Histograms, pie charts, and regression analyses are very helpful to managers attempting to spot trends and inequities and come to grips with complex resource allocation and other questions.

The Project Team should be careful not to suggest that the personnel system exist solely via the online mode, however, since experience has shown that many line managers and certain personnel applications may still require lists of employees in hard-copy form.

## 6.2. INTERFACES: LINKS WITH PAYROLL AND OTHER SYSTEMS

Virtually no personnel systems are developed these days that do not have data entering from at least one existing system and being fed by the HRIS to one or more other systems or subsystems. These linkages are called "interfaces" and must be precisely defined in the Specifications Stage in order that the systems operate correctly. The data to be shared between systems must be delivered in the proper format, on the right schedule, and in the correct sequence.

The first step for the Project Team in specifying interfaces is to obtain a set list of "Required Interface Specifications" (6.2.1) and become familiar with each of the systems by examining its inputs, data base element formats, cycles, and requirements. This analysis will assure that the Team has devised the best mode of meeting the interfacing requirements, and it provides the background needed to decide whether to "Interface or Absorb" (6.2.2). In some cases the new HRIS will simply absorb the functions of existing systems, eliminating altogether the need for interfaces.

It is more likely, however, that the HRIS will have several subsystems to feed and one or two that will supply it with data. "Payroll System Interfaces" (6.2.3) are nearly inevitable, and this sometimes controversial subject is explored in greater detail later in this section.

### 6.2.1. Required Interface Specifications

The basic information gathered for analysis of each interface should provide the Team with at least the following specifications, with more specs required for a particularly complicated interface:

## Required Interface Specs

1. Name of interfaced system or subsystem
2. Purpose of interface
3. Direction of interface
4. Frequency of interface
5. Data elements involved
6. Volume per cycle
7. Format of data
8. Medium of interface

### 6.2.2. Interface or Absorb?

If the cost of including the functions of an existing subsystem in the HRIS (the cost of absorbing the subsystem) is less than the cost of interfacing the subsystem over the useful life of the HRIS, *perhaps* the Team should make a case for absorbing it, but only perhaps. Remember, the larger a system becomes, the more difficult it will be to build and operate. If the project is being pursued in workable phases (as recommended in Chapter 2), this may be the overriding concern. The HRIS will simply become too big and unwieldy if there are too many subsystems built into it.

Therefore, if a subsystem already exists and is working correctly and need not be reprogrammed, the Team should usually try to keep it intact and try to establish a link or interface to the subsystem rather than absorb it.

Subsystems that are not working correctly, of course, should be replaced. The purpose of the HRIS is to correct as many needs and solve as many operational difficulties as possible.

In most cases, the Project Team will be faced by a situation in which the interfaced subsystem in question appears to be working adequately. One reason it appears to be sufficient, perhaps, is that no one has done a cost/benefits study to compare its effectiveness with the proposed HRIS. However, a decision has to be made by the Project Team whether to interface the subsystem or let the HRIS take over its functions. These are some of the questions that should be examined:

- Would incorporation into the HRIS improve the performance of the subsystem? By how much? Can this improvement be justified against the cost of reprogramming the subsystem?
- Does the HRIS have the data to feed the subsystem, or does the HRIS need data from the other system?
- How much would it cost to incorporate the subsystem into the HRIS? Over the next five years?
- Would the inclusion of the subsystem's functions make the HRIS project too big?
- Are the frequencies and timings similar?
- Are the functions of the systems compatible?
- Does the economic justification of the HRIS rest importantly on the inclusion of this subsystem?
- Which option do user groups favor?

As a rule, the Team should try to limit the scope of the HRIS to those things which matter most — that is, the major problems and needs — and avoid any tendency to "fix things that ain't broke." In the case of operationally sound subsystems, this means building interfaces rather than absorbing.

### 6.2.3. The Payroll System Interface

The discussion of the payroll interface is always a lively one. It seems that in building a personnel system, the same set of problems emerges with regard to the payroll interface, whether the company is large or small, on the West Coast or East Coast. The main problem stems from the very fact that the Team will want to alter the payroll system in some fashion.

As a rule, the payroll group fears that any interference in the flow of payroll data is to be avoided at all costs. The operations in Payroll have usually been established for years and are seen as a well-oiled engine. Tampering can only prove harmful. Procedures are in place, and all managers in the organization are familiar with authorizing payroll-related documents in order to hire a new employee, transfer an employee, or change a rate of pay. The employees most likely receive their pay on time, with few problems encountered with respect to deductions or incorrect pay amounts. These procedures work well, and from the Payroll standpoint there is no reason to alter any of the operations.

However, many of the outputs that the HRIS will produce will contain data already captured by the Payroll system. The employee's name, salary, department, service date, and other information are data that both the payroll system and the HRIS will need. Clearly, an organization will try to avoid the time and expense of collecting, key entering, editing, and storing these data twice when they already are contained in machine-readable form. The Team is then faced with the options of:

1. Building the HRIS to absorb the Payroll functions.
2. Modifying the Payroll Systems to perform the needed HRIS functions.
3. Interfacing the two systems as appropriate.
4. Leaving the two systems separate, without any computerized link between them.

Let us review the absorption and integration options.

In today's atmosphere of data base management systems, there are powerful and persuasive arguments to be made for arriving at one common data base for Payroll and Personnel's use. These usually center on such themes as:

- Standardization of data definitions
- Reduction of data redundancy
- Consolidation of update procedures
- Independence of data between application programs and file storage
- Reduction of the need for program maintenance

These have proven to be quite successful in some cases and disastrous in others. However, utilization of data base technology and the ability to determine the best data base structure have eluded most companies in the payroll and personnel areas. Unless the Team has had prior experience building data base systems, it may be best to avoid mixing the two applications. The resulting system may be too large to implement. Therefore, I suggest that the KISS principle (Keep It Simple, Stupid) should not be ignored.

As far as data base architecture is concerned, there may be a problem in trying to build a system to accommodate differing needs. Whereas one data structure may be appropriate for Personnel's use, it will usually not be efficient for Payroll's purposes. Personnel's accesses tend to be ad hoc, one-of-a-kind reports, whereas Payroll has a large number of fixed reports and production runs. The two data structures tend to be different, since one is structured for access and the other for update.

In examining the problem of data redundancy, the Team should first determine as precisely as possible the information elements that appear to be common between the systems. This can be done by matching the payroll data elements to the HRIS data elements on a one-by-one basis. The following is a list of the most frequently chosen "common" elements between payroll systems and personnel systems:

**Potentially Common Elements**

| | |
|---|---|
| Social Security Number | Department Code |
| Employee Name | Base Pay Rate |
| Date of Birth | Base Pay Frequency |
| Sex | Adjusted Service Date |
| Hire Date | Scheduled Hours |
| Employment Status | Location Code |
| Job Number | |

The list could be longer, of course, depending on the functions that are performed by each system. The smallest list of common elements is normally found when the payroll system is restricted to pay and accounting functions, and the HRIS is relegated purely personnel functions. In any case, the list should be drawn up, since these "common" elements form the basis for discussion of redundancy between the two systems.

As we can see, the list of common elements is quite short — thirteen elements in this example — and the number of common elements would rarely total more than twenty-five elements. This leaves at least 100 or so payroll elements and at least the same number of personnel elements — depending on the modules chosen — for which there is no match. Therefore, the commonality between systems is only about 10 to 20%. Although there are common data when both data bases are viewed in their entirety, there is only a small redundancy factor with which to contend. Since this is usually the main argument that proponents of integration will use, it turns out to be less than compelling in itself.

Another problem in combining these systems and integrating the data base items is data definitions. The payroll system may have its own definitions of base pay, hire date, or even employee name, which are unacceptable to the Personnel Department. The payroll system may keep only the last name and initials of an employee, since that is sufficient for pay purposes. Personnel, however, may wish to carry the complete first names of all employees. Thus, in some cases when the elements on the surface appear similar, they actually are different. The elements must be very carefully matched to determine which elements are common.

Furthermore, in reviewing the considerations mentioned above in Section 6.2.2, the Team will usually find that there are sound economic and development reasons to keep the two systems separate as well. In the development cycle, if the Team were to try to combine the two systems into one, trade-offs and compromises would have to be made, since there is never enough time or money to satisfy all user needs to the nth degree. Payroll can define their needs more precisely; because the payroll system is sensitive and vital to the business, its development will take priority in just about every situation. Resources will be expended for Payroll's needs, and the personnel system's objectives will be given a subordinate role, with the possible result that the new payroll system will be built and the Personnel Department will still be without a system. The Payroll Department will make all decisions in favor of the payroll system, and the Team has no choice but to satisfy payroll needs first. Knowing this ahead of time may save a lot of anguish and internal meeting time.

The Team will also find that while there is a dependency between the two systems because of the common data, the payroll system has different timing problems. Payroll will have to be concerned with update cycles, year-to-date fields, and accounting registers, whereas the personnel system will not. Clearly, a very large area of difference between the two systems is apparent in the timing area.

The objectives of the two systems are also dissimilar. The payroll system is a financial system whose primary mission is to issue paychecks and to account for the pay. The objectives of the HRIS will be to monitor and control certain personnel plans and to produce information for decisions. These objectives call for widely disparate systems in terms of inputs, outputs, and internal calculations.

In summary, then, options 1 and 2, calling for integration of systems and a common data base, have serious problems. Rejection of a common data base does not imply rejection of the use of data base technology. It only means that the two data bases should not usually be combined.

The option of leaving the two systems apart has merit in situations where a mechanical interface cannot be drawn up. This is usually the case, for example, where there is no centralized payroll system, as in a multiplant or otherwise widely distributed system, and it would be highly impractical or impossible to arrange a linkage between the systems. In this situation, the Team should still explore the merits of a single input form for the common data elements. One copy of this multipurpose change form would be sent to the Payroll Department and one copy to the Personnel Department. Although the two systems are not linked physically, the objective of minimizing data collection by the providers of the data is achieved. While this does not solve all the redundancy problems, there is at least some saving, although data discrepancies between the systems will occur.

The final option of interfacing the two systems is generally the option chosen, since it represents the best method of allowing the two systems to function independently while still sharing common data. The choice of having Payroll feed Personnel, Personnel feed Payroll, or both systems feeding from a mechanized input file is left to the Team. Also, this interface approach is usually the least expensive way of linking the systems mechanically, since it is normally an easy program to write. The benefits and savings of collecting and editing the data only once are achieved, and the payroll cycle can be left untouched.

Discrepancies of data between the systems should be minimized by using this approach, since the data common to both systems are being entered only once. Those in the systems area know, however, that when there are two files with the same information, there is a very high probability of the data being different. This inaccuracy between files occurs for many reasons: The user groups submit changes to one system and not the other; the two systems may have different edit parameters, and the incoming data may fail one set of edits and pass the other; internal processes may alter the data in one and not the other; and so forth. These problems, though, will not be as severe as they would be if there were no interface at all.

Having an automated front end to the payroll system can actually speed the processing in some cases. In situations where changes to the payroll stream are submitted and the payroll group manually "pends" them until the proper run cycle nears, there is often little or no time left in which to correct complex errors. In these circumstances, it is often a help to the payroll group to have a front-end system — either an HRIS or an edit program — built for this purpose, process the change as soon as they receive it, and subject it to the most rigorous edits available. If the change should fail this edit procedure, there is sufficient time to correct the offending piece of information. This edit program can then send the changes to the payroll system when it is ready to receive them, with all changes passing the payroll edit. Handling the HRIS to payroll interface in this fashion helps all parties and makes the relationship with Payroll mutually beneficial.

As a rule, the integration option will make sense only if (1) both existing systems are seriously deficient and (2) user groups are competent in both Personnel and Payroll and can adapt to a totally new system. In these circumstances, a new HRIS that absorbs Payroll offers its strongest advantages.

Organizations differ, however, as well as payroll systems. Questions of decentralized versus centralized processing may influence the interface/absorb decision as well as the condition of present systems.

To summarize, the question of whether to interface the HRIS with an existing payroll system or absorb the system in the HRIS depends on circumstances of individual organizations, although the paramount concern in making this decision should be the goal of collecting and processing information only once. As long as data that are used by both systems can be gathered, edited, and put in machine-readable form only once, economies of time and money will be realized, and there is no preferred method of accomplishing this goal.

## 6.2. TABLES

The use of tables in some ways epitomizes the efficiency of computerized personnel systems: vastly simplifying record keeping, permitting automatic changes in whole classes of employees' records, and standardizing certain kinds of personnel data. In addition, tables can usually be controlled and updated by users in the Personnel Department, making them "user-oriented."

Tables in an HRIS store data that are common to a class of employees. A Work Location table, for example, shows that all employees with a certain location code have the same work address, which means that full work addresses need not be part of individual records. A Benefit Plan table might code a series of different plans with varying premiums, enrollments, vesting periods, and other characteristics; or a Salary Grade table might contain an associated range of salaries (minimum, midpoint, and maximum) permitted for each grade.

The efficiency of such tables stems from the fact that a certain grade may be held by many people; it may be changed for all of those people at once, but it needs to be stored and changed only once in the HRIS. Each employee's individual record will contain a code, and the computer will use the table to line up the salary or range. When a change in salary is made for a certain title or function, or when annual changes such as cost-of-living increases are made, this can be accomplished by simply altering the table rather than altering each employee's record. Should an inquiry be made on an individual employee, the HRIS will access the table and make the requested information available for analysis or display.

The labor-saving advantages of tables when mass changes have to be made in employee records, such as when departments are being reorganized or large numbers of employees are transferred to a new location, make tables an important feature of modern personnel information systems.

Tables also ensure the standardization of data. In the typical HRIS tables listed below, for example, all employees with a given key code have the same information, reducing the possibility of errors through uniformity.

Some of the tables found frequently in computerized personnel systems, and their usual contents, are shown below:

## Typical HRIS Tables

| Table Name | Possible Contents |
|---|---|
| Job table | Job Number (key to the table)<br>Job Title<br>EEO Job Category Indicator<br>Job Evaluation Point Scores<br>Exempt Status |
| Salary Grade table | Grade Level (key)<br>Minimum Salary<br>Midpoint Salary<br>Maximum Salary |
| Work Location table | Location Code (key)<br>Location Address<br>Street    State<br>City      Zip Code |
| Department table | Department Code (key)<br>Department Name<br>Authorized Head count |
| Benefit Plan table | Benefit Plan Number (key)<br>Eligibility Code<br>Benefit Coverage Amount<br>Premium Amounts-Employee/Company |
| Skill Code table | Skill Code (key)<br>Alphabetic Translation |

Depending on the scope of the HRIS and organizational needs, there may be other tables as well. These should be outlined and requested in the Specifications Stage so that their final number and particular format can be determined by the design team.

Very often, tables can be user-controlled and updated, reducing the need for programming assistance in this area. In most cases, the Personnel Department should be able to add values to tables, change current values, or delete some values entirely — all without involving the data systems organization. This not only reduces overall administration costs but makes the HRIS more responsive to users.

One additional kind of table particularly suited to user control is the Edit table. This table will store the edit requirements for each data element as well as the error messages that will be displayed if an incoming transaction fails to meet the specified edits. The user can change these requirements as the need arises, minimizing programming needs. Not all edits can be put into tables, but a typical edit table might include:

### Edit Table

- Input number (key)
- Field length
- Type of edit
- Range values
- Allowable code sets
- Error condition to be displayed

This type of flexibility in the HRIS helps keep the system flexible and enables the user to add data criteria without having to reprogram the function.

## 6.4. PROCESSING ROUTINES

Processing routines are by definition individual to each HRIS. They are the routines that make the system fit into the organization, and they must be specified for all of the internal calculations, derivations, and transformations that the HRIS must perform once the data have cleared the edits.

If your organization requires benefit enrollment after ninety days of employment, for example, the processing routines must specify this. The Project Team must work in close concert with users in developing processing routine specifications and be alert to all possible calculations and derivitives as they go through the I/P/O process. The absence of a needed routine will affect the performance of the system critically.

For each processing routine that the HRIS design team will be asked to develop, the following information should be provided:

### *Processing Routine Specifications*

1. Process name
2. Process description and purpose
3. Elements needed to perform process
4. Elements derived from process
5. Files and/or reports produced

6. Process rules, formula used, and complete specifications
7. Volume of processes per year
8. Frequency of calculation
9. Supporting tables

If possible, the specifications should include any examples of routines and copies of current activities that may be available to further assist the design team.

As in the case of data element specifications, a recording form will help organize and collect information relating to processing routines.

In seeking to identify and describe internal processing routines, it may be useful to classify them into three groups normally found in computerized personnel systems:

1. Data Element Derivations
2. History Maintenance
3. Output Processing.

These are often arbitrary classifications, however, with some overlap. The important point is to consider such categorization to ensure that no routines have been overlooked.

**CONCLUSION**

In addition to specifications for the data base elements, codes, and edits, the Team will have to prepare specs for the use of the HRIS designers on items covered in this chapter: output reports, interfaces with other systems, tables, and internal processing routines. Checklists are provided to help the Team include all the required information in these specifications.

Specifications in these areas will continue to shape the operating characteristics of the final HRIS. The format, timeliness, and frequency of output reports, for example, will affect system design fundamentally. If many reports are need on a real-time basis, with the latest data available whenever requested, the system will be built differently from what it would be if reports were needed only on a monthly schedule, for example. It is the Project Team's responsibility to make sure that users specify only what they actually need in the way of reports rather than specify features that add developmental and operational costs.

Because so many HRIS installations occur in organizations that already have a computerized payroll system, the question of whether to interface with this system or absorb it in the new HRIS is often crucial in personnel system development. Guidelines that will help the Team answer this question are presented. Whatever approach is used, the two systems should be linked in a way that achieves the benefits and savings of collecting and processing data only once. As long as data that will be used by both systems can be gathered, edited, and put into machine-readable form once for both systems, economies of time and money will be realized. There is no preferred method of accomplishing this objective.

The use of tables, which standardize certain kinds of personnel data, simplify record keeping, and permit changes to whole classes of records automatically, exemplifies the efficiency made possible by the HRIS. Typical HRIS tables and the specifications needed for both tables and processing routines are presented for the Project Team's guidance.

# 7
# Design Considerations: Major Influences on HRIS Design

Data base design is a subject frequently cloaked in mystery. In part this is a natural consequence of some of the technical language used to describe data systems. Non-technical readers have what has been called a MEGO (my eyes glaze over) reaction when confronted with prose densely packed with terms that have special meanings in systems design and that often define only one kind of system.

A more fundamental cause of the mystery, I think, is that most prescriptive works on systems design attempt to generalize beyond their means. Design is treated as an art form or a scientific discipline, depending on the author's leanings, but almost always the student will find a body of precepts — guiding rules or commandments that good designers will always obey.

Paradoxically, much design literature is obscure because it focuses too much on design. Thus, this chapter will attempt to avoid unnecessary abstraction by demonstrating that HRIS design — specifically the design of the data base, its file arrangement, and retrieval methodology — is part of the overall continuum of HRIS development rather than a completely separate function. In fact, much design work has already been done by the end of the Specifications Stage, if users' needs for specific kinds of tables, reports, and other information have been identified explicitly.

The job of the design team is to work with users in examining these requirements, which may include extensive government regulatory needs as discussed in Chapter 10, in light of constraints such as cost

## DESIGN CONSIDERATION: MAJOR INFLUENCES ON HRIS DESIGN 121

and computer technology. In a number of specific cases, the users may have specified that certain reports are needed, but the manner of producing those reports — whether online or in a batch mode, for example — will depend on cost and other considerations developed and clarified by the design team.

Conceptually, the design process will usually follow the path of iterations roughly shown in Figure 7A, beginning with the broadest possible "General Design," proceeding through a series of user reviews, and becoming increasingly detailed until acceptance is reached. The final results of the Design Stage will be a set of subfunction tasks, detailed in every respect, from which the personnel and data systems organizations can develop their products, as discussed in Chapter 8. For Personnel, this product is the user instruction and training programs. The product of the data systems organization will be the actual computer programs.

The important overall concept to keep in mind in setting up the work of the design stage, as shown in Figure 7B, is that this stage is to a large extent a joint effort among Team members working with

A. Start — *General Design*

   *User Review/Modifications*
   *Subfunction Tasks*

B. Next Level of Design (many iterations)

   *User Reviews/Modifications*
   *Subfunction Tasks*

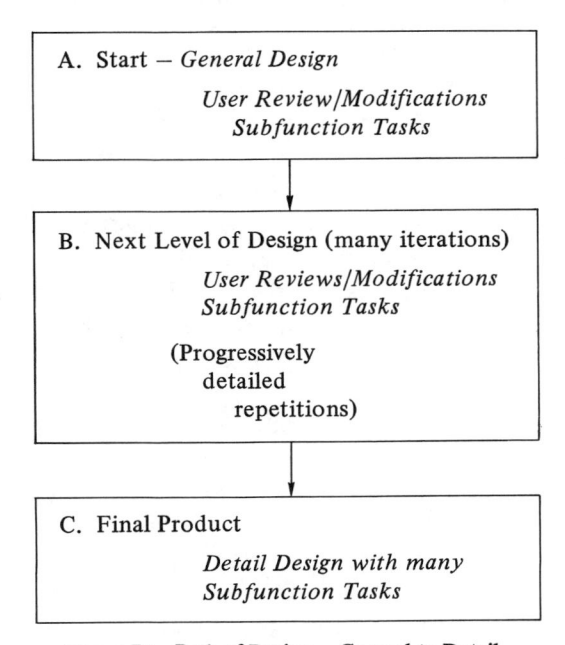

   (Progressively
      detailed
         repetitions)

C. Final Product

   *Detail Design with many*
   *Subfunction Tasks*

Figure 7A. Path of Design — General to Detail.

## 122   III/DESIGN AND INSTALLATION

*User Functions*
- Prepare Input
- Data Entry

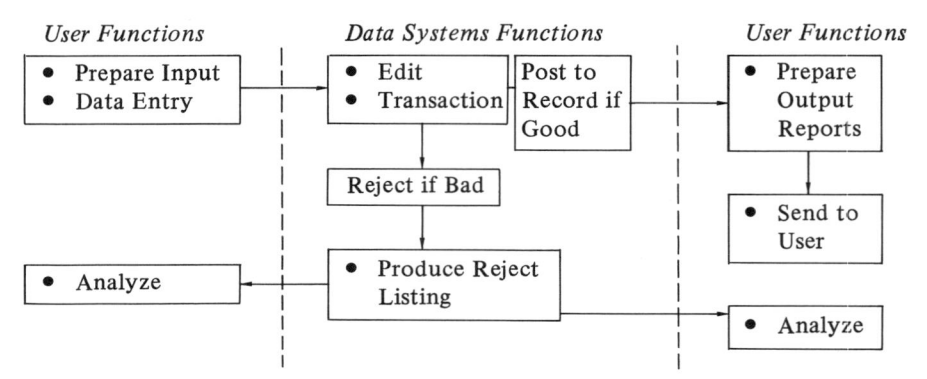

*Data Systems Functions*
- Edit
- Transaction
- Post to Record if Good
- Reject if Bad
- Produce Reject Listing

*User Functions*
- Prepare Output Reports
- Send to User
- Analyze

- Analyze

**Figure 7B. Personnel (User) Functions and Data Systems Functions.**

users. There is a tendency on the part of HRIS developers to hand over the system to data people at this point. This can be a fateful mistake.

### 7.1. HUMAN FUNCTIONS MUST BE CONSIDERED

In the design stage, the Project Team will be deciding which development functions are human functions and which will be performed by computer. Human processes must be designed as well as computer processes. For example, suppose the production of next year's salary increases has been identified as a needed function in the system. The task of preparing an output listing with ranges of salaries is a data systems output, and the design work could end there. However, an input sheet, with instructions and some code requirements, also needs to be designed. These instructions are designed for people to use — managers who are putting in the proposed salary increases.

Another case is the edit and error control process. In any system this process is one of the most complex and intricate to design, and this is certainly true in an HRIS. The function of monitoring and controlling the edit and error process may be designed only as far as building the internal edits and producing the list of codes for the HRIC to use. While this list is important and vital, it is not sufficient by itself to control the system. There must be an explanation of the causes of each error code and instructions on how to clear the error and correct the entry.

## DESIGN CONSIDERATION: MAJOR INFLUENCES ON HRIS DESIGN

*Personnel Designers*          *Data Systems Designers*

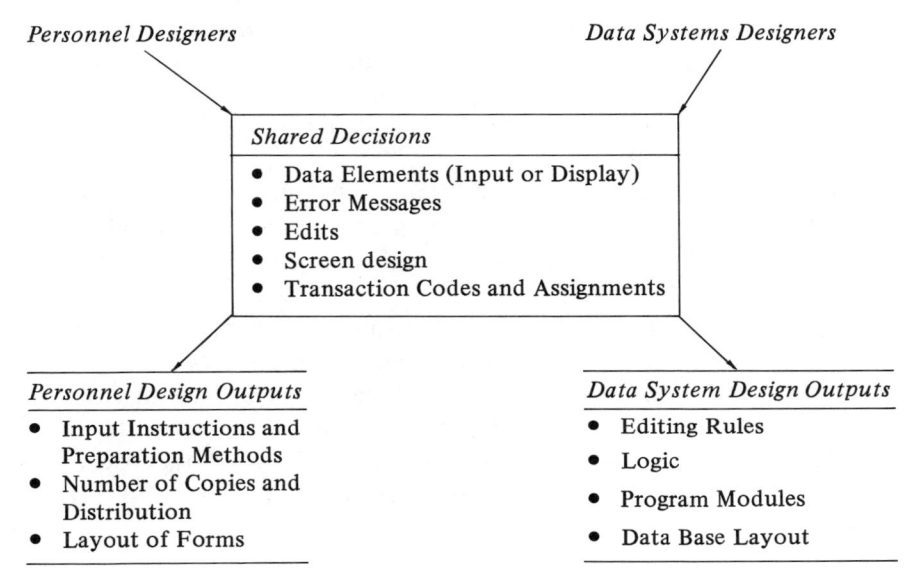

**Shared Decisions**
- Data Elements (Input or Display)
- Error Messages
- Edits
- Screen design
- Transaction Codes and Assignments

*Personnel Design Outputs*
- Input Instructions and Preparation Methods
- Number of Copies and Distribution
- Layout of Forms

*Data System Design Outputs*
- Editing Rules
- Logic
- Program Modules
- Data Base Layout

**Figure 7C.**

These are human processes that must be designed in order to administer the HRIS properly. Failure to design these functions and allocate them will produce a computer system that cannot be administered properly. Data systems Team members should design the computerized portions of the system, and the personnel members the people side. Sufficient interaction should take place to ensure that the system will operate smoothly. Tasks such as input forms design, data entry screens, and masks should be shared, since both groups design them. A recommended functional allocation of tasks is shown in Figure 7C.

*Design Considerations.* This chapter uses the word "considerations" in its title for good reason. It is simply not feasible to attempt to present a single design or set of design rules that will result in an optimum data base configuration for your HRIS. To begin with, many data base management systems are available in the marketplace, and each has its own file arrangement, data storage, and retrieval methodology. Computer equipment differs as well, and its characteristics can have important impacts on systems design.

Even more important, there is no optimum design that covers every organization's personnel needs. The uniqueness of each set of employees, and differences among organizational goals and objectives and other factors that will shape the HRIS, defy any attempt to prescribe a detailed design.

Demands for access, storage, editing, and updates — all key issues in design — vary widely among organizations. Thus, the actual plans, schemes and subschemes, and file layouts and hierarchies are left to the Project Team to devise.

Certain major considerations and influences on data base design should be examined by any HRIS Project Team, however. Some, in fact, may determine whether you will want to enhance an existing personnel system, build a new HRIS from scratch, or purchase a prepackaged system from a vendor and modify it for your own use.

These general considerations are discussed in the sections that follow:

7.2. *Designing for Historical Change,* with guidelines to assure that the design permits you to take full advantage of one of the chief benefits of having a computerized personnel system.
7.3. *Determining Data Base Activity and Size,* presenting detailed examples of how to estimate the total storage capacity you will need for different module configurations and employee coverages.
7.4. *Analysis of Reports,* describing categories of reports and key factors in report requirements that will shape the final HRIS.
7.5. *Distributed Processing,* a discussion of the capabilities of recently developed minicomputers and the uses of local processing and retrieval to meet certain HRIS design needs.
7.6. *External Files and Interfaces,* reviewing the question of whether to absorb or interface systems and subsystems in the HRIS.

## 7.2. DESIGNING FOR HISTORICAL CHANGE

One of the distinguishing characteristics of a computerized personnel system, and in many cases the most important benefit of having an HRIS, is the system's ability to provide a readily accessible history of data on people, events, and organizational relationships. History is important in virtually every area of personnel administration, since it is through the analysis of change over time that salary treatment, pension accruals, possible EEO imbalances, and other key functions are examined and acted upon. Six of the basic uses of data element history that should be considered by the HRIS design team are discussed later in this section.

As a rule, the Project Team in the design stage should make provisions to keep as much history as possible about every data element in the HRIS. Fortunately, modern computer systems are able to store increasingly extensive amounts of data at increasingly cheaper rates, a trend welcomed by personnel systems designers, since there is apparently no end to the demand for data analyses and statistics regarding employee and applicant movement and flow.

Common sense will tell the Team that there are some data elements for which no history need be provided, however. Data elements denoting sex, barring the isolated sex change operation, or a person's race (except perhaps when a woman acquires a Hispanic surname through marriage) do not change over time or change so infrequently and for such a small percentage of the population that it makes little sense to provide for change.

Most data elements in the personnel system have historical importance, however, and the HRIS should be designed to retain the changes that make up that history.

*Key Questions.* The Team may wish to classify data elements according to their importance as history, and this will vary according to organizational needs and the purposes of the HRIS. For the most part, however, organizations will require history on certain basic elements that reflect each employee's place in the organization — "then" as compared with now.

To do this, the system's design must permit you to answer certain key questions about employees' history:

- Where they were, physically and organizationally
- What they were doing, by job title and function
- What they were paid, or salary, grade, and Compa ratio
- When they were doing it, with effective dates and ending dates.

*Watch Changing Values.* One of the most important factors to consider in designing for historical change is that data and relationships change over time. Job title 1234 may not stand for the same job that it stood for a few years back; Company Unit 456 may have meant Engineering in 1978 and now be part of the Marketing Department. Organizations change to meet the needs of new environments, and the HRIS must reflect rather than impede such desirable change. The way to accomplish this is to design the HRIS so that sufficient supporting information and tables are retained and available to the new system.

The problems that come up in this regard emerge when reports are needed that will use both the "old" and "new" data base views, and identical code values have been used for different purposes and meanings. If current table files are used to derive elements in such cases, the picture mapped by historical data will be false. Without the old reference files or tables, accurate history on derived values will not be available.

For example, it may be obvious to the Team that all changes to the data element Job Title should be saved. But Job Title may be a key to files on Salary Grade and EEO Job Category. Merely keeping the changes to the Job Title code will not be of much use five years from now if the relationships to the derived salary grades and EEO categories have changed. The Job Title code itself does not have the information on pay and EEO you want — the table files do. The solution is to keep all changes and files indefinitely or to periodically do a dump and "freeze" on the data base to preserve the history that will be required.

*Basic Uses of History.* The design team should ensure that the HRIS will be capable of providing the data for at least the following kinds of analysis of historical data:

1. *Total Record of Each Employee*
   All changes to employee records, from initial hire to the current date, are essential if the HRIS is going to replace manual record keeping in the organization. This primary historical record, sometimes known as the "Employee Record" or "Service Record," keeps length-of-service documentation and is the source of benefits calculations and other functions. In many organizations, this record is the official compnay personnel record for

each employee. This record, which must have all entries and changes to all fields to be complete, is also needed to meet privacy requirements and for proper data base administration (as in cases where a total "dump" of a record is required).

2. *Statutory Requirements*

   By law, certain records are needed to explain hiring, firing, promotion, and training decisions in an organization. These requirements vary by organization, industry, and state as well as by classes of employees. As a rule, a complete history of all changes in an employee's status is sufficient to meet all needs, although where pay is concerned, actual time worked must be included — including overtime — and deductions accounted for.

   It is worth noting that in cases of disciplinary discharges, complete documentation, including supervisors' notes, may be necessary. Any case where a problem might emerge requires more than a mere notation on the HRIS stating that the employee was discharged. Detailed records of both the employee's actions and management's actions are vital in such instances, and the HRIS cannot be viewed as the total record keeper in an organization unless it includes this kind of information.

3. *Reconstruct Work Groups*

   There are instances when the Personnel Department may need to reconstruct a work group or the condition of a class of employee for a certain period of time in the past. This type of analysis is done, for example, to study possible disparate representation of minorities or women. A study of this type may involve a request for data from the Marketing Department between September 1, 1980, and August 31, 1981, such as the average starting salaries of men versus women or their average promotional increase amounts over that period.

4. *Year-to-Date and Year-Over-Year Studies*

   A fairly common use of history is the production of year-to-date and year-over-year studies, reports especially important in manpower planning, EEO, salary administration, and force control studies. Such reports show the numbers of hires, transfers, and terminations on an annual basis and display the same statistics for a corresponding time period of the previous year.

5. *Longitudinal Studies*

    To meet research and other needs, the progress (or lack of it) of a fixed control group of employees in the organization should be available in the HRIS. An example would be to identify all black females hired as secretaries in 1972 and to study them over a five- or ten-year time frame. Obviously, you can go back only as far as history permits.

6. *Employment and EEO Analyses*

    Over and above the foregoing requirements and uses of history, there is a growing demand for a review of the overall employment process in many organizations, usually covering a number of years and requiring breakdowns by race, sex, and other factors. A typical request is shown below:

*Sample Request*

1. Number of hires over the past five years — display by year
   Number of White Males
   Number of White Females
   Number of Black Males
   Number of Black Females
   Number of Hispanic Males, etc.
2. Average starting salaries for each group
3. Average starting salaries by highest level of education for each group
4. Average age of each group

Total movement — including upgrades, downgrades, lateral moves, hires, fires, and to and from leaves of absence — is required for detailed EEO analysis. Furthermore, it may be necessary to analyze each personnel plan — such as salary, training, and career development — with these statistics.

## 7.3. DETERMINING DATA BASE ACTIVITY AND SIZE

The activity and size of the data base — defined as the total number of characters or bytes of storage that the HRIS will have to process and maintain — can be crucial design factors for the Project Team, and some detail is provided in this section on ways of estimating needs and limitations.

The limitations occur for the most part in such equipment configurations as mini or microcomputers; although the sure progress of advancing technology is expanding the boundaries of equipment storage year by year, certain size limitations are very real and should be examined closely by the Team. In major computer centers, the ratings or storage that can be accessed at one time run into the billions and represent boundaries that will probably never be reached.

*Types of HRIS Data Storage.* In sizing the HRIS, there are two types of data with which to contend: active online data and offline data. The active online data is the data base that is presented to the user for reports and analysis on a regular basis. This is also the data base that the HRIS will access for its editing functions.

In smaller systems, this could be all of the data that the HRIS has ever handled, including data on active employees, inactive employees, and applicants. When the number of records is small, the designers may not have to contend with segmenting the data base in order to optimize its design.

The secondary storage, or offline data, includes everything else that is not in the primary or active online data base.

**7.3.1. Methods of Segmentation**

In order to reduce the size of the files that are processed, the designers should try to balance the needs of the users and the system requirements with the attendant costs and run times that will be associated with each function. For example, to update the data base, it might take twenty minutes of wall clock time in a stand-alone environment under version A of the data base and 30 minutes under version B, where version A represents the HRIS with no inactive records and version B has all records, active and inactive. These time and cost estimates are very useful for the users, since they can now make trade-offs with respect to operating costs. These decisions obviously influence HRIS design.

There are ways to segment or stratify the data base to reduce its size. The most frequent methods of partitioning the HRIS data base are by type of record and type of data.

*By Type of Record.* This is done by keeping employment applicants or inactive employees in a separate file. This technique can easily cut the size of the data base in half.

*By Type of Data.* This approach keeps different record configurations and layouts, depending on the coverage of a given personnel program and status of an employee. Hourly employees, for instance, usually do not need the same number of data elements that salaried employees do. Benefit plans for hourly employees normally lend themselves to tables (much more so than plans for salaried employees, as a rule), and the Team may therefore decide that the only elements needed for these records are the "keys" to the tables. In this way the designers would be developing two or more record types, and this approach would keep the data base within manageable bounds.

In large systems, where storage and processing costs are a factor to be considered in design, it is usually beneficial to segment the data base by both methods: record type and data type. The matrix in Figure 7D shows one way of segmenting an HRIS.

For illustrative purposes in these sections on data base activity and sizing, a fictitious company's needs will be analyzed. This company, the Ajax Corporation, is presumed to be ready to design an HRIS, and has the following characteristics:

**Ajax Corporation**

| | |
|---|---|
| Size | 5,000 employees |
| Salaried/Hourly | 1,000/4,000 |
| Turnover (10–30%) | 500–1,500 new hires |
| HRIS Module Requirements | Basic, Career Development, Benefits, and Applicant modules |

The factors of employee type and turnover are extremely important, since they represent the criteria for segmentation. The module to be installed is important, since it determines the type of elements that need to be retained.

### 7.3.2. Active Employee Data Requirements

The number of bytes of data needed on an active employee's record depends on the module and whether that module will be extended to

# DESIGN CONSIDERATION: MAJOR INFLUENCES ON HRIS DESIGN 131

| Type of Record | Basic Module || Benefits Module || Career Development Module || Applicant Module ||
| --- | --- | --- | --- | --- | --- | --- | --- | --- |
|  | Coverage | History | Coverage | History | Coverage | History | Coverage | History |
| 1. Active Employee |  |  |  |  |  |  |  |  |
| • Hourly | Y | Y | Y | Y | N | N | N | N |
| • Salaried | Y | Y | Y | Y | Y | Y | N | N |
| 2. Inactive |  |  |  |  |  |  |  |  |
| • Terminated | Y | N | N | N | N | N | N | N |
| • Terminated Vested | Y | N | Y | Y | N | N | N | N |
| • Retired | Y | N | Y | Y | N | N | N | N |
| 3. Applicant | N | N | N | N | N | N | Y | Y |

Figure 7D. Design Matrix Segmenting an HRIS

the population that includes the employee. The range varies, based on a low value for a new hire to an employee who will have been in the data base for several years.

The bearing of history on data base storage is very crucial, since keeping all changes to every field on the active or online data base can easily double the amount of current data kept in any year.

*Current Data Elements.* The requirements for current data can be determined by analyzing the normal amount of data it would take to describe a given employee's current status in the company. This would range from a minimum of information, such as for a new hire, who is not yet in any benefit programs and is without any formal education, to a mature employee, who is in all benefit programs, has a degree and has been with the organization for some years, and has an entry in most or all elements.

**Ajax Corporation**

| Module | Number of Bytes of Data* | | | History | Employee Type |
|---|---|---|---|---|---|
| | Low | High | Avg. | | |
| Basic | 50 | 400 | 300 | Yes | All |
| Car. Dev. | 100 | 350 | 300 | Yes | All Salaried + Some Hourly |
| Benefits | 10 | 200 | 100 | Yes | Hourly |
| | 10 | 1,000 | 400 | Yes | Salaried |

| Total per current employee: | | | Average Bytes per Record |
|---|---|---|---|
| | Low | High | |
| Hourly | 160 | 950 | 700 |
| Salaried | 160 | 1,750 | 1,000 |

| | Low | High | Average |
|---|---|---|---|
| 4,000 Hourly | 640,000 | 3,800,000 | 2,800,000 |
| 1,000 Salaried | 160,000 | 1,750,000 | 1,000,000 |
| Total current Storage | 800,000 | 5,550,000 | 3,800,000 |

*The "Low" estimate is for new hires; "High" is for employees with at least five years of service in this example.

*History Data: Three Options.* The historical record-keeping requirements of the HRIS can be estimated after first deciding which of three options the design team will pursue with respect to maintaining history. These options are to:

1. Keep all changes to all items on the online data base and keep all derived elements that change when the basic element changes. In this option, not only would values such as a salary change be maintained, but derived elements dependent on salary, such as Compa Ratio, would be stored.

    Saving all historical changes to all elements is the safest of all options, since the future needs for data cannot always be predicted. Obviously, however, it is the most expensive and cumbersome approach.
2. Keep little or no history on the online data base; purge it to offline storage on a periodic basis. Under this option, the user is limited to retrieving current data only, or only as much history as has occurred since the last purge. If there is to be little call for immediate analysis of past events, this option will keep the data base lean, but clearly it is the most limiting approach from the user's standpoint.
3. Some combination of the above, based on the need for access to key or critical fields. This approach requires a prior categorization of elements based on thier criticality. For example:

### Type of Data Based on Criticality

Class I. *Most Critical.* This type is made up of a selected number of key data elements for which all changes should always be available. Among these key data elements should be job title, salary, location, and department. Effective dates are required. With or without derived data, all past occurrences to key elements must be accessible in the same manner as current data.

Class II. *Recent History.* In addition to class I history items, the last two or three years of data for selected fields may be required. Data such as career development changes unique to salaried employees might fall into this class.

## 134   III / DESIGN AND INSTALLATION

Class III. *Storable.* The rest of the changes to other elements, changes not covered in class I or class II, do not need to be retained in an active mode beyond a purge date. This class is a rising and falling category of items awaiting purge. It might include home addresses or skills inventory changes that were in effect at the time but are no longer applicable to an employee's evaluation.

*History Analysis: Size Per Option.* For this analysis we will assume a ten-year history horizon and estimate the number of bytes of storage necessary under each of the three options described earlier: (1) keeping all changes to all elements, (2) keeping little or no history online, and (3) keeping certain element changes, based on criticality.

1. *Keep Data Changes to All Elements*

   As noted earlier, key elements such as salary, job, organization, and location are usually driver elements and are keys to tables. In these cases the related elements must be stored as well.

**Basic Module**

| Elements | Changes/Year | No. of Other Elements That Must Be Saved | Total Chtrs Each Change |
|---|---|---|---|
| **Driver Elements** | | | |
| Job | 1 | 10 | 120 |
| Organization | 1 | 5 | 100 |
| Location | .5 | 5 | 100 |
| Salary | 1 | 5 | 80 |
|  | 3.5 | | 400 |
| **Basic Other** | | | |
| Name, Address | 1 | 3 | 70 |
| Others (Education Service Dates) | 1 | 2 | 30 |
|  | 2 | | 100 |

**Benefits Module**

| Elements | Changes/Year | No. of Other Elements That Must Be Saved | Total Chtrs Each Change |
|---|---|---|---|
| **Driver Elements** | | | |
| Plan Codes | 2 | 6 | 80 |
| **Benefits – Others** | | | |
| Salary History | 1 | 4 | 50 |
| Others (Dependents) Beneficiaries, etc. | 2 | 2 | 100 |
|  | 5 | | 230 |

DESIGN CONSIDERATION: MAJOR INFLUENCES ON HRIS DESIGN 135

**Career Module**

|  | Element Changes | Changes per Year | No. of Elements | Total Characters |
|---|---|---|---|---|
|  | New Skills/Devel. Codes | 1 Update | 125 | 500 |

Totals

| Employee Type | Type Change | Changes per Year | No. of Characters per Year |
|---|---|---|---|
| Hourly Employees | Basic, Driver | 3.5 | 400 |
|  | Basic, Other | 2 | 100 |
|  | Benefits | 5 | 230 |
|  |  | 8.5 | 730 |
| Salaried Employees | Career Module | 1 | 500 |
|  |  | 9.5 | 1,230 |

Summation for all Employees

5,000 × 730 = 3,650,000 per year
1,000 × 500 =   500,000 per year (salaried only)
                4,150,000 bytes per year
For 10 years = 40,150,000 bytes of storage

2. *Keep Little or No History Until Purged*

    Assuming an annual purge, the maximum requirement would be one full year of history as calculated above, or 3,650,000 bytes of storage. There would not necessarily be one year's worth of changes, however.

3. *Combination Based on Criticality*

    This option uses some combination, based on class of element, to keep all changes to most essential items available at all times. In addition, there would be the current history on all items until purges. Following the same logic as above, but paring the list to the minimum, we get:

**136** III/DESIGN AND INSTALLATION

### Basic Module

| Driver Elements | Changes | No. of Other Elements Which Must Be Saved | Total Characters |
|---|---|---|---|
| Job | 1 | 2 | 30 |
| Organization | 1 | 1 | 20 |
| Location | .5 | 1 | 30 |
| Salary | 1 | 2 | 30 |
|  | 3.5 |  | 110 |
| Others | 0 | 0 | 0 |

### Benefits Module

| | | | |
|---|---|---|---|
| Plan Codes | 2 | 2 | 30 |
| Others | 1 | 4 | 50 |
|  | 3 |  | 80 |

### Career Module

| | | | |
|---|---|---|---|
| None | 0 | 0 | 0 |

### Total for Combination Employee Type, All

| Type Change | No. | Type per Year |
|---|---|---|
| Basic Driver | 3.5 | 110 |
| Benefits | 3 | 80 |
|  | 6.5 | 190 |

5,000 Employees × 190 bytes = 950,000 bytes per year for all years beyond the first.

| | |
|---|---|
| Year 1 – All Changes | 3,650,000 |
| Year 2 – 10 – Same changes only 950,000 × 9 years | + 8,550,000 |
|  | 12,200,000 |

*History Summary.* The number of bytes of storage for history needs ranges from a low to a high as follows:

Low – Keep one year only. . . . . . . . . . . . . . . . . . . . . . . . . . .3,650,000
High – Keep all (10 years). . . . . . . . . . . . . . . . . . . . . . . . . .40,150,000
Average – Combination. . . . . . . . . . . . . . . . . . . . . . . . . . . .12,200,000

*Current and History.* Combined view of the requirements per employee is shown below.

|  | \multicolumn{3}{c|}{Hourly} | \multicolumn{3}{c}{Salaried} |
| | Low | High | Most Likely or Average | Low | High | Most Likely or Average |
|---|---|---|---|---|---|---|
| Current | 160 | 950 | 700 | 160 | 1,750 | 1,000 |
| History | 190 | 730 | 190 | 190 | 1,230 | 190 |
| 1 Year View | 350 | 1,680 | 890 | 350 | 2,980 | 1,190 |

### 7.3.3. Tables and Reference Files

The number and size of any and all tables necessary to operate the HRIS must be included in the design discussions and computations.

| Table | Number of Records | Size | Total |
|---|---|---|---|
| Job table | 600 | 175 | 105,000 |
| Location table | 150 | 80 | 12,000 |
| Benefits table | 45 | 40 | 1,800 |
| Education table | 800 | 65 | 52,000 |
| Organization table | 350 | 95 | 33,250 |
| | | | 204,050 |

### 7.3.4. Applicant Records

The number and size of the applicant records must also be calculated by the design team. Like the employee records, these can vary widely, depending on the functions performed and the amount of time the organization wishes to maintain an applicant record before purging it to an inactive state. Also, an applicant who moves all the way through the preemployment process will generate many more data elements than an applicant who is rejected early.

On a recruiting/employment year basis, the records of applicants will be of three types: those who were rejected early and about whom little data is known; those who secured employment and about whom many data are captured; and those in between, who were rejected or who dropped out during the preemployment process. The size can be estimated based on an estimate of the data requirements for these three types, together with the applicant volume, or number of applicants.

## Ajax Corp. Applicant Records

| Applicant Type | Data Requirements | Applicant Volume Low Year | High Year | Average Year |
|---|---|---|---|---|
| Early Reject | 100 Chrts | 3,000 | 7,000 | 4,000 |
| Completed Process | 1,000 Chrts | 500 | 1,500 | 1,000 |
| In-Process Reject | 350 Chrts | 2,500 | 6,500 | 3,000 |
|  |  | 6,000 | 15,000 | 8,000 |

The number of bytes of data can then be calculated as follows:

| Applicant Type | Low Year | High Year | Average Year |
|---|---|---|---|
| Early Reject | 300,000 | 700,000 | 400,000 |
| Completed Process | 500,000 | 1,500,000 | 1,000,000 |
| In-Process Reject | 875,000 | 2,275,000 | 1,050,000 |
|  | 1,675,000 | 4,475,000 | 2,450,000 |

### 7.3.5. Inactive Employee Records

An analysis of the types of data necessary for inactive records should be performed. The segmentation should be based on the type of inactive status, i.e., terminated without vesting, terminated with vesting, and retired, deceased, etc.

If the design team chooses to create a different type of record format from the format used for an active employee, care must be taken not to purge needed data. A very effective way of handling the design is to keep a skeletal record on the online system and the complete record in an inactive state.

The task of determining the storage requirements for inactive becomes a matter of determining how many records of a basic or skeletal variety are necessary and how many vested terminated or retired employees records must be kept and for how long.

A low estimate may involve only one year of skeletal records along with retired and vested terminated. The high estimate could reflect that all data are kept in the full context — the way the data were at termination for a ten-year period with no purging. An average could represent a compromise along the lines of the last two years of full records and skeletal records beyond that, say for for eight years. If

## DESIGN CONSIDERATION: MAJOR INFLUENCES ON HRIS DESIGN

the inactive employee is a vested terminated or retiree, however, all data should be kept for ten years.

All figures will be factored in the volume of turnover and number of retirees. In the examples, the estimates are used:

*Turnover*  Low Turnover       = 500/year
            Moderate Turnover  = 1,000
            High Turnover      = 1,500

It should be noted that leaves of absence should be treated as active employees.

The estimate of data storage for inactive records could yield the following estimate:

A. Low Estimate – One Year Skeletal, only Low turnover, then purge

| Year | Numbers | Type | Bytes | Requirements Storage |
|---|---|---|---|---|
| 1 | 400 | Terminations – Not Vested/ Retired Hourly and Salaried | 350 | 140,000 |
| 1 | 70 | Vested Terminated/Retirees, Hourly | 730 | 51,100 |
| 1 | 30 | Vested Terminated/Retirees, Salaried | 1,230 | 36,900 |
|   | 500 | Turnover Annually |  | 228,000 |

B. High Estimate – Ten-Year Estimate of all data, high turnover

| Year | Numbers | Type | Bytes |  |
|---|---|---|---|---|
| 10 | 1,100 | Terminations, Not Vested/ Retired, Hourly | 1,680 | 18,480,000 |
| 10 | 200 | Terminations, Not Vested/ Retired, Salaried | 2,980 | 5,960,000 |
| 10 | 150 | Vested Terminated/Retired Hourly | 1,680 | 2,520,000 |
| 10 | 50 | Vested Terminated/Retired Salaried | 2,980 | 1,490,000 |
|   | 1,500 |  |  | 28,450,000 |

## 140  III / DESIGN AND INSTALLATION

C. Most Likely Estimate – Two Years of Most Likely, Moderate turnover plus eight years skeleton/full retirees

| Years | Numbers | Type | Bytes | Requirements Storage |
|---|---|---|---|---|
| 2 | 800 | Terminations, Not Vested/ Retired, Hourly Avg | 890 | 1,424,000 |
| 2 | 100 | Terminations, Not Vested/ Retired, Salaried | 1,190 | 238,000 |
| 2 | 70 | Vested Terminated/Retired Hourly | 890 | 1,246,000 |
| 2 | 30 | Vested Terminated/Retired Salaried | 1,190 | 71,400 |
|  | 1,000 | Turnover Annually |  | 2,979,400 |

| Years | Numbers | Type |  |  |
|---|---|---|---|---|
| 8 | 900 | Terminations, Not Vested/ Retired, Hourly/Sal, Skel | 350 | 2,520,000 |
| 8 | 70 | Terminations, Not Vested/ Retired, Hourly | 890 | 498,400 |
| 8 | 30 | Vested Terminated/Retired Salaried | 1,190 | 285,600 |
|  |  |  |  | 3,304,000 |
|  |  |  |  | 6,283,400 |

The total average estimate for a ten-year period for inactives is:

$$17,098,000$$
$$\underline{9,632,000}$$
$$26,730,000$$

The range of data storage necessary in an online mode for inactive records becomes:

|  | Bytes |
|---|---|
| Low Estimate | 1,079,000 |
| High Estimate | 150,750,000 |
| Average Estimate | 9,632,000 |

## 7.3.6. Total Storage Requirements

Total HRIS data storage requirements for the online data base for the Ajax Corporation are as follows:

|  | Low | High | Most Likely or Average |
|---|---|---|---|
| 1. Active Employees (current history) |  |  |  |
| Hourly Employees | 350 | 1,680 | 890 |
| × 4,000 | 1,400,000 | 6,720,000 | 3,560,000 |
| Salaried Employees | 350 | 2,980 | 1,190 |
| × 1,000 | 350,000 | 2,980,000 | 1,190,000 |
| 2. Tables | 204,050 | 204,050 | 204,050 |
| 3. Applicants | 1,675,000 | 4,475,000 | 2,450,000 |
| 4. Inactive Employees | 228,000 | 28,450,000 | 6,283,400 |
| Total Storage Needed | 3,857,050 | 42,829,050 | 13,687,450 |

## 7.4. ANALYSIS OF REPORTS

The overall design of any HRIS will to a large degree also depend on the type and volume of reports required by users. If there is a heavy demand for reports that have year-to-date statistics, the design of the system and its data base must be able to respond to that need. If, on the other hand, there is a great demand for rapid response and interactive query capability, a different file design and access method will be chosen. Thus, in fundamental ways, the HRIS design will be shaped by reports.

In reviewing the reports called for in the specifications stage, the design team should first categorize these outputs in terms of the computations that will have to be performed and the data base elements that will have to be calculated in order to produce them. This is necessary to determine whether an element should be present at all times or only calculated at output time.

### 7.4.1. Categories of Reports

The classifications of specified reports shown here will assist the design team in understanding the type, volume, frequency, and destination of reports, as well as point to the data elements necessary to support the system. While not a rigid classification scheme and not intended to categorically isolate any one report in a definitional pigeonhole, this is rather a suggested way of looking at user requests.

## *Report Categories*

- *Summary Statistical Output.* Included here are all outputs that have purely aggregated counts, where no individual data are needed.
  Example: Departmental count by age or level.
- *Time against Time.* (Year end 19___ versus Year end 19___) These are reports that compare two or more employee group counts at different time intervals.
  Example: Year end 1980 versus Year end 1981 count.
- *Time to Date.* (Year to date or month to date) These reports count activity from a benchmarked employee population.
  Example: New hires or terminations from the beginning of the year to the current date.
- *Combination of Time against Time and Time-to-Date.* These reports count activity from a benchmark and compare these counts to a previous period's activity.
  Example: Salary increases of a given level employee group, year-to-date, versus activity in similar period last year.
- *Employee Listings.* Simple lists of employees who meet certain parameters. The data content is obviously important, as is the sequency of the report.
  Example: Employees elegible for merit increases next month.
- *Employee Profile.* All meaningful data about an individual displayed in a readable format.
  Example: Career Development profile.
- *Graphical and Statistical Output.* Reports that utilize statistical or graphic analysis. These normally are histograms, regressions, and similar displays.
  Example: Average salary by education level; number of employees by department.
- *Multifile Outputs.* Reports that utilize extraneous files as an input.
  Example: EEO target-setting report

### 7.4.2. Design Considerations of Reports

When the file medium was tape or disk and the only type of file layout was a sequential file, there was no real discussion or analysis of HRIS design beyond making sure that the data elements were there to produce the output. However, with the various access methods now available and with data base management systems in use, there are other factors that the design team must account for when reviewing these reports.

Each output or report should be examined in the light of the factors that were developed during the systems specification stage. These factors are:

- Population covered
- Volume
- Media
- Format
- Interface
- Time frame
- Destination
- Retention rules
- Security/privacy
- Frequency of production

And, most important, the data content, including an analysis of the need for historical data.

These are not necessarily all the factors involved, but they do provide a starting point from which to assess the impact that the production of the reports will have on the design of the system. Several are especially important, such as time frame.

*Report Time Frame.* The time frame should be closely examined with the users, since it may well be that a user is requesting reports containing data current as of the moment or the previous day. This implies a system that must process immediately, or at least daily, and not only have all changes to data posted each day but employ a delivery vehicle to get the output to each user within the same time frame. This need for a real-time or pseudo-real-time system obviously increases the operating costs of a personnel system to such an extent that it would become prohibitive in all but a few situations. For instance, an online training course enrollment and registration system would need to be current on at least a daily basis, or even more frequently in a heavy training environment. This online feature demands a very rigorous design. Each transaction to the system must be edited and posted to the employee master data base and counters, statistical summaries, and other auxilliary files as well. In a company of any size, this means that the data base, its programs, and supporting tables or reference files must be in available storage during prime time. The costs for this storage, communications costs, and other expenses will be quite a bit higher than if the system were operated in a batch mode or some combination of batch updating and online editing.

Examination of the year-to-date and month-to-date requirements must be made at this time to ensure that the data base has, or is capable of producing, the elements necessary for these calculations and that the costs do not become prohibitive.

*Volume, Destination, and Media.* The users should be discouraged from receiving too many copies of fixed outputs on a regularly scheduled basis. Designers should make available prepackaged, or "canned," routines that users can call up on request. Display terminals with printers are very useful in this setting, and if the user sees a report or wants a listing of a given population, he or she can scan the report visually and print it when desired.

This method of handling report distribution is preferable to designing a system that produces mountains of printouts that wind up on office windowsills. Even if these reports are used, they do not usually lend themselves to easy analysis of problem situations.

Trends, possible trouble areas in EEO, salary distributions, relevant labor pool shifts, and other similar uses and analyses are very difficult to find or study with paper listings and standard outputs. These analyses are better suited to graphic and statistical outputs, and the design team should be alert to these considerations.

Microfilm and microfiche should also be explored and perhaps suggested in office settings where retention and storage of large printouts is essential. End-of-year printouts of the entire population and other situations in which the data base is dumped are potential beneficiaries of this technology.

*Data Usage Mapping.* All the reports that the users specified in the Needs Analysis must be analyzed to see the expected usage. A way to do this is to establish a matrix or usage map. This map would depict each data element and show which reports would use which elements. The high-usage elements, of course, become prime candidates for the nodes on a hierarchy in a DBMS environment.

As shown in Figure 7E, the data elements "department" and "status" are high-usage elements, since they are used in most reports. (This example is very simplistic, since there are only eight elements and seven reports.) If these elements are put in the hierarchial path, the search becomes much more efficient for the system, since fewer records need to be searched.

The same concept is used as far as updates are concerned. Information on which data elements are changed most frequently will help the designers as well, since they need to develop the structure from both the access and the update aspects.

If a trade-off has to be made on where to place items, it usually is a good idea to favor retrieval rather than update, unless it is a very one-sided argument. The access has a higher visibility index and usually will involve higher-ranking users than the update does. From a public relations standpoint, therefore, if it is a close call, decisions should be made in favor of access speed.

|  | Report 1 | Report 2 | Report 3 | Report 4 | Report 5 | Report 6 | Report 7 |
|---|---|---|---|---|---|---|---|
| Birth Date |  |  | x |  |  |  |  |
| Class |  | x | x |  | x |  |  |
| Department | x | x | x | x | x |  | x |
| Location | x |  | x |  |  | x |  |
| Name | x |  | x |  | x |  |  |
| Race | x | x |  |  | x |  | x |
| Sex | x | x |  |  | x |  | x |
| Status | x |  | x | x | x | x |  |
| •        |   |   |   |   |   |   |   |
| •        |   |   |   |   |   |   |   |
| •        |   |   |   |   |   |   |   |
| •        |   |   |   |   |   |   |   |
| •        |   |   |   |   |   |   |   |
| •        |   |   |   |   |   |   |   |
| Zip Code |  | x |  | x |  | x |  |

**Figure 7E. Data Usage Map Access**

## 7.5. DISTRIBUTED PROCESSING

Should your organization have a number of outlying locations or intermediate collection points through which personnel information flows in the normal course of operations, the concept of distributed processing may be important in your HRIS design. There exist an almost limitless number of possible configurations of distributed networks, each with somewhat different dependencies between the outlying equipment and data bases and the central mainframe and overall data base, but the main trend in recent years has been to deliver more and more power to outlying locations, using higher-capacity minicomputers.

In the past, the standard way of distributing the power of the central computer or mainframe to many remote users was to provide each user with a terminal and output device and provide for direct access to a central time-sharing system. Each user at a remote location would have a dial-up or leased line and would engage the host computer directly to perform input or output functions. The computer would interact with the user directly, and each user would have access to all of the central mainframe's functions.

This approach to online time sharing provides the quick data input and error correction needed by remote users and easy interaction with data bases that are relatively small and not elaborately structured. Also, the mainframe processing time, the salaries of central staff people, and other expenses can be prorated over users, based on their usage of the facilities. The cost of operating a personnel system in this environment tends to be on the high side, however; and if the central data base is large and complex, this separation of data from users can lead to communication problems. Data may not always be available when required.

The recent advances in microprocessing that have spurred the growth of mini or microcomputers for remote locations have provided a broad range of options for HRIS designers interested in distributed processing. While there is no one design especially suited for personnel systems, the new capabilities of mini or microcomputers offer a number of improved options and trade-offs to systems designers requiring online distributed networks.

Utilizing the more powerful minis, designers can shed some of the more routine tasks of the HRIS to cheaper machines. This not only reduces overall costs but frees the mainframe host computer for larger, more important tasks that cannot be shifted.

This environment works best when the employee data base does not have to be updated immediately. The user can enter data at the remote site, where a less expensive device — an intelligent terminal or microcomputer — would perform some edits and store the data for later transmission to the host computer. The host might be designed to poll the remote locations — hourly, daily, or weekly, depending on the urgency of data needs — and take in the input data for processing and posting to the centralized data base. Teleprocessing costs are reduced, since there is only one link to the host per location instead of many.

For many tasks, the local sites can be completely decoupled from the main computer. Routine jobs such as data entry can be performed locally, never engaging the host computer. If it is captive to Personnel, these smaller machines can be used twenty-four hours a day, seven days a week, at no additional computer cost. A distributed system such as that depicted in Figure 7F can be considerably less expensive than a totally user-to-mainframe system.

These standalone systems very often come with word processing capabilities now making it possible to have a self-contained office system which will handle routine correspondance, documentation as well as input and retrieval.

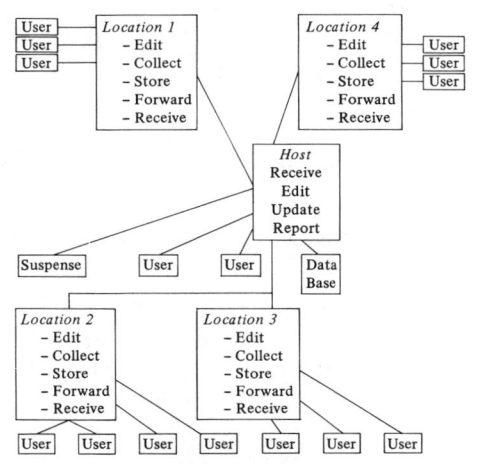

Figure 7F. Distributed Processing System

If the local system is large enough to accept data down stream from the host and print it, the outlying location can produce reports. This type of network will further save users. Instead of direct-accessing the expensive host and keeping it engaged in printing and transmission, users can formulate requests locally and have the mini engage the host. The host then scans the data base, arranges the data, and transmits the final output to the mini — all at an extremely fast rate. The mini can then print or otherwise display the data at the user's discretion. Time on the host has been minimized through automation.

For Project Teams making design choices, the relative costs of remote hardware versus mainframe and transmission costs will have to be weighed. If, as expected, present trends continue and mini and microcomputer costs keep coming down, designers of personnel systems requiring remote processing will no doubt adopt them increasingly in distributed systems. More powerful, less expensive minis will also have the DBMS technology needed, along with graphics, storage, and other features.

## 7.6. EXTERNAL FILES AND INTERFACES

Finally, system designers should make a review that is necessary at each step of the development cycle — an analysis of the scope and boundaries of the HRIS — to ensure that the Team is not designing a system that is too large and monolithic.

Experience has shown that it is easier to develop and operate separate systems or subsystems than to bite off too much at one time. Although it may be obvious that the Payroll System and Career Development modules should be treated as separate systems, it may not be so clear that there are other pieces of an HRIS that can be separated as well and possibly should be.

The possibility of separating these systems should not be overlooked:

- *Wage and Salary Administration,* with its annual salary surveys, production of merit increase schedules, and budget control.
- *Job Evaluation Systems,* including benchmark job analyses and point score factors.
- *Labor Relations,* producing union membership lists, grievances, bidding and bumping rosters, and preparations for bargaining.

- *Medical and Safety,* including such items as accidents and illnesses, employee physicals, exposure to toxic chemicals, or automotive fleet maintenance.

## CONCLUSION

The design of the data base, the file arrangement, and retrieval methodology represent part of a continuum of HRIS development rather than a completely separate discipline. Much design work has already been done in the specifications stage, for example, if users' needs for specific kinds of reports, tables, and other requirements have been identified and specified accruately. And although the design stage of HRIS development is customarily thought of as data systems responsibility, human functions should also be considered by the Project Team in this stage. Items such as input forms and edit instructions must be designed with users in mind to assure that the system can be operated and administered.

The design stage proceeds from an overall "grand design" concept to a series of increasingly detailed user reviews with many iterations. Its final product will be a detailed array of subfunction tasks that will serve as the basis for implementation and conversion.

Key design considerations explored in this chapter include the need for history in the HRIS, how to determine data base activity and size, reports, the nature of modern distributed processing, and external files and interfaces. In each of these areas, guidelines are presented to improve the Project Team's understanding of options rather than recommendations of choices that will necessarily depend on individual organizational and user needs.

# 8
# Program Development and Conversion

After the design of the HRIS, the actual coding for program development and conversion to the new personnel system can take place. Two distinct products will be delivered at the end of this implementation stage: the computer programs themselves and the user instructions and procedures.

The development of each of these products, it should be remembered, is a joint effort between the technical data systems members of the Project Team and personnel and user members. It is especially important not to overlook the need for user involvement in the development of procedures and instructions.

The creation of a centralized Human Resource Information Center (HRIC) at this stage of system development, with specific development, conversion, and operating functions, will greatly facilitate the job of getting your system "up and running" and help assure the integrity and quality of the data base in the new HRIS environment. In relatively small system installations, the HRIC need comprise only one or two people, but its existence will help the transition from a Project Team environment to the HRIC-administrated situation of normal operation. The HRIC and some of its more important functions are discussed in Chapter 9.

In this chapter, general guidelines are provided on program development for personnel (8.1), the test plan and user tests are discussed (8.2), steps in the conversion plan are outlined (8.3), and certain key operating considerations, notably data base accuracy, are examined for their implications at this stage (8.4).

## 8.1 PROGRAM DEVELOPMENT FOR PERSONNEL: FIVE GUIDELINES

Computer programming is obviously a field of study in itself, and much has been written about how to develop effective programs. In developing programs specifically for computerized personnel systems, however, my experience is that the following guidelines are especially applicable to HRIS program development:

1. *Break the Job Up Into Manageable Pieces*
   Just as the overall HRIS has been broken up into modules for ease of design and development, each module or separable function should be broken down to simplify program specification and coding. The first separation may be by specific computer functions — e.g., data base I/O, report generation, interfaces — based on machine and system operating efficiencies.
   
   The next stratum of split should be by module. If the HRIS is to have Basic, EEO, Benefits, and HRU modules, program development should proceed independently for each of the four modules.
   
   In some cases, it may appear that strong enough relationships exist in the usage, timing, and processing areas between modules to permit two or more to be combined for development. This choice should be examined rigorously, however, since what looks like a fairly easy task of integrating objectives and processes invariably winds up being more complex.
   
   Separate development teams for each module, made up of cross-sections of the Project Team, can work to deliver several modules concurrently, while at the same time joint work takes place on developing common input-output modules and similar routines that can be shared.
   
   Moreover, if funding permits, separate groups can simultaneously work on separate tasks within each module, further accelerating the implementation process. These tasks, identified and designed in the design stage, include the table file updates, edit and posting, file handling, historical record processing, data base backup and recovery, mass updates, interfacing programs, and retrieval and report programs. These tasks can be further broken down into subtasks in the scheduling of the development cycle.

2. *Start Early on the Most Difficult Tasks*

   It is axiomatic in systems development that the last 10 percent of a system takes anywhere from 30 to 50 percent of total development time. Another tongue-in-cheek "rule" asserts that the first 90 percent of the task takes 90 percent of the time, and the last 10 percent takes the other 90 percent.

   This need not be so. By doing the difficult work early, the Project Team will improve its chances of coming in on schedule, because troubles encountered early obviously have more time to be worked out. But it is human nature to put difficult work off, and this must be guarded against, especially in this stage.

   In HRIS development, the most difficult program modules are invariably those involving edits, processing, and history. The Team should get to work early on these functions and specify precise routines as soon as possible in the development stage.

3. *Put the Best People on the Most Difficult Tasks*

   The most difficult tasks, specifically history and edits, should be assigned to the most competent and experienced people to avoid bottlenecks in the development cycle. Even though the best people may not always welcome the jobs that the Team ranks as potentially the most troublesome, the Team should resist the common tendency to give difficult work to "the newest kid on the block," which courts disaster.

4. *Develop Complete Coding Specifications*

   Each sub task should be developed into a programmable module with its own specific inputs, processes, and outputs. Most of the edit routines, update processes, and outputs can be handled in this way, and the work can be broken up for distribution to several programmers. The administration of this work is extremely important; Team leaders must be attentive supervisors in this area and stay on top of the project on a daily basis.

5. *Program Coding*

   Programmers should deliver fully tested, fully operational and documented programs with data layouts, program folders, listings, data labels, catalogues, utility usage, and descriptions of each program.

## 8.2. DEVELOP SYSTEM TEST PLAN: USER TESTS KEY

Each programming module should be fully tested with as severe a test as possible. All possible cases and combinations of data should be hypothesized and prepared for input to the system. Reference files and tables should be tested as well as the master file programs, and the interrelationships between the files should be explored. Volume tests as well as single-entry tests should be performed. Interfaces between files should also be tested. Every situation that can be thought of should be tested by the systems group before the users are granted delivery.

When these preliminary tests have been completed to the Team's satisfaction, the development process can move to user acceptance tests, a crucial stage in any HRIS and the main subject of this section. After some general guidelines on user tests, several of the more important kinds of tests — table/master file interaction, history, and derived data — are discussed and examples are provided.

*Need for User Test.* It is extremely important for the users as well as the programmers and systems group to test and accept the system. Some companies actually have a third party develop the test plan in order to provide an independent, outside test of the system. Whether or not third parties are called in, however, the full user acceptance must be performed, since there inevitably will be problems encountered with the systems; it is highly preferrable to encounter them in this stage when they can be corrected than at a time when the system is operational.

*Development of User Test.* The user test should be constructed around the framework of the HRIS specifications. These specifications, of course, outlined exactly what the system should do in the way of functions: what data to edit, how to edit the data, how to process the data, and what files and output reports to build.

The users can now demonstrate that the HRIS performs these functions as specified. Users can enter data with predictable outcomes and see that what should have happened indeed did. They expect to ascertain that the functions and processes are working to their specifications, and this is the time for that certification. If there are any problems or shortcomings, this is the time when they should be discovered.

In a sense this is akin to what happens when an architect lays out specifications for a builder to construct a bridge able to hold ten tons. Once built, there must be a test to see if it can actually hold those ten tons, before the general public begins using it with possibly tragic results.

*User Involvement.* The Project Team naturally assumes a leadership role in this effort by drawing up an overall work plan for the acceptance test.

The user community must provide the Team or the users on the project team with sufficient examples of test cases for their data elements.

| User Test Examples: | | Salary Changes Are Submitted - Some Correct And Some Incorrect Additions | | |
|---|---|---|---|---|
| Employee | Current Salary | User Supplies the Following: Salary Change Transactions Amount  New Sal. | The HRIS Calculates the Following Result | The Following Disposition Should Result |
| 1234 | 100 | +10   110 | 110 | Accept |
| 1235 | 100 | +10   120 | 110 | Reject |
| 1236 | 100 | +10   100 | 110 | Reject |

Figure 8A.

Example: Salary Amounts Are Changed To Grade 6.

| | Grade | Salary Table Range | Employee Salary/Wk | Compa Ratio Percent |
|---|---|---|---|---|
| | 6 | 110 – 120 – 130 | 110 | 91.6 |
| Change | 6 | 120 – 130 – 140 | 110 | 84.6 |

Figure 8B.

Each case should be given to the team with a brief notation as to what the test is for and what the user expects the HRIS to do with the transaction — i.e., accept it or reject it — and with which error message.

In the examples in Figure 8A, the system is being tested to see not only whether bad transactions are rejected but whether good transactions are accepted. Both cases must be reviewed by the user.

*Table/Master File Interaction.* The users should also test the update and change routines on tables and their efforts on incoming data. If the tables and master file are not in proper alignment, the system cannot function properly.

The effect of a change to the table in Figure 8B caused the employee to go from 91.6 percent to 84.6 percent. The system must be tested to ensure that this and other functions that interrelate data between files are working correctly.

*History Testing.* The storage and handling of historical changes to data elements must also be checked. One of the most crucial tests is the proper data sequencing of the historical data elements. Quite often it will be necessary to correct a particular piece of historical data; therefore, the sequencing routines must be verified to ensure that the dates of the entries are in sequence. Failure to assure this sequence may result in erroneous searches of the data base, since the logic of searches is such that a date-sensitive search would stop at the wrong element.

Under the example in Figure 8C, a search of Employee A's record for a 1981 average salary would be different from a search of Employee B's salary. To get Employee A's total salary in 1981, the computer would take a decending look down A, stop when it encountered 1980, and work backward until it hit 1982. Then it could calculate the 1981 salary. Under this logic the computer would add five months at $120 a week and seven months at $125 (assuming an effective date of June 1 for both).

Employee B's 1981 salary, however, because of a bad sequence, would yield a full twelve months at $120, since the computer would read backward from 1982 down to 1979 and assume the $120 amount, since it encountered no change in 1981.

| Employee A<br>Correct History Alignment | | Employee B<br>Incorrect History Alignment | |
|---|---|---|---|
| Weekly Salary | Date | Weekly Salary | Date |
| $130 | 6/82 | $130 | 6/82 |
| 125 | 6/81 | 120 | 6/80 |
| 120 | 6/80 | 115 | 6/79 |
| 115 | 6/79 | 125 | 6/81 |

Figure 8C.

*Derived Data Element Testing and Logic Problems.* There will be several key derived elements that should be closely evaluated, since it is in this area that certain logic problems may appear. This is especially true where there is more than one "trigger" field. The Team should watch for error correction, cleanup, and other tough-to-control situations during periods such as after a system purge, year-end processing, or other nonroutine situations. Sometimes the combined effect of these runs may throw the HRIS into a major bind from which normality may be difficult to regain. An example is that either a salary change or a change to grade will recalculate a new Compa-Ratio. The Team should check both "trigger" fields singly or in tandem for errors of logic.

*Backup and Recovery Tests.* The system should be put through extensive tests of interrupted operations, incomplete data, wrong file loads, and even complete "disaster" situations. Fortunately, these problems are not encountered frequently, but they are terribly difficult to correct and should be planned for.

## 8.3. CONVERSION AND IMPLEMENTATION PLAN

A conversion plan is a detailed, step-by-step guide to the implementation of the HRIS. If a HRIC is going to be established to coordinate the system centrally, as recommended in Chapter 9, it is advantageous that this organization be responsible for the design and implementation of the conversion plan. In any case, and whether the current system that will be replaced or enhanced is manual or computerized, the Project Team must assure that a comprehensive conversion plan is devised that will permit a smooth transition of operations from the old mode to the new and that certain guidelines will be applicable to all HRIS conversions.

The most crucial considerations in devising a conversion plan are the timing and marshaling of the necessary human resources and machine resources to carry out the plan. The overall plan will have to outline specific functions, to whom they are assigned, with beginning dates and targeted completion dates.

A conversion plan is by nature a succession of jobs that must be carried out in progression, which means that each job must be lined up in a sequential manner. The file must be created, and changes must be added to it in sequence.

### 8.3.1. Conversion Plan Considerations

Several considerations apply particularly to HRIS conversion plans and should be noted before proceeding to trial testing. Singled out here are problems related to historical data and the issue of when to undertake the conversion itself, which are separate timing questions.

*Data and File Initialization: When to Begin.* One of the most important decisions that the Project Team faces is whether to go back in time for the data it will collect and initiate files with or to start fresh with current data and only go forward. This is a decision usually made in the design stage on the basis of specifications that came out of the Needs Analysis. Usually, the choice depends on whether the system will be expected to go back and gain historical data for reports and analysis. However, in the conversion process, the Team may encounter insurmountable problems that call for a review of this decision. The most common problems of this type are:

1. *Unavailability.* In some cases, past data are simply not available. This may happen if the data were never collected in the first place; have been destroyed, lost, or discarded; or are unreadable in the current form.
2. *Data Do Not Match Current Interpretation.* Organizations change with time, and the new code values, job titles, work locations, organizational alignments, and departments may not match the current company or organization codes. In order to properly enter, edit, and store the data, all the tables would have to have

matching entries and the deviations and processing routines would have to be examined to ensure that they are compatible. In most cases, these tasks border on the unfeasible, since the HRIS ordinarily would not be able to be programmed for every edit situation, nor could the users supply the table values for all situations, say for the last three or five years.
3. *Economics.* The time and cost of collecting, entering, and processing the data may just not be worth the payback that is derived for the few reports that can be produced with the data. In some rare cases, such EEO or ERISA, the cost may be worth the effort, however; if the data are available and can be collected, the Team can go back in time.
4. *Timing of Conversion.* The best time to convert the system is when the people involved can work for some weeks in a fairly uninterrupted manner. Normally this is in the periods of March through May or September through November, avoiding year-end processing and the summer vacation periods. Key people should be available for the entire conversion effort, since they are the ones who guide the process. Keep in mind that the current system, whether computerized or manual, must be kept running until the HRIS has been cut over and accepted.

### 8.3.2. Field Trial: First Step in Implementation

Having applied the same principles of modularity, and following the completion of tasks in their proper sequence, the project Team has by now detailed the conversion plan and is ready to switch to a pilot test or a field trial mode.

A field trial is a process in which the HRIS is installed in a small location or branch office and then is watched closely to see whether every part functions properly. Changes are made where necessary. In this way, a good feel can be had as to the operational characteristics of the HRIS. Mistakes are confined to a smaller percentage of the company, and firsthand knowledge of how to install the system is gained.

It is usually advisable to have volunteers for the trial, since false starts and problems may be encountered. The trial population should be as representative as possible to maximize the Team's understanding of the system and help the Team see as many operational situations and problem areas as possible.

Both the technical and nontechnical parts of the system should be trialed, including all input forms, user instructions, reports, and ad hoc retrievals.

It should be noted that the field trial is not a systems test or a user test. That testing must have been completed by this time by both the systems group and the users. Rather, the field trial is the first operational phase of the implementation in a live environment.

### 8.3.3. Parallel or "Quick Cut"

Usually some parallel processing is advisable, at least until the Team is sure that the new system is operating correctly. In some situations, though, such as when the HRIS is a first-time system and there is no basis for comparison, a "quick-cut" approach may be best.

Moreover, a staggered or phased approach, taking one department or a location at a time, is usually best from a workload and machine constraint basis.

### 8.3.4. Field Collection

One of the most widely used methods of initializing data fields in an HRIS installation is to do an employee-by-employee canvass. This method should be avoided or at least highly controlled. The problem with this approach is the amount of data being collected, the questions that the employees inevitably have, and the limited amount of resources in the HRIC with which to respond. If there is simply no other way, as in employee skills or work experiences, a location-by-location or department-by-department approach is advisable to limit the volume. Easy-to-read, unambiguous user instructions are invaluable, and the HRIC needs to be prepared for an initial high rate of rejections.

### 8.3.5. Treatment of Initial Errors

The importance of getting off to a good start regarding errors cannot be overstressed. Unless the users are conditioned from the outset to good work habits, file integrity will degrade.

When the system is first processed, there will inevitably be a high number of errors, especially in data that have not previously been machine-processed. In some cases this percentage may reach 40 percent or more. Users may be disheartened and may not want to apply the resources to clean up these errors. This initial load and the resulting errors must be planned for and managed effectively or the file will never get better.

## 8.4. OPERATING CONSIDERATIONS

Among the major operational factors that should be at the forefront of the Team's thinking during the program development and conversion stage are measures that can be taken to assure privacy and security and data base accuracy. Privacy issues are discussed in detail in Chapter 9, but some of the basic precautions that should be taken to assure the security of the data base — technical considerations that should be covered in the conversion plan — are summarized here.

### 8.4.1. Privacy and Security

Two kinds of data base security measures should be built into the system or provided for in its operations: automatic screening of users and backup for files and documentation.

*Password and User Lockout.* Only authorized users should be allowed to access the HRIS, and each user should be required to pass a two-level security check with a unique password. Once into the HRIS, each user should be limited to those elements which the user "needs to know." This limitation can be performed by most data base management systems in a technical manner — by the software — and does not necessarily inhibit any other operational characteristics. In essence, each user is granted access only to those elements needed to perform the user's functions.

*File Backup.* In addition to screening users, provision should be made for certain file backups to ensure HRIS security:

- At least eight previous update files of transactions input should be retained for batch systems.
- Copies of all quarter-ending HRIS master files and tables should be retained.
- Every master file should be copied and retained.
- Totally online data bases should be backed up each day when update activity occurs or if documentation is stored online.

*Documentation Backup.* All copies of original documentation should be kept for at least a year, since the instructions, code values, and other interpretations of the system are as important as the data.

#### 8.4.2. Data Base Accuracy

The most serious operational problem encountered in most personnel systems is that of inaccurate data. Errors in the HRIS data base can lead to so many inaccuracies in reports that the reports are virtually useless. Even minor errors can erode users' confidence to the point where they consider the old manual or computerized system more authoritative than the HRIS. The task of keeping errors to a minimum is one of the most important jobs the HRIC has.

On a more personal level, data accuracy and integrity become matters of intense pride with many people. The HRIS is, after all, a record keeper; just as supervisors would not tolerate any correctable errors in a "kardex" or McBee card system, that attitude should apply to the HRIS.

*Self-Checking Features of an HRIS.* One of the most dramatic differences between automated and nonautomated systems is the rapid, inexpensive ability of the former to run cross-checks — to compare items in the system with other items. Data elements such as employment status as full- or part-time, for example, can be cross-referenced with hours worked or pay rate. College codes can be checked against acceptable table values.

The ability to perform these edit checks automatically assures that from the initial file load onward, the data base will be subjected to a rigorous set of logic rules that will improve the quality of information to a degree not possible before with limited resources.

Self-checking edits and cross-comparisons, although vital for the full utilization of the HRIS, bring with them a necessary burden — correcting a rejected entry. This task must be done as promptly and conscientiously as possible because users expect accuracy to mean a complete as well as an error-free data base.

*Error Types and Causes.* There are many reasons for errors in a data base, some easier to detect than others. The kinds of errors range from entering data on the wrong employee (or even a nonexistent employee) to simple arithmetical errors in a change to base pay. Data being changed may have changed again before entry, or a clerical error such as the transposition of digits may cause problems. These kinds of errors can be reviewed and corrected relatively easily by users and the HRIC staff, especially if error correction is pursued regularly and not allowed to pile up. Presented with hundreds of thousands of errors to correct, HRIS users and coordinators may become demoralized, and the situation can go from bad to worse. Resources must be applied at all times to keep the error problem within bounds.

A more serious situation may emerge when it becomes apparent that a significant number of wrong entries to the data base have been accepted by the HRIS, have been passed by the edits, and have gone into the data base. These could be incorrect work location codes, department codes, hours of work, benefit plan status codes, or other groups of data that fall within the acceptable ranges but are wrong in fact. These errors are virtually undetectable by the HRIS without elaborate relational edits. Some cannot be detected by the system under any circumstances, and the HRIC may not spot these errors because of lack of familiarity with the subject matter or the employees involved.

Only constant reviews and usage by line personnel and departmental user representatives can prevent this type of error, since some elements of data are known only to employees themselves and their supervisors.

*Error Correction Assistance to Users: At the Source.* The HRIC people should try to deliver as much error correction assistance as they can to the users who are inputting data, at the source of the data. Time and effort spent on supporting the error correction function pays for itself in a cleaner and more accurate file. The HRIC should be available with training programs, examples of error message interpretation, good readable documentation, and any other help in this area. The best help may be an online edit module as explained in 5.2.5 that will allow users to input changes directly and have the system interact with the users if there are further errors or problems with the incoming transaction.

*Periodic Audit.* It is good data base operations practice to develop a program that will compare the HRIS data base to the payroll data base or any other data base that can be used for audit purposes.

Key data fields such as salary, job, department, employee class, or status should be compared, and discrepancies should be noted. Keep in mind that differences in effective dates can cause mismatches, and so the effective data of the file and the data should be as close as possible.

Other ad hoc audits of the HRIS file should be developed as well. These programs, which can be developed by the users or the HRIC, would list any unusual data elements or unallowable events just to ensure the integrity of the file.

Example
- Part time employees working 30 or more hours per week
- Employees at less than VP level earning more than $80,000/year
- Sales employees in other than the Marketing Department

*Sampling.* An extremely worthwhile activity for the HRIC is a sample of the input documents as they are passed into the HRIS stream. The input documents are compared with the truth, and errors are noted. The sampling plan should set up allowable error rates for each user; when they are exceeded, help is called for.

The more editing and auditing, the more time will be spent on cleanup and accuracy. The result, though, is an HRIS you can use with confidence.

**CONCLUSION**

In this chapter on coding and conversion, guidelines are presented on program development for human resource needs, test plan and user tests, and recommended steps in the conversion plan. Several operating considerations, in particular data base accuracy, are also covered.

Special attention is given to the development of strict tests for each programming module. Crucial in this process are user acceptance tests, and guidelines on the more important kinds of user tests are provided in some detail.

The conversion plan, which is a detailed guide to HRIS implementation, should be designed and put into effect by the Human Resource Information Center, a key organization described further in Chapter 9.

# 9
# The Human Resource Information Center; Privacy Issues; and Skills Inventory Guidelines

Three further subjects affecting decisions made on HRIS design and implementation are discussed in this chapter. Chapter 10 will deal with the major regulatory requirements that may affect HRIS design significantly.

The first of these is the Human Resource Information Center (HRIC), a centralized training and control organization that serves as the administrative link between users in various personnel organizations and the HRIS. As indicated in Chapter 8, the HRIC should be set up early in the conversion stage of system development to help with user training, error correction procedures, and other vital matters in the transition from the old to the new system. Ideally, the HRIC staff will not change greatly once the system is in operation, providing users with a familiar and experienced administrative organization that they will deal with on a daily basis.

One of the key functions of the HRIC is the implementation of data base security and privacy policies. Certain basic concepts of privacy that apply to HRIS design are discussed in Section 9.2, with a suggested approach to meeting government-endorsed Fair Information Practice principles.

Finally, guidelines for setting up a Human Resource Inventory for use in a Career Development or Human Resource Utilization module are presented in Section 9.3. This key application of an HRIS may essentially justify the system.

## 9.1. THE HUMAN RESOURCE INFORMATION CENTER (HRIC)

As indicated in Chapter 2 and mentioned throughout this book, the establishment of an HRIC to oversee the day-to-day operation of the HRIS is essential. The HRIC may consist of a single person or a large department — staffing levels are discussed at the end of this section — but the functions of the HRIC require the kind of objective oversight and intervention best performed by a separate organizational entity with the human resources organization.

### 9.1.1. Timing of HRIC Installation

The Project Team should develop the specifications for the HRIC at the same time that the systems group is developing the program modules for the HRIS. The HRIC must be installed prior to or coincident with the conversion and implementation phase so that incumbents who will be working in the center are fully trained, can assist the Team with implementation, and are prepared to carry on with the subsequent operation of the HRIS.

### 9.1.2. HRIC Functions

Different organizational requirements and constraints can create an almost limitless array of possible specific functions for the HRIC, but usually these functions will include both specific tasks and continuing data base administration activities.

*HRIC Functional Duties.* The following are some of the more common tasks performed by the HRIC:

- Preparing data for data entry
- Data entry and editing of data
- Interpreting data error messages
- Error correction guidance
- Handling requests for information
- Handling employee access requests
- Distribution of output to users
- Preparing reports
- Preparing HRIS program operating schedules

- Answering HRIS questions of field managers
- Balancing the HRIS with interfaced systems
- Training HRIS users
- Developing specifications for system changes
- Providing for proper privacy and security
- Maintaining tables

*HRIS Data Administration.* With the emergence of data base management systems has come increased attention to the overall area of data purity, integrity, and interpretation. To this end, the Personnel Department will be called upon to provide administrative control and guidance on the operation of the HRIS. In addition to these functions, HRIC administrative functions may include:

- Precise definitions of each data element
- Impact statements regarding discontinuance of data elements
- Backup and recovery administration
- File structure and hierarchy control
- Data dictionary administration
- Budgeting and billing for system usage
- Balancing systems usage
- Frequency and timing of HRIS update
- Accuracy and integrity of data elements

### 9.1.3. Documentation and Training of the HRIC

The level to which users are trained by the HRIC or the level to which the center's staff is trained depends on the size of the HRIC, the number of satellite locations, and the overall number of users. The costs involved are also a factor, of course.

Generally speaking, the more widespread and geographically dispersed an organization, the greater the need for good documentation and training in order to operate the system properly.

*Documentation.* The normal set of documents needed in an HRIS include the following:

- *Field User's Manual.* This should be an easy-to-understand "event-oriented" manual that describes "how to" information for the user:

how to set up a new employee, how to enter a job or salary change, or how to make a request for information from the system.
- *Error Correction Manual.* This is a complete guide on how to correct data and keep the data base accurate. It is written for the clerical employee or data originator.
- *Retrieval Manual.* This document is a complete indepth manual on how to exercise the retrieval programs and generate online or ad hoc requests for data.
- *HRIC Manual.* This is a complete guide on the system overview: complete data descriptions, error messages and error correction instructions, operations and control advice and retrieval instructions, user access rules, and procedures documentation. This is directed to the HRIC organization itself.
- *Technical Documentation.* This includes run books, flow charts or other program logic diagrams, program listings, and complete operational and control documentation meant for the data systems organization.
- *Online Documentation.* With online systems, there are advantages to having as much error correction and element definition as possible on the system itself. In this way the HRIS can provide a self-contained system in many respects for the user population without referring to written material. The online documentation is also easier to change, since there need only be entry of the data into the system for the users to gain access to it.
- *Training.* The HRIC staff will be trained by the Project Team, based on the user acceptance testing that takes place. The Team should be documenting the HRIS performance as the testing takes place so that a more formalized training program can emerge.

The HRIC is normally responsible for the user training as well; therefore, a description of the requirements in this area are in order.

### 9.1.4. User Training

The users should be trained both initially and on an ongoing basis in two areas: input and error correction, and information retrieval.

*Data Input Training.* The input and error correction functions are normally performed by clerical and administrative employees. One aspect of the work that makes the delivery of training easier is that data entry is normally clustered around user areas. This means that the Benefits clerks normally prepare benefits data, the Salary clerks prepare their own, and so forth. In this way, fairly specific user training and input procedures can be developed. Subject matter experts from the user areas are vitally important to this process and should assist in user training.

*Data Retrieval Training.* The HRIC should develop at least two training programs for users with respect to retrieval.

First, a very simple method of data retrieval for the simple requests must be explained to the user community. This training program normally would take no longer than a half day and should stress the online prepackaged routines or other already programmed data requests that exist now as outputs from the HRIS. The normal usage of these reports would be explained, and the procedures used to get the reports would be reviewed.

The second type of training for information retrieval involves the high-level language usage that the HRIS would employ. This language, usually very powerful and interactive in nature, is normally available with an already developed and structured training package. The users who will be most heavily engaged in data searches and analysis should be trained. However, it is quite common to have only selected members of the HRIC trained, for efficiency and privacy reasons. All that the users would do under this arrangement is call the HRIC, which would in turn execute the request.

### 9.1.5. Staffing Levels of the HRIC

The level of staffing of the HRIC necessarily depends on a number of issues, primarily the number of modules in the HRIS, the volume of inputs and errors, and the number of data requests that will be made. As a rule of thumb, however, one employee in the HRIC per thousand employees in the organization provides a general estimate. This is to be considered a benchmark rather than a hard and fast rule, since a high error rate or a high turnover in the organization would cause the

## 170   III/DESIGN AND INSTALLATION

number of clerks needed for data entry or error correction to escalate.

Similarly, if all or most users do their own data retreivals, support in that area may drop. In an online mode, however, the HRIC would be devoting many hours to the development of online searches or documentation, and this takes resources.

### 9.2. PRIVACY

Although the subject of privacy has been widely discussed since the early 1970s, it is still misinterpreted by many in the data field as a synonym for data security. Data base security — essentially the protection of a valuable resource from competitors and other unauthorized people — is indeed an aspect of privacy, but there are many more facets of personnel information privacy that relate to HRIS design, the Project Team, and all HRIS users — both those who supply data to the system and those who administer or access it.

Most major corporations have by this time developed a comprehensive set of policies and procedures regarding employee data and the HRIS. The HRIC — whose functions include the implementation of privacy policies — should follow these closely if they exist. Also, many states have passed privacy laws affecting personnel information, and the Project Team must ensure that the HRIS conforms to these laws.

*Fair Information Practice Principles.* Should there be no state laws or fully developed organizational policies, certain basic guidelines should be considered by the Project Team. First and foremost, these should include the following Fair Information Practice principles, first set out in a landmark HEW study published in 1973*:

- There must be no personal-data record-keeping systems whose very existence is secret.
- There must be a way for an individual to find out what information about him is in a record and how it is used.

---

*Records, Computers, and the Rights of Citizens,* Report of the Secretary's Advisory Committee on Automated Personal Data Systems, U.S. Department of Health, Education and Welfare, DHEW Publication No. (OS) 73-97, 1973, p. 41.

- There must be a way for an individual to prevent information about him obtained for one purpose from being used or made available for other purposes without his consent.
- There must be a way for an individual to correct or amend a record of identifiable information about him.
- Any organization creating, maintaining, using, or disseminating records of identifiable personal data must assure the reliability of the data for their intended use and must take reasonable precautions to prevent misuse of the data.

*Relevance to the HRIS.* One of the key questions regarding privacy issues is, What really belongs to the individual and what belongs to the organization? As can be inferred from the above guidelines, the inescapable answer to this question is that information must be relegated to an employee if it can be indexed to or identified with that employee. Thus, any data stored by name, Social Security number, or other unique identifier clearly is relevant to the privacy issue. The HRIS will in virtually all cases be maintaining data by some sort of employee identifier and therefore is subject to the requirements of any state or federal laws covering employee or applicant data.

At this writing, there is no federal law governing the privacy issue with regard to employee records in the personnel area in the private sector. There are many state laws, though, and it makes good sense to proceed as if there were a comprehensive set of laws in the privacy area. Compliance with the Fair Information Practice principles, along the following guidelines, is strongly recommended.

### 9.2.1. Data Base Elements Limited to "Need to Know"

The data base should include only those items of information clearly needed by management for business reasons, including items required by laws and regulatory rulings.

For example, do not include unsupported items or elements that "have always been asked for." Items regarding an employee's political beliefs, religion, or sexual preference are almost always outside the boundary lines of privacy and should be excluded. Items regarding marital status and whether someone rents or owns a home must have a valid reason for inclusion. Sex, race, and age are needed for EEO reporting purposes and should not be used in a job selection or salary setting. Their use is governed by EEO or Salary administrators, and this is generally not a privacy issue.

### 9.2.2. The HRIC as Watchdog

The HRIC must act as the responsible body over the administration of the HRIS and as such must be the day-to-day unit that monitors the usage of the system. This role, though, will expand to include requests for new elements after the disbanding of the Project Team. The duties would include at least the following functions:

| Activity | HRIC Involvement |
| --- | --- |
| Input of data to HRIS | • Only essential data elements included in the data base |
|  | • Data must be accurate, complete, and timely; tight edits and good error control are essential |
| Output of data | • Valid requests only allowed |
|  | • Users are authorized users only |
|  | • Data base to be kept secure with proper backup and recovery procedures |
|  | • Output is marked confidential |
|  | • Access logged |
| Uses | • "Routine" uses only; others reviewed for legality |
|  | • Transfers of data must be watched |
|  | • Users briefed on their responsibility |
|  | • Audit programs run periodically |

### 9.2.3. All Data are Private: Access Limited

There should be some distinction between various classes of data elements when the data base is in use. One way to do this is to declare some "sensitive" data items — e.g., salary and performance evaluation — as limited-access fields and to allow access to all the others by all personnel data users. Since the privacy advocates declare all data that are personally identifiable as private, a better way is to establish user views by user area and to review the need for each data item, limiting each user to only those items essential for his or her work function. An example of this stratified access policy would be:

| User | Element Access |
|---|---|
| • Benefits | General items and Benefit items only |
| • EEO | General items and EEO items only |
| • Salary Administration | General items and Salary items |
| • Telephone Directory | General items only |

Most data base and online systems are able to offer various views of the data base and can secure a data element down to the field level. This level of security is needed to exclude certain items from unauthorized users.

### 9.2.4. Disclosures to Outside Agencies

A major area with a potential for misuse of employee data is the unauthorized release of information to outsiders. These may be law enforcement officials, unions, federal government agencies, insurance companies, credit bureaus, or others who do not have the employee's permission to receive the information provided to the employer in good faith. The organization must maintain that trust and establish safeguards over information. If there is a need for these agencies to obtain the information, it should either be by a valid court order or legal summons or with the employee's written permission.

### 9.3. KEY APPLICATION: SKILLS INVENTORY NEEDS

While growing privacy concerns over the last decade have had the effect of eliminating certain nonessential personal data from personnel information systems, another incipient trend has resulted in the expansion of more detailed information on employees: important work-related data on individuals' skills, talents, and interests that can be more efficiently collected, stored, and used by organizations operating a Human Resource Inventory (HRI) as part of the HRIS.*

The HRI, often called a skills inventory, is an essential part of an organization's Human Resource Utilization plan, an area of personnel management gaining increasing attention as a means of making the most out of human resources now and in the future. Human resource utilization involves much more than the HRI. Its components include strategic planning by product, market, or function; employee evaluation systems; management development; career pathing; selection standards; reassignment procedures and monitoring; and other programs. However, most of its functions require the creation of a usable Human Resource Inventory: an in-depth survey of the work experience, education, skills, and interests of employees.

This section describes the prupose of such inventories as well as procedures for developing this key ingredient of the Human Resource Utilization module in the HRIS.

### 9.3.1. Need for the Human Resource Inventory

The staffing group and individual managers need to have a detailed description of an employee's education, training, work experience, particular skills and knowledge, interests and goals, geographic preferences, and other information that might be of relevance in a job-matching setting. The HRI is the vehicle that can collect, store, and present this information to management.

There are several components of the HRI: a booklet of instructions containing the vocabulary of work experience codes, school codes, training course codes, and the like; a data collection procedure to collect, codify, and verify the information; and HRIS programs to edit, store, and retrieve the needed information.

The HRI gives each employee an opportunity to describe his or her background and interests to the company in a standard vocabulary that will allow computer interrogations. This permits each employee to be "reviewed" for openings, training classes, task force assignments, and other situations. No one is overlooked, the imperfections of personal biases can be overcome, and the fact that some supervisors won't submit certain employees for openings can be ignored.

---

*See, e.g., "Management Selection Systems that Meet the Challenges of the '80s," Alfred J. Walker, *Personnel Journal,* October 1981, p. 775 FF.

Based on job-related criteria, staffers can examine the work flow and obtain a list of employees whose background and qualifications meet those criteria. Individuals may then be interviewed by the supervisor of the open job to determine their specific strengths and suitability.

Without such an inventory, there is no organized way for a middle- to large-size company to determine the particular skills and education of its employees. A given supervisor can get to know his or her workers and suggest the best utilization of those employees. But how does this supervisor evaluate employees in other work units? This problem is compounded in larger or geographically dispersed companies. The supervisor should discuss particular candidates with the candidate's past supervisor if at all possible. But how can the list of the most qualified candidates be developed in the first place? An HRI provides this facility economically in the HRIS.

The HRI allows the search to take place in a highly efficient and structured manner without overlooking anyone. The degree to which the HRI can assist the staffers is determined by the vocabulary with which the requestor describes the job and the employee describes his or her background.

### 9.3.2. Work Experience (Skills) Vocabulary

A standard set of work experiences, skills, and other factors is necessary to provide a common basis for comparison of employee background and interests with potential job openings. This standardized set of codes provides a method for the employee to list the types of work he or she can perform. The vocabulary of terms should provide codes both for activities that are now being performed in the organization and for activities that the organization may need at some future time.

Obviously, one cannot present the employee with a list of every job performed in America. However, a meaningful and relevant set can be derived by appointing subject matter experts in each department and developing an overall set of job experiences that the department can use to perform job placement. It should then be used by the department to describe an opening, and it should become part of the requisition. The staffers will have the department's statement regarding the work-related skills they would like a canddate to possess.

The basic construction of a Work Experience is accomplished by developing a computer-searchable code defined so that an employee can enter both broad areas of knowledge and specific skills. A method to accomplish this has been developed over the years and has been found to be fairly effective.

Broad knowledge of an area is depicted by an overall code, with subordinate levels using the same primary and/or secondary digits. For example:

| Work Experience Code | Level of Detail |
|---|---|
| For Code – AB100 | AB = Primary Job family |
| | 1 = Intermediate classification |
| | 00 = Detail of Job (Code 00 depicts general knowledge) |
| DP 408 | DP = Data Processing family |
| | 4 = Programming languages |
| | 08 = COBOL |

With this coding scheme, the organization can develop a set of codes that will enable management to canvass its employees and find out their particular abilities as well as interests. In the example, an employee could enter DP400 as general knowledge of all DP languages or any subset to show specific language skill. The codes for the data processing overall structure might be set up as follows:

| | |
|---|---|
| DP 000 | Data Processing, General |
| DP 100 | Data Processing Operations |
| DP 102 | CRT Operations |
| DP 104 | I/O Setup |
| | |
| DP 200 | Programming Environment |
| DP 300 | Systems Design |
| DP 400 | Programming Languages |
| DP 410 | COBOL |
| DP 420 | Fortran |

Each department and user area would develop a similar set of codes, covering all internal functions that are likely to be present in a job placement situation.

In addition to the code itself, it is useful to use the coding structure to obtain a feel for certain attributes with respect to work experience or skill. Items such as years of experience, how recently the skill was used, where the skill was obtained, and level of skill are vital to the success of the inventory. These modifiers should be entered along with the code, and they will help make the code usable to those searching the HRIS data base. For example, an employee who was in the Data Systems Department for four years, who last used COBOL in 1981, and who was a programming supervisor would code that as follows:

DP 408   E   04   81   S   DS

- E  – Depicts experience (E), knowledge (K), or interest (I)
- 04 – Number of years skill was used
- 81 – Last year skill was used
- S  – Level of skill (S = supervisor skill)
- DS – Department where skill was used (DS = data systems)

In addition to the work experience codes, the HRI vocabulary should provide a method to collect training courses taken, formal college information, foreign languages the employee can use, specific development activities that may be planned, and relocation limitations.

It is also highly important to allow employees to enter areas of work in which they are interested as future assignments become available. All things being equal (admittedly, rarely the case), it is preferable to have someone in a job who wants to work in that area rather than someone who does not particularly want the job.

Thus, the areas of information that the vocabulary should cover are:

1. *Work Experience Codes (Skill Codes):* Encompassing company and external work activities.
2. *Formal Education:* College-level education including school, major course, degree level, and year. In-progress education may be included.

3. *Training Course:* All formal work-related company-sponsored courses of at least two or three days' duration. Course number, title, date, and location should be recorded.
4. *Foreign Language Skill:* Needed only for multilingual situations. It may include some indication of whether language is native and whether employee can act as an interpreter.
5. *Career Interests:* Indications of the two or three preferred areas in which the employee would like to work or have an assignment.
6. *Relocation Limitations:* A listing of any areas to which employee would not want to be transferred.
7. *Development Plan:* A list of the training courses or next assignments or experiences that have been planned for the employee.

The data shown above will be added to the other HRIS data to be used along with performance data for job selections.

The work experience and skill data are collected separately from job title data or job function data for several reasons. Titles or functions are usually broad in nature and not specific enough for placement. They change over time where skill codes usually do not. And finally, titles and functions cover company jobs only.

### 9.3.3. Collection of the Inventory Data

The technique most commonly used to capture these data is a form that is sent out with the work experience vocabulary. A copy of this form should be distributed at least annually to all employees for whom the data are to be collected. It may be mailed or distributed through the supervisor. Regardless of the method chosen for distribution, it is important to show that the supervisor is the link for any job movement in the organization. Satisfactory performance on the current job is normally mandatory for upward mobility, and the distribution of forms through supervisors strengthens this connection.

The employee, following instructions in the booklet, completes the form to the best of his or her ability and submits it to the supervisor for review. The supervisor examines the form for completeness and appropriateness of codes and then sends it to the staffing group for their review. If the supervisor should note any unclear areas or possible miscoding of entries, the form should be corrected.

It has been determined that most employees can be fairly effective in accomplishing this task and will normally require between fifteen and twenty-five codes in the work experience area to cover the last seven to eight years. Newer employees may have fewer than fifteen, and more mature employees more, depending on the number of assignments in different areas of the business, promotions, etc. An upper limit of choices should be established to force the employee to make a selection regarding the more important codes. The instructions should clearly state that the codes to be entered should be restricted to those which are related to potential work assignments.

The collection would normally be on a voluntary basis, but circumstances may arise that require it to be made mandatory. For example, a firm undergoing reorganization may require such data for the ongoing operation of the business. Or skills data may be needed for contract bidding.

As part of the canvass, employees should be asked whether they would object to transferring their work locations and residences.

The reviewing supervisor would also be responsible for entering or updating career development and training course information, thereby achieving a highly critical phase of the HRU process: preparing an individual development plan for each employee. The kind of specific, detailed information on employees made possible by a computerized HRI is especially valuable to staffing groups in a nonhierachical environment, such as when managers work in an organizational matrix with complex responsibilities or when a special task force needs to be assembled.

### 9.3.4. Selection Standards and Support Procedures

The final components of the HRI are the staffing and selection standards that must be established to make the HRI operational. These selection standards will cover administrative procedures for such items as treatment of surplus, interdivisional or other transfers, mix of new hires to promotions, which jobs are eligible for relocation expenses, how the EEO goals and targets will be attained, and how the staffing group will fill vacancies.

These standards should also provide a method by which employees can learn about career advancement opportunities. These opportunities will be a by-product of the planning activities occurring in each department. The planning cycles will generate data relative to the type and number of openings and opportunities that will be available, and these data will then be used both for staffers and individual employees to make more informal career decisions.

The evaluation of performance information is one of the most important selection criteria. Without this information, the company cannot determine the skills of its people and properly compensate and reward them. Potential appraisal is also a key index, since it is an estimate of an employee's ability to handle the responsibility of the next higher management level.

These evaluations of performance and potential for advancement should be conducted in as uniform a manner as possible. The staffing group should endeavor to supply guidelines on how to rate employees consistently and fairly. They may utilize case examples and any other helpful tools. Obviously, the overall selection process will never get acceptance by organizations unless they can be assured that an employee ranked "outstanding" by another group meets their criteria for that same rating. This data must be monitored and validated continually for accuracy and completeness.

The staffing group should invite comments and advice from departments in order to most effectively develop the operating search criteria without violating the law. There should be general acceptance of the procedures the staffing group will use when filling a vacancy. While these rules should be meant as guidelines rather than construed as being rigidly inviolate, they should seldom be broken, or the process will be bypassed. They should include such items as whether employees can self-nominate themselves for jobs, whether all jobs must be sent to staffers for searches, or how long the staffers can take in examining inside candidates before a vacancy request can be filled from the outside marketplace.

Often the available pool of candidates for certain jobs is quite large, yet other positions may find few or even no qualified candidates. The latter situation makes it very important that a report be prepared as soon as the planning cycle is completed, to determine the available, promotable, or movable people over the next six months or year. This will provide information regarding positions that have or do not have potential candidates. A further comparison can be made on the HRI by skill levels so that organizations can determine whether a deficiency exists in any critical skills. If voids in skills do exist, the training groups must develop programs to overcome the problem. Similarly, the staffers must ascertain whether people need to be reassigned and retrained to fill these gaps. These computer analyses are extremely important, since it takes lengthy lead times to fill or train people for highly technical or other critical jobs.

Furthermore, this information on skills shortages or large pools of qualified people should be shared with the employees involved so that they are informed about advancement opportunities in these areas. They in turn may redirect their career interests into areas where there are fewer contenders for jobs. This knowledge not only helps employees with their own career management it also tends to disperse employees and make them more available for staffers in other areas of the business.

The selection standards must provide for a sequence of selection criteria. This sequence should handle such questions as how to place surplus employees or dislocated employees, how to handle returns from leaves of absence and recalls from layoffs, rectifying EEO imbalances or deficiencies, managing downgrades, and whether an employee is protected in his or her old job and can return without prejudice for a certain period of time. If these operating procedures are not specified at the beginning of the program, problems may develop after implementation.

With the HRI data in the HRIS data base, the staffers can interrogate the system and select all employees whose backgrounds and interests meet job requirements as posted on the requisition. By utilizing other data elements in the system — such as performance, status, department, level, and service data — the selection criteria can be as complex as desired. In a matter of minutes, the HRIS can provide the names of those who meet the criteria. If the list is too long, the search criteria can be narrowed; if it is too short or there are no candidates, criteria can be dropped — all based on the job requirements, organizational policies, and the department's approval.

**CONCLUSION**

The establishment of an HRIC is vital to the successful implementation of the HRIS programs. The training and overall administrative aspects of the system are every bit as important as the computer programs.

An integral part of the administrative guidelines are organizational privacy policies, which must be in place in order to protect each employee's data in the system. Although there are now no federal laws requiring specific procedures and reports in this area for the private sector, the protection of sensitive information in the data base is both sound business policy and an important reflection of the organization's respect for the rights to privacy of its employees.

The HRU program is an umbrella plan to identify, through integrated Human Resources Planning, skills and talents needed in the business. The HRI is a method to collect data about skills and abilities from employees themselves and present it to the staffing group in a computer format. Selection standards and operational guidelines provide uniform rules on how people get moved and vacancies get filled. The HRU, with an effective skills inventory or HRI, helps to make the very difficult task of finding the right person for a job a day-to-day, normal activity, thereby ensuring the quality and continuity of the work force.

Without this type of process, companies will find it very difficult to move into new markets with any assurance that they can fill key jobs or provide continuity of employment to their employees.

The key to the HRU function is an HRIS that not only has the ability to collect and store needed data about employees but also can create models to assess the impact of new programs in the organization. In this way, organizations can truly utilize their human resources and prevent their employees from losing their individual identities or from being misused by an arbitrary bureaucracy.

# 10
# Using the HRIS to Ensure Compliance with Federal Regulatory Requirements — and More

In many respects, modern computerized personnel systems have been shaped by federal regulatory requirements. Laws passed since the mid-1960s apply horizontally to all but the smallest local employers, public as well as private. These laws have enormously escalated the legal need for employee data respecting equal employment, health and safety, and pensions — in addition to expanded coverage of wage and hour laws on the books since the 1930s.

At the same time, employers today must comply with the reporting requirements of a broad range of state laws and the frequently uneven interpretations of regulatory law made by courts and quasi-judicial administrative agencies at various levels. Failure to comply can lead to massive financial penalties in addition to lost contracts, and there is no substitute for competent legal counsel when regulations or rulings appear ambiguous.

The modern HRIS cannot ensure compliance with all the provisions of wage and hour laws, EEO regulations, pension plan requirements, or health and safety standards. Only the organization's practices can ensure that.

On the other hand, the organization's practices must include record keeping in the regulatory environment that has emerged in the last two decades. Moreover, to prove that your organization's practices have been in compliance, should an employee or government agency bring suit, you will need the kind of detailed, comprehensive data best recorded and stored by a computerized personnel system.

More is involved here than mere compliance with government regulations, however, as important as this compliance has become and as much as a computerized personnel system reduces the costs of compliance. Leaving aside the adversarial aspects of the need for records, most organizations can gain important insights and information from the records required by law — data that should have been sought and analyzed whether the government requires it or not.

No modern company wants to deliberately discriminate on the basis of sex or race. It's simply too costly to hold good people back for the wrong reason, and even moral idiots know that these are nonbusiness reasons. The reports turned out to comply with EEO requirements may uncover inadvertent discriminatory practices, say in a department or job title, that management may wish to correct.

Similarly, no modern organization is unconcerned about its employees' job-related illnesses or safety in the workplace. Given the costs of accidents and the rising costs of medical insurance, HRIS data in these areas may conceivably provide the basis for safety and health measures that end up paying for the cost of HRIS development.

In the benefits area, the HRIS not only facilitates and reduces the costs of the calculations and record keeping necessary to meet ERISA requirements, it offers the means to improve benefits administration in a host of specific areas. In an era when the Social Security system's long-range financial stability is a matter of increasing concern, the confidence that employees have in employers' pension plans is likely to be a growing issue in human resource management.

Thus, while this chapter on federal regulatory requirements focuses on the reporting requirements of the major legislation affecting personnel practices, there are ways to make necessity a virtue in meeting these requirements with the HRIS.

The legislation and requirements detailed in this chapter include the following federal laws:

- 10.1. *Wage and Hour Laws:* specifically the Fair Labor Standards Act and its amendments.
- 10.2. *Fair Employment Laws:* including various EEO laws and executive orders.

- 10.3. *OSHA:* the Occupational Safety and Health Act of 1970, with its record-keeping and posting requirements.
- 10.4. *ERISA:* the Employee Retirement Income Security Act of 1974.

**10.1. WAGE AND HOUR LAWS**

The basic federal laws regarding wages and hours are the Fair Labor Standards Act (FLSA), requiring overtime for work in excess of forty hours per week and setting the minimum wage; and the Equal Pay Act, an FLSA amendment intended to prevent discriminatory pay practices. In addition, the Walsh-Healy Public Contracts Acts of 1936 provides that the Secretary of Labor can require that prevailing minimum wages be incorporated in government contracts exceeding $10,000, and specifies premium pay of time-and-one-half for work over eight hours per day or forty hours per week.

**10.1.1. Fair Labor Standards Act of 1938 (as amended in 1949, 1966, 1974, and 1977).**

This legislation, setting minimum wage levels for firms engaged in interstate commerce, grew out of state laws — the first in 1893 and later in Massachusetts in 1912 — originally intended to protect women and children. More generally applicable state laws on hours and wages emerged with the Depression, culminating in the Federal FLSA in 1938, which set a 25-cents-an-hour minimum wage and, within a few years, the forty-hour week.

A determination must be made for each job in the organization as to whether the overtime/pay provisions of the FLSA apply. If they do not apply, the rationale establishing that position (e.g., the job is executive, administrative, and professional or outside sales) must be recorded and documented.

*FLSA Required Records.* The following is a list of information that every employer must maintain and preserve for all employees subject to minimum wage and/or overtime provisions of the Fair Labor Standards Act (Sections 6–7 (a) FLSA). Retention is required for two years.

1. Full name (as filed with Social Security)
2. Home address (including zip code)
3. Date of birth, if under 19
4. Sex
5. Occupation
6. Time and day work week begins
7. Regular hourly pay rate
8. Hours worked each workday
9. Hours worked each work week
10. Total straight time earnings, daily or weekly
11. Total overtime earnings
12. Total additions to or deductions from each pay period
13. Total wages paid each pay period
14. Date of payment and pay period
15. Retroactive payments

For fixed weekly workers or fixed schedule workers, items 8 and 9 need not be kept, but a notation or statement showing that they did work the schedule in a given period must appear. If the employee worked more or fewer each day or week, the exact number of hours worked must be recorded.

For bona fide executive, administrative, and professional employees, including teachers and academic personnel plus outside sales employees, items 7 through 12 need not be kept. However, the basis for total pay sufficient to calculate pay in each pay period must be kept, e.g., $1,000 per month plus 5 percent commission on gross sales. This information should include fringes and perquisites.

In addition to the above records, employers must keep for three years all payrolls, individual contracts or collective bargaining agreements, applicable certificates, and notices of the wage-hour administrators as well as sales and purchase records.

These records must be kept at the place of employment, unless they are kept centrally for decentralized facilities, and must be made available within seventy-two hours if requested by a Department of Labor representative.

These requirements permit retention using microfilm or computerization if the required records can be readily converted to reviewable form.

## 10.1.2. Equal Pay Act of 1963

This act is an amendment to the FLSA and states that both men and women should receive equal pay for work that is substantially equal in terms of "skills, effort and responsibility" performed under similar working conditions. Exemptions pursuant to seniority, merit, or quantity or quality of production are allowed.

Since the EPA is directed toward producing equality of pay for women and men, the key to compliance is to keep information relating to employees' sex, pay records, hiring and seniority dates, performance, work location, and job duties.

The primary issue addressed by this act involves job content, not just titles associated with jobs. Clearly, titles may be examined to determine whether there is a disparate pay treatment between men and women for the same work if there are no data regarding job descriptions or job content.

Without the EEO aspects of underutilization or equal employment opportunity, the Equal Pay Act says that if the work people do is the same in terms of skill, effort, or responsibility, they should be paid accordingly. Therefore, any data supporting the pay or job areas are helpful.

*Equal Pay Record-Keeping Requirements.* Although only FLSA reports are mandated, the following analyses could be helpful to the Salary Administrator or EEO Coordinator to determine whether there is a potential equal pay problem:

A. Analysis of starting salaries by sex, by job family, by experience.
B. Analysis of performance appraisal categories by sex.
C. Analysis of pay rate by sex.
D. Analysis of percent of pay range by sex.
E. Analysis of percent of pay range by sex and by length of time in job.

These and other analyses can reveal the extent to which company management may be vulnerable to equal pay litigation and may suggest areas for remedial action.

Obviously, a clearly defined job structure and grading system that is not sex-based will provide an effective foundation for a standard job evaluation system.

An HRIS can help an employer by keeping all the essential data elements for producing the reports described above. The HRIS also provides the resource to monitor the job and salary structure in such a way as to minimize disparate pay treatment.

Should there be an inequality, the Salary Administrator will be able to ask that the HRIS produce needed audit reports on a regular basis and have the data available within days or a week of the pay treatment. Using this resource, new guidelines or policies can be established to forestall future problems in this area.

Analyses in the comparable worth area which is highly complex also will require this data.

### 10.2. FAIR EMPLOYMENT LAWS

Fair employment laws came with full force onto the American business scene in the mid-1960s, as the power of the federal government was put behind efforts to redress long-standing imbalances between job opportunities for blacks and for other Americans. Within a few years of passage of the 1964 Civil Rights Act, amendments to that law and court rulings had broadened the purview of government oversight of employment practices and added the regulatory machinery to enforce this new body of law, which now covers a range of situations from sexual harassment to premature mandatory retirement.

The primary purpose of agencies such as the Equal Employment Opportunity Commission (EEOC) and the Labor Department's Office of Federal Contract Compliance Programs (OFCCP) has remained to correct all racial discrimination in the workplace. Despite the expansion of the original mandates to include women and the flurry of legislative and judicial activity on behalf of the employment rights of the aged, the handicapped, and religious minorities, the main thrust of Washington's fair employment enforcement effort continues to be directed toward equal employment of minorities.

#### 10.2.1. Title VII of the Civil Rights Act of 1964

Title VII, as amended by the Equal Employment Opportunity Act of 1972, is the major piece of legislation in the EEO area and contains most of the basic language and concepts that are referenced and amplified in related legislation. Title VII makes it unlawful for an employer to fail to consider or refuse to hire, to discharge, or to otherwise discriminate against any individual with respect to compensation, terms, or conditions or privileges of employment because of the individual's race, color, religion, sex, or national origin.

*Title VII Record-Keeping Requirements.* For all employers with fifteen or more employees, the following data retention rules exist:

A. Records to be retained for six months include any personnel or employment record made or kept by the employer, including application forms and records having to do with hiring, promotion, transfer, layoff or termination, rates of pay or other terms of compensation, and selection for training or apprenticeship.
B. Records to be retained until final disposition of any charge or action, including personnel records relevant to any charge of discrimination or any action brought by the Attorney General against the employer. For example, this would include records relating to the party initiating the suit and to all other employees holding similar positions and would include application forms or test papers completed by the unsuccessful applicant or candidate and by all other candidates for the same position.
C. Records to be retained that relate to apprenticeship programs include:
  1. For two years, a chronological list of names and addresses, dates of application, sex, and minority group identification for all applicants, or a file of written applications containing the same information. It also includes other records pertaining to apprenticeship applicants, e.g., test papers and interview records.
  2. For one year, any other record made solely for completing report EEO-2 or similar reports.
D. Employers with 100 or more employees must file a special annual report, usually by March 31 for the proceeding year. This Employer Information Report (EEO-1) asks for basic employee statistics by EEO-1 category, race, and sex for each establishment of twenty-five or more employees. Similar EEO Reports (EEO-2, 3, 4, 5, and 6) pertain to apprenticeships, unions, state and local governments, and higher educational institutions.

Basically, the intent of the EEOC record-keeping requirements is to have employers make and keep records relevant to the determinations of whether unlawful employment practices have been or are being committed. Care should be taken to not utilize the data captured for compliance reasons in a discriminatory manner. For instance, it is legally required to record each employee or applicant's race and sex. However, this should be done in such a fashion that the information is not passed to the interviewer or supervisor who has the opening. In short, only the applicant's qualifications should be considered for employment, and extraneous data (particularly items such as race, sex, or age) should be kept out of employment considerations.

**10.2.2. Executive Order #11246 (1964), Revised Order #4 (1972), and #14 (1974)**

These executive orders prohibit discrimination by government contractors or subcontractors because of race, color, religion, sex, or national origin and specify the requirements for an Affirmative Action plan and standardized compliance measures in order to determine compliance with EO #11246.

These orders specifically direct each federal contractor covered to develop a comprehensive Affirmative Action program to remedy any and all aspects of past discrimination and to lay out specific measures enabling minorities to compete for jobs on an equal basis.

*Affirmative Action Record-Keeping Requirements.* For the last twelve months each employer is required to produce on demand the following documentation by EEO-1 category:

- *Availability Data.* Required for each establishment's relevant labor area — national, regional, state, SMSA, county, or city — the numbers of people by EEO-1 Job Classification in the available labor pool.
- *Work Force Analysis.* Requires an analysis of a company's work force distributed by race/sex groups by job title within salary grades. Lists all employees by job title; listed in high to low pay title; includes name, job title, EEO-1 Category, race, sex, hire date, and salary or pay.

- *Utilization Reports.* Requires an analysis of the relevant labor pool or the civilian labor force (CLF) as compared to the work force analysis data. The number of people in the work force for each job classification are matched with the relevant CLF, and possible underutilized areas are noted.
- *Goals and Targets.* Breaks the actual goals and targets for each EEO job classification by race and sex into specific numerical objectives. The goals are usually identified by such groupings as immediate action, long-range goals, and annual intermediate goals.
- *Applicant Flow Records.* Specifies for each job applicant the name, race, sex, national origin, referral source, date of offer, hiring action or reason for nonhire, and job title or job grouping for which the applicant was considered.
- *Process Data.* Specifies for each establishment or internal departmental unit that the following data should be kept for all hires, terminations, laterals and transfers, layoffs, and recalls: name; race; sex; salary, job, and grade; prior salary, job, and grade; and reason for termination with date (if possible).
- *Upgrade and Promotion Data.* For each successful and unsuccessful job bidder: name, job title, race, sex, department, date of hire, reason for selection/rejection, plantwide seniority date, and department or job group seniority date.
- *Trainees.* Includes meaningful training that increased the employee's qualifications for higher-level positions or would allow the employee to move laterally to a position resulting in career progression. Includes name, race, sex, and titles of courses taken in the last twelve months.
- *Job Titles and Descriptions.* Requires a listing of all job titles indicating job groupings with written job descriptions. Organization charts may be required as well.
- *Other Documentation Possibly Needed.* All recruitment advertising, lists of community leaders contacted, list of all training programs in which employees participated, internal or external, by race, by sex, and by program.

Over the past few years, the compliance aspect of the Affirmative Action regulations has shifted from ensuring numerical parity to requiring a deep examination of a company's hiring, transfer, and promotional policies and procedures.

The large data requirements of EEO legislation have made an HRIS almost mandatory. Information is needed by the organizational unit for EEO-1 reports and includes pay categories, race, and sex. It also concerns applicants, current employees, and ex-employees. Manual production of these data for companies of any size is highly inefficient.

### 10.2.3. Age Discrimination in Employment Act of 1967, as Amended in 1977

This legislation prohibits discriminatory practices in the hiring, compensation, terms, conditions, or privileges of employment because of age, protecting workers between the ages of forty and seventy. Effective in 1979, the law prohibits mandatory retirement of all but certain high-pensioned executives before the age of seventy and eliminates mandatory retirement for federal employees at any age. Some state laws have no upper age limit in age discrimination laws.

One of the personnel areas most affected by the age discrimination laws involves benefit plan participation. Care must be taken to track the funding and costs of various plans and to ensure parity between older and younger workers. (ERISA laws, discussed in Section 10.4, are also involved here.)

*Age Discrimination Record-Keeping Requirements.* In general, records that must be kept to assure compliance with the ADEA can be categorized by the time the employer must keep them or their tenure as records:

A. Records to be retained for three years include payroll records containing each employee's name, address, date of birth, occupation, rate of pay, and weekly compensation.
B. Records to be retained for one year include personnel records relating to (1) job applications, résumés, or other replies to job advertisements, including applications for temporary positions and records pertaining to failure to hire, (2) promotion, demotion, transfer, selection for training, layoff, recall, or discharge, (3) job orders submitted to an employment agency or union, (4) test papers in connection with employer-administered aptitude or other employment tests, (5) physical examination

results, (6) job advertisements or notices to employees regarding openings, promotions, training programs, or opportunities for overtime work.
C. Records to be retained for the period of the plan plus one year, including a description of employee benefit plans and written seniority or merit rating systems.

In addition to the above records, it would be very beneficial for the EEO Coordinator, Salary Administrator, Benefits Manager, and any other involved management personnel to continually monitor the promotions, layoffs, salary increases, retirements, and other benefit programs to ensure that older workers are being treated fairly. Analyses such as those listed under the equal pay area could be designed to analyze a company's compliance with age discrimination requirements as well.

Some of these reports are:

- Analysis of new hires by age
- Retirements and other terminations by age and reason, i.e., forced retirement or voluntary
- Salary increase analysis: average wage increase of workers in five-year bands, e.g., 25 to 29, 30 to 34, etc.

The HRIS can produce most if not all of the needed records in this area on an ongoing basis. Utilization of this system can eliminate the need for manual records that would otherwise have to be generated. An additional advantage of the HRIS is that the system administrator will have the option of generating reports on either a regular or an ad hoc basis.

**10.2.4. Vocational Rehabilitation Act of 1973 (Handicapped)**

This legislation makes it illegal to deny an applicant or employee any "right, privilege, advantage or opportunity of employment" solely because of a handicap.

Employers must not discriminate against anyone able to perform the essential functions of a job. Accommodations have to be made, and each job situation should be examined to determine whether any restrictions would apply.

*Handicap Record-Keeping Requirement.* Employers are required to keep a listing of applicants and employees with known handicaps. These candidates and employees should be treated fairly and on an equal basis with others seeking promotions or employment. At this time there is no requirement for an Affirmative Action program with goals and targets, underutilization reports, or other analyses. It may be prudent, though, to recognize that this type of reporting may be necessary in the future.

A code should be developed that describes the type of handicap or illness. This code should be treated with a high degree of confidentiality, since this type of information is highly private and sensitive.

An HRIS would contain the handicap code and would produce monitoring reports of the numbers of job promotions, transfers, training assignments, compensation treatment, and other activities for involved personnel to ensure that there is no discrimination.

### 10.2.5. Vietnam Era Veterans Readjustment Act of 1974 and Executive Order #11701

This legislation requires all federal contractors to implement Affirmative Action programs on behalf of disabled veterans and veterans of the Vietnam era.

*Vietnam Era Veterans Record-Keeping Requirements for Federal Contractors.* Records to be retained for one year after final payment under the contract include copies of reports made to state employment service regarding number of individuals and veterans hired as well as related documentation such as personnel records respecting job openings, recruitment, and placement.

Other records to be retained for one year include records regarding complaints and actions taken under the act.

### 10.2.6. Other Fair Employment Areas

*Religious discrimination is prohibited under equal employment law.* The primary record-keeping requirements relate to instances where observance of the sabbath may cause a problem for required work on either Saturday or Sunday. This work restriction may be noted in the employee's record, but no reference should be made to the nature of the religion.

## 10.3. OCCUPATIONAL SAFETY AND HEALTH ACT OF 1970

The Williams-Steiger Act of 1970, commonly known as the Occupational Safety and Health Act (OSHA), requires the provision of safe and healthful working conditions for virtually every employee in the United States.

The act sets minimum safety standards for operation of equipment, exposure to harmful agents and chemicals, acceptable noise levels, and many other areas of safe office and plant operation. The Department of Labor is the primary enforcement agency in the safety area and sets the record-keeping requirements.

The National Institute for Occupational Safety and Health (NIOSH) conducts research, training, and education activities in the field of workplace safety and health. NIOSH is a unit of the Department of Health and Human Services and interacts with the Department of Labor in this field.

Most of the emphasis of the OSHA legislation and its related enforcement activities is directed toward efforts to ensure that employers create an environment for the safe and healthy operation of their businesses, not toward employee records directly. The record-keeping aspect of OSHA begins when an accident, illness, or exposure to a toxic substance occurs. It is conceivable that some employers would have no extensive employee record keeping to perform if there were no accidents, occupational illnesses, or exposure to toxic or harmful substances. In this case, the company would only need to note the fact that there were no recordable activities. This circumstance is quite rare, however, and most companies will have OSHA records to keep. It should also be noted that each state will also have its own standards in the OSHA area that must also be met.

*OSHA Record-Keeping Requirements.* Any employer who has had eleven employees at any time during the reporting year is subject to the record-keeping requirements. A separate set of records must be kept for each establishment of the employer. Two basic record-keeping forms, Nos. 200 and 101, may be required.

I. *Log and Summary of Occupational Injuries and Illnesses* (OSHA Form No. 200)

This form has two purposes: to record injuries and illnesses during the calendar year and to serve as an annual summary.

The employer must enter each recordable case on the log within six workdays after learning of its occurrence. If the log is prepared elsewhere, using data processing equipment, the copy retained at the central location must be updated within forty-five calendar days of the occurrence. Logs must be updated as the data changes — e.g., if a person's condition requiring only medical treatment changes, and the person later loses more time on the job; of if a person whose records indicate a certain number of lost-time days later dies from the condition being tracked.

The logs must be maintained and retained for each establishment for five years after the end of the calendar year to which they relate.

Any employee or former employee must be given access to the log for the establishment where he or she worked.

Employers are required by OSHA to record information about every occupational death, every nonfatal occupational illness, and those nonfatal occupational injuries which involve one or more of the following: loss of consciousness, restriction of work or motion, transfer to another job, or medical treatment other than first aid. The employer must enter the following data on each case:

A. Case or file number
B. Date of injury or onset of illness (mo/day)
C. Employee's name
D. Employee's job title
E. Employee's department
F. Description of injury or illness

*For Injuries: Extent and Outcome of Injury plus*

1. For fatal injuries: date of death.
2. Notation if injury involved days away from work, or days of restricted work activity, or both.
3. Notation only if injury involved days away from work.
4. Number of days away from work.
5. Number of days of restricted work activity.

6. Notation if there were no days away from work or restricted days but if injury is still considered reportable.
(Items 2 to 6 apply to nonfatal injuries only.)

*For Illnesses: Type, Extent of, and Outcome of Illness plus*

7. Illness category
   a. Occupational skin diseases or disorders
   b. Dust diseases of the lungs
   c. Respiratory conditions resulting from toxic agents
   d. Poisoning (systemic effects of toxic materials)
   e. Disorders resulting from physical agents
   f. Disorders associated with repeated trauma
   g. All other occupational illnesses
8. For fatal illness, date of death
9. Notation if illness involved days away from work, days of restricted work activity, or both.
10. Notation if illness only involved days away from work.
11. Number of days away from work.
12. Number of days of restricted work activity.
13. Notation if there was no death, lost time, or work restriction.

Employers are required to report any incident or accident that results in a fatality or hospitalization of five or more employees to OSHA within forty-eight hours. (Items 9 to 13 apply to nonfatal illnesses only.)

II. *Supplementary Record of Occupational Injuries and Illnesses* (OSHA Form 101)

For each recordable occupational injury or illness entered in the log, the employer must complete a supplementary form (OSHA Form 101) giving more detailed information about the employer, employee, accident or illness, and physician.

The employee data requested includes name, Social Security number, home address, age, sex, occupation, and department.

*Monitoring Employee Exposure to Potentially Toxic or Harmful Physical Agents.* In addition to record keeping and reporting for injury and illness data, some OSHA standards require maintenance of accurate records of employee exposure to certain potentially toxic or harmful physical agents. Based on the standard, the employer may be required to advise the employee of the excessive exposure, remove the employee from the exposure workplace, provide the employee with medical examination and treatment, or take other corrective action.

The specific treatment and action differs according to the substance involved. In all cases, however, the record retention requirements range from twenty to forty years, or in many cases the duration of the exposed individual's employment plus twenty years. The dates, numbers, duration, and results of all medical tests given should also be maintained.

Some of the more critical substances and agents for which employee exposure must be monitored are:

- Asbestos
- Coke oven emissions
- Vinyl chloride
- Arsenic
- Lead
- Carcinogens
- Cotton dust
- Acrylonitrile
- DBCP

Other legislation applies to certain industries with uniquely hazardous situations. Samples are:

- Atomic Energy Act of 1954 as amended
- Federal Mine Safety and Health Act of 1977

As mentioned above, most of the regulations are geared to the establishment of workplace standards. OSHA representatives will concentrate primarily on the equipment and operational aspects of an industry during inspection. However, records will usually be audited.

The area of managing safety programs within a company offers an excellent example of an HRIS module that can assist a unique area of personnel with new input forms and reports designed for one set of users.

The safety module is entirely capable of maintaining all data required to produce the log, and of recording the exposures to the toxic substance. Some records can be automatically generated by the HRIS. With good input procedures, the HRIS can offer valuable labor savings by not only keeping the required logs but also producing the annual summary that must be filed with OSHA offices. The module will also keep records of other incidents and medical visits as these inputs are submitted. Also, by analyzing the work units based upon differing criteria — such as type of equipment, time of day, level of employee, etc. — the HRIS can become a valuable decision-support system assisting a company's Safety Administration system.

Comparisons and interfaces with other internal systems, such as the Medical or Attendance Control modules, should also be explored by the designers to see whether there are duplicate functions that could be eliminated by the Safety module. This module would then be able to provide key data on unsafe practices, excessive lost days by location or work units, and other useful data to help the employer cope with the very costly aspects of accidents and lost time. The HRIS can help prevent lost time by identifying potentially injurious situations before they become accidents.

### 10.4. EMPLOYEE RETIREMENT INCOME SECURITY ACT (ERISA)

The Employee Retirement Income Security Act of 1974 covers all employee benefit plans established or maintained by an employer engaged in interstate commerce or in an activity affecting interstate commerce; it also covers union plans for members so employed. Not covered by ERISA are government plans, those of railroads and churches, Workmen's Compensation, Disability Insurance, and plans for nonresident aliens. Also excluded are unfunded excess benefit plans and certain "tax sheltered annuities." Under ERISA, all other U.S. employers with benefit plans must file a number of reports with the Department of Labor, the Internal Revenue Service, and the Pension Benefit Guaranty Corporation (PBGC).

There are a great many calculations and much record keeping — relating to compensation, breaks in service, and benefit eligibility, for instance — that need to be performed in order to determine the population covered by each benefit plan, the funding involved, premiums to be paid, and benefits to employees. In any organization large enough to have even a single plan, these calculations and the record keeping required by ERISA can impose a significant strain on information processes and record administration groups — a strain that might be intolerable without a computerized system.

Viewed from the broadest perspective, ERISA is a comprehensive law with wide-ranging impacts on many aspects of the benefit field beyond pure record keeping. The act covers the funding arrangements, tax implications, investment standards, contribution limits, fiduciary responsibilities, and other nondata issues of benefit programs. While an HRIS is not intended to directly or entirely accomplish these functions, a data system can become a valuable tool for the benefit administration aspects of ERISA.

### 10.4.1. Eligibility and Vesting Calculations

Some basic calculations must be performed on each employee's record to determine employee participation, extent of employee coverage, and contributions to employee benefits. Most of these calculations address the issue of whether an employee is a participant in the program or is vested in the plan.

The first calculation necessary to establish plan participation will determine eligibility. The minimum requirements ERISA establishes are that an employee must be at least age twenty-five, with one year of service. Plans can exclude those employees who are within five years of normal retirement. A year of service for ERISA purposes is any calendar or plan year in which the participant has 1,000 hours of service. Some rulings have interpreted a week of forty hours for twenty-five weeks to be sufficient service to satisfy the requirement. A break in service occurs in any year in which an employee has less than 500 hours of service.

Vesting implies that a pension participant will, after meeting one of the requirements listed below, retain a right to all or part of the benefits accrued during that time period, even though the employee may leave the job before retirement.

Upon certification and establishment of the plan, an employer *must* adopt one of the following vesting options:

1. Obtainment of ten years of service, known as "cliff vesting." No vesting occurs until the ten-year requirement is met.

2. Graded vesting on a five- to fifteen-year basis; 25 percent at five years service, 50 percent at ten years thereafter, and 10 percent more per year until the employee has 100 percent at fifteen years.
3. When age and number of years of service equal forty-five, the employee is 50 percent vested. Thereafter, the vesting is increased be 10 percent per year.
4. Vesting separately in each year, and the year is fully vested by the fifth succeeding year — known as class-year vesting — is available for certain plans.

It is obvious that detailed records of service and employee demographic information must be retained in order to produce the data calculations listed above for eligibility and vesting.

### 10.4.2. Pension Plan Calculations

Once the employee has reached a vested status, it is clear that the employer has an ongoing liability to produce a benefit for that employee under the particular provisions of the benefit plan. The employer should ensure that all needed compensation and service-related and personal statistics are retained in order to calculate a precise benefit under the plan. The complete retirement formulas are necessary as well as any prior or grandfather provision, ruling, or frozen benefits.

Social Security benefit amounts and levels of coverage may also be needed if these are offsets used in plan calculations or if a "Benefacts" report is to be produced.

### 10.4.3. Plans Covered

Although the intent of ERISA was to strengthen the pension plans in existence and to afford a level of protection to the American worker, the law extends to most other benefit plans as well. Included are deferred profit-sharing plans; savings, thrift, and stock ownership plans; simplified employee pension (SEP) plans; and individual retirement accounts (IRA), Keogh plans, employee stock ownership plans (ESOP), Tax Reduction Act stock ownership plans (TRASOP), and tax-deferred annuities (TDAs). These, as well as other plans such as welfare and insurance plans, all include tax and disclosure provisions that are required by law.

The Age Discrimination in Employment Act had a significant impact on benefit plans by including the provisions that the upper limit for mandatory retirement be raised from sixty-five to seventy. The act has now imposed limitations on the amount that plan benefits can be reduced for older workers. Basically, it requires that reductions can be made as long as the same amount of premiums are being spent on the older worker as the younger. There are age-bracketing restrictions that must be watched closely in the insurance and benefit area.

As with the other employment laws, many states have their own requirements that must be applied in addition to the federal laws.

**10.4.4. Benefit Guarantees**

ERISA established the Pension Benefit Guaranty Corporation (PBGC) to guarantee payment of benefits to plan participants in the event that their pension plan terminates. Only benefits under defined benefit pension plans that meet IRS qualification standards are guaranteed by PBGC. Operating similarly to an insurance policy, there is a mandatory program for employers that guarantees that a certain percentage of the employee's basic pension benefits are now forfeitable. The current premium rate is $2.60 per year for each individual who was a participant of the plan on the last day of the year. Participants are defined to be any of the following:

1. An individual accruing benefits on earnings or retaining service.
2. A vested former employee or a retiree receiving or eligible to receive benefits.
3. A deceased participant whose survivors are receiving or are eligible to receive benefits from the plan.
4. Anyone else who is a participant.
5. An employee participating in more than one plan is counted as a participant in each plan for which he or she is currently in or has retained benefits.

*ERISA Record-Keeping and Reporting.* ERISA requires benefit plan administration to provide each plan participant and beneficiary with a written description of the plan, a copy of the statements and schedules from the annual report, and a statement of accrued and vested benefits. It also requires that information on their vested benefits be provided to participants whose employment was terminated during the year.

The major annual reports that are required are:
1. PBGC-1 Annual Premium Filing report, which is required by the Pension Benefit Guaranty Corporation and transmits the premiums due with participant counts.
2. Form 5500 Annual Return/Report of Employee Benefit Plan (with more than 100 participants); sent to the Labor Department, IRS, and PBGC with statistical data on each plan detail.
3. Form 5500, Schedule A for insurance information.
4. Form 5500, Schedule B for actuarial information.
5. Form 5500, Schedule SSA, Annual Registration Statement Identifying Separated Participants with Deferred Vested Benefits.

There are other reports necessary to terminate or start a plan. Also, each participant may request certain reports once a year.

The utilization of an HRIS in the benefit area is highly recommended for both the calculation and the record-keeping aspects of ERISA.

It is also recommended that an HRIS be utilized to assist in the management of benefit programs by accomplishing various calculation and record-keeping functions as well as providing data to support the overall administration of the various plans. This can and should include enrollment, deductions, premium billing, claims verification, and many other aspects of benefits administration.

**CONCLUSION**

As can be seen, the federal regulatory requirements of personnel record keeping alone have made the installation of automated human resource systems a virtual necessity for most sizable employers in this country. This chapter has covered these requirements in some detail, in an effort to assure that systems developers consider all the requirements of current legislation and rulings. Oversights in this area can be extremely costly.

At the same time, it is recognized that the specific requirements of government regulation are subject to change. In the early and mid 1980s, the mood of the country seems to favor deregulation, a climate that may result in less governmental intrusion into human resource functions. Still, bureaucracies have ways of protecting themselves, and laws and rulings that have evolved over two decades and have been supported by all three branches of government — and frequently have been supplemented by state and local laws — will not disappear overnight. More likely, certain requirements of federal law will change in their specifics. Most of these laws are, after all, relatively new, and internal reforms in many of the agencies that enforce them have been under way since the late 1970s. In addition to hoped-for simplification of the requirements, however, changes to existing requirements may include additional governmental incursion, in the areas of privacy restriction and handicapped persons, for example.

Perhaps most important, however, the personnel information required by the government may turn out to be a blessing in disguise. Many organizations that began using an HRIS to comply with federal laws have progressed well beyond mere compliance, using data and methods of analysis that would not have been available without the pressure of government regulation.

# Part IV
# Corporate Perspectives and Profitability

# 11
# HRIS Savings, Benefits, and Cost Justification

The decision on how to present the HRIS to top management, both initially (as discussed in Chapter 3) and throughout the development stages as the Project Team reminds ultimate decision makers of the benefits of the new system, should be closely reviewed with user management in order to avoid a potentially fatal blunder in the "selling" of the HRIS. User groups and the Team must decide on what basis the HRIS should be put forward — as an information system, cost saver, processing streamliner, etc. — and then build their case.

Invariably, some sort of cost/benefit analysis will have to be done, if only to determine how strong the cost/benefit case really is. The objective of such an analysis is always to see where the actual savings are and how much they amount to; in the case of an HRIS, the analysis should allow for at least a five-year payback. The overall time frame should cover both the development period and an equal period of operational time in any case.

Before conducting a thorough cost/benefit analysis, however, the Project Team should first be clear about the relative significance of dollar savings: whether it is absolutely necessary to rest the justification of the HRIS entirely or primarily on cost savings. Because actual cost savings may in part rely on indirect savings and intangible benefits, it may be preferable to base justification on the need for better data, legal compliance, or provision of more information for management's decision making, instead of attempting to justify the HRIS on a 100 percent direct-savings basis. Since it is often difficult

## 208  IV/CORPORATE PERSPECTIVES AND PROFITABILITY

to actually offset all HRIS costs with direct savings, a justification that combines several kinds of benefits, including costs, is usually in order.

In most cases, top management will accept the fact that the HRIS can upgrade the level of personnel information throughout the organization, and they will not make high payback ratios a precondition of system approval and their continuing support. If they do require "bottom line" answers early, however, the Project Team should be prepared to conduct a very thorough review of all potential areas of saving in order to project the HRIS in its most favorable cost-saving light.

This chapter presents overall guidelines and specific checklists that will help the Team measure and identify these savings, which may occur in many areas of organizational activity and should be watched for from the beginning of the Needs Analysis.

### 11.1. GENERAL GUIDELINES ON COST/BENEFIT ANALYSES

Before proceeding to specific areas in which savings usually occur through HRIS installation, some general guidelines on the definition and measurement of cost savings that apply to computerized personnel systems should be underscored. These relate to the nature of most HRIS savings, which is in people-time; the often overlooked area of cost-avoidance; and the always troublesome question of direct versus indirect savings.

*People Savings.* The most likely place to find substantial savings through installation of an HRIS is in people-time savings. In estimating these savings for management, there is no need to do more than identify estimated savings by type of employee, e.g., clerical, administrative, or management.

For purposes of analysis, each type of employee can be given a coverage-loaded salary rate. This rate is then used to determine the total impact of the HRIS insofar as manual savings are concerned. This impact is calculated by subtracting the estimated new cost of a function from the current estimated cost of that function, as shown in this example of producing salary administration worksheets:

**Production of Salary Administration Worksheets**

| Employee Level | Average Salary | Current Time | Est. Time Post HRIS | Annual Savings |
|---|---|---|---|---|
| Management | $25/hr | 100 hrs/yr | 50 hrs/yr | $1,250 |
| Clerical | $ 8/hr | 500 hrs/yr | 70 hrs/yr | $3,440 |
| Administrative | $12.50/hr | 200 hrs/yr | 100 hrs/yr | $1,250 |
|  |  |  |  | $5,940 |

These cost-saving functions are described by the user during the Needs Analysis stage. The Project Team should get the user's best estimate of the time it takes to perform a given function over a suitable time frame and then estimate, with the user, how much help the HRIS will be in reducing that time. This difference — in hours, days, weeks, or months — is then multiplied by the average salary of that level of employee. The result is the amount of net savings in current dollars for that function. This total amount of savings will have to be offset by system operating costs to get a true estimate of the impact.

Some organizations allow this approach of partial people savings, and some do not, arguing that it is impossible to reduce a staff by a piece of a person. The counter to this argument is that it does free up some hours, and this allows more work to be performed with the same resources. As long as the overall costs of the new system do not exceed the overall savings, there is an increase in productivity.

Also, one can argue that in some cases a fixed-expense resource — e.g., a computer — is being utilized to offset an increasingly expensive resource — people. Therefore, one should, wherever possible, substitute machines for people. That way, the overall information-handling expenses will be kept at a relatively lower cost than if the entire job were done with human resources. Obviously, a dilemma occurs when the machine cost is incurred and the human cost is also incurred. This produces the worst possible case and the situation management most wants to avoid — incurring the expense of the existing work force and the added cost of the system as well.

*Cost Avoidance.* One cost-saving area that sometimes goes overlooked is the costs that would ensue if the HRIS were *not* developed and installed. These costs can be quite substantial and can extend from the cost of continuing with their current outmoded system — perhaps even hiring more people to do the work manually — to the development of a similar computer-based system. In some cases, multiple, redundant systems may have to be developed if the HRIS is not approved. Many more people, or more systems and people to operate them, may mean more space, furniture, etc., as well. Thus the ramifications of the cost-avoidance area in a cost/benefit analysis should not be glossed over lightly.

*Direct Versus Indirect Saving.* The issue of whether a particular cost-saving item is direct or indirect can often be quite controversial. First of all, the entire topic of whether a function or process can be impacted upon by the HRIS may be based on a biased viewpoint, since the estimates are rendered by the Project Team. Second, the estimates are rarely given a point-to-point examination by the experts. Third, the estimates are almost never reviewed after the fact to see whether they have taken place. Therefore, the entire direct/indirect discussion has to be placed in context. An item that is a direct savings to the Project Team may appear to be an indirect savings to others; thus the entire cost/benefit analysis may be suspect.

The best approach to this problem is to have some very clear and unambiguous instructions with examples of what a direct saving is and what an indirect saving is. The Project Team can then follow these instructions and present a more plausible report to management.

For instance, an example of a direct saving might be the elimination of a time-sharing system now used to produce EEO statistics. An example of an indirect saving might be the production of more accurate data for the staffing function, or increased employee morale resulting from a Career Development module. Obviously, any savings associated with indirect examples are going to be tough to prove. As a general rule, it is wise to limit the number of indirect cost savings in the rationale and to base the overall justification on hard cost savings, increased productivity, and better service to the users.

## 11.2. POSSIBLE SAVINGS IN USER AREAS: CHECKLISTS

The following checklists of examples of possible user savings that may result from HRIS installation are presented to help assure that the Project Team overlooks none of the major savings in functional areas of personnel. Not all will apply, of course, but each has occurred in at least some HRIS installations, and the Team should at least be alert to these possibilities for user savings in these areas.

### 11.2.1. Benefits Administration

- More accurate insurance premium billings from carriers instead of estimates that are always in the carrier's favor.
- On-time premium collection from employees, reducing employer expense and deductions.
- Errors such as double Social Security payments on the same employee after transfers are reduced or eliminated.
- Reduced time in calculating estimated benefits and vested benefit amounts under ERISA.
- Reduced time in posting salary changes, transfers, new hires, and terminations on benefit records.
- More precise actuarial data, which can reduce pension payments.
- More precise data on the employee population can yield better quotes in new plan coverages and expenses.
- Reduced time in tracking costs and payments to pensioners.
- Easier preparation of data for an annual statement of benefits or "Benefacts" report, or the actual production of the report itself.
- More accurate Pension Benefit Guarantee Corporation annual premiums.
- Tighter claims control on group insurance claims for dependents.

### 11.2.2. Wage and Salary Administration

- Reduced clerical time in producing salary increase sheets for line department managers, and reducing the time each department keeps its own records.
- Better data to compare to salary surveys. These produce more competitive wage scales.
- Reduced clerical and management time in preparation of salary survey participant data.
- Reduced clerical and management time in tracking performance appraisals with pay.

- Reduced clerical and administrative time in tracking each pay increase for guideline deviations.
- Better data for forecasting the effects of salary plan changes, and reduced time in producing the forecasts.
- Reduced time producing Compa-Ratio studies.
- Tracking equal-pay-for-equal-work compliance can avoid noncompliance costs, including back pay awards, legal fees, etc.

### 11.2.3. General Personnel Administration

- Vacation eligibility listings can be produced more cheaply, and vacation usage can be tracked easily and inexpensively.
- Turnover analysis can spot weak points in supervision.
- Attendance tracking can identify trends or patterns by length of service, departments, locations, reasons for absence, or other factors.
- Reduced clerical time to produce service anniversary listing.
- Reduced clerical time to keep the switchboard and telephone directories up to date.
- Audit use of part-time or term employees.
- Reduced time to produce basic departmental name and address lists.
- Monitoring employee usage of tuition aid programs can identify abuses.
- Reduced time in individual preparation of payroll change notices and backup records maintained to support them.
- Reduced time to produce reports and analyses that utilize manual search of records, such as historical trends and year-over-year statistics.
- Turnaround documents will save the organization thousands of hours of posting time in all departments.
- Car pool listings based on ZIP Code and department or work location.

### 11.2.4. Force Planning

- Reduced time to produce authorized manning levels by department or location, and easier tracking against those levels.
- Audit and control of hiring into unauthorized jobs or unevaluated jobs.

- Reduced time and expense to project openings and force imbalances by levels or functions, thereby identifying more accurately training, promotion, lateral hiring, and other expenses.
- Easier and more accurate comparison of departmental projections with corporate projections.

**11.2.5. Staffing and Career Development**

- Complete inventory of interests, abilities, and "skills" of employees allows more orderly development and placement of employees into openings and next assignments.
- Reduced delay in filling jobs to minimize loss of productivity owing to understaffed positions.
- Reduced clerical time devoted to manufacturing lengthy and cumbersome manual employee background files.
- Better employee morale because of a smoothly functioning career development system.
- Quicker and less costly preparation of hard-to-find skills and language specialties for task force assignments.
- Reduced time to prepare "promotable" lists, and tracking of those promotable on an easier basis.
- More uniform selection standards yield more consistent, defendable positions and fewer lawsuits.
- Key employee log, for succession planning and emergency or strike planning, saves many hours of record keeping.

**11.2.6. Training**

- Reduced clerical and administrative time to produce employee training records for employees, supervisors, or training departments.
- Fewer mismatches between employees and training classes because of better identification of employees who need training.
- Better site and date selection for training classes.
- Reduced time to monitor training taken versus performance, output, or other measurements.
- Easier comparison of course content for possible duplication of courses.

### 11.2.7. EEO Administration

- Reduced clerical and administrative time to set annual targets and track opportunities against targets.
- Reduced clerical time to produce EEO-1 reports.
- Reduced clerical and administrative time to produce disparate impact reports by race, sex, age, or other factors.
- Easier monitoring of test results and applicant flow.
- Reduced time and expense to track locations, departments, and other units on pay, promotions, training courses, tuition aid, benefit sign-ups, and other company programs.
- Readily identifiable pools of promotables or others ready for movement allows more accurate assessment of target population percentages and goal setting.

### 11.2.8. Medical and Safety Administration

- Reduced time to maintain illness, accident logs, and reports (OSHA-200).
- Reduced time to keep records on exposure to toxic chemicals.
- Automobile accident statistics easier to produce.
- Physical exams for executives or those exposed to potentially harmful substances less costly to produce.
- Safety analyses can pinpoint chronic offenders or potentially dangerous situations.

### 11.2.9. Other User Areas of Personnel Savings

- Labor relations can do prenegotiation planning more easily.
- Grievance data and bid-and-bump rosters can be produced more easily and at less expense.
- Applicant tracking can be accomplished at a fraction of manual costs, and candidate retention and match-ups can be performed much more cheaply.
- Offer of employment and applicant reject letters can be produced via word processing at a much cheaper rate than manual typing allows.
- Personnel researchers can save many dollars by not having to individually collect data from the field for every analysis.

## 11.3. SAVINGS OUTSIDE USER AREAS

Depending on circumstances within the organization installing the HRIS, past practices, and information procedures, certain major savings may be realized that are not specifically related to user areas such as Benefits and EEO. These include savings in the computer expenses of systems that will be replaced, reductions in temporary help needed for one-time reports, and savings that result from data and usage standardization and uniformity.

### 11.3.1. Computer-Related Expenses

Very often, the organization will have been gathering and processing personnel information with a fragmented system or partially computerized system that the HRIS will absorb, replace, or otherwise make obsolete. The costs of any system that will be replaced by the HRIS should be included in the cost/benefit analysis of savings. Care should be taken to include the following costs if applicable:

- Hardware costs if dedicated portions of the old system can be identified and reduced
- Annual run charges
- Telecommunications expenses
- Programmer maintenance
- Storage costs
- Miscellaneous supplies and forms

### 11.3.2. Temporary Help

Because of the comparative inefficiency of the present manual or partially mechanized system, a great deal of expensive short-term help and resources may have been required to turn out annual or periodic reports that will now be generated without additional expense in a fraction of the time. At times, the old system may have required the programming of fixed reports and whole subsystems to answer one set of questions. This type of programming can be reduced dramatically in an HRIS because of its complete data base and data retrieval capabilities.

The temporary help required in the past may have included clerical people used for manual posting, programming help to write programs, data surveyors, and collectors or statisticians to help prepare reports.

The HRIS may be replacing a number of annual projects that separately required complete collection, file load, program development, and reporting; the additional costs incurred in each case should be included in HRIS savings.

### 11.3.3. Standardization and Uniformity

While it is difficult to put an exact dollar amount on the value of the standardized terms, definitions, and codes that the HRIS brings to the organization, the Team can make some estimates based on the number of users who are currently keeping records, producing reports, or using the data.

Almost assuredly, each of these users will have his or her own definitions and set of usage parameters in the absense of overriding rules for employee information usage and interpretation. Cutoff dates, employee group definition, collection rules, or error correction methods are probably not being employed or enforced. Indeed, such basic personnel events such as promotions (not to mention temporary promotions) have no rigid informational standards in all likelihood.

This lack of discipline in personnel areas naturally leads to inaccurate salaries, inconsistent performance appraisals, discrimination, and other abuses. An HRIS may not be able to correct all these problems, but it does provide a framework for change through its overall systematic approach and ability to review all areas of personnel record keeping. It also has a very powerful retrieval, analysis, and tracking capability that will pinpoint and expose policies that may be unlawful as well as error-prone.

### 11.4. HRIS COSTS

The operational cost of the HRIS must next be computed, since this will have to be compared with cost savings in the cost/benefit analysis. In examining costs, the Project Team should as a rule include as many costs as are reasonable, although there may be differing opinions on how to treat certain items. The costs that should be included are listed below in three categories.

### 11.4.1. Development Costs of the HRIS

- Hardware purchases
- Project Team salaries and expenses
- Analyst and programming salaries and expenses
- Software purchases
- Forms design
- Documentation development
- Training development

### 11.4.2. Conversion and Installation Costs

- Initial data collection
- File loading
- Systems test
- User acceptance test
- Training
- Forms and booklet printing
- Parallel run costs

### 11.4.3. Ongoing Costs

- HRIC staff salaries and expenses
- HRIS run costs for update
- HRIS retrieval costs
- Programmer maintenance and enhancements
- Annual hardware/software leases
- Training costs
- Forms and booklets

## 11.5. OVERALL JUSTIFICATION

In addition to the direct and indirect cost savings identified in the five-year cost/benefit analysis, there are usually several areas of justification that the Project Team should include in its report to management. These will vary from industry to industry, and there may be many more than are listed here. However, some of the more common are the following:

- *Compliance with federal, state, and local Legal and Statutory Requirements.* In many cases, the fear of being in noncompliance and the protection that good, consistent data bring can be the decisive factors in management's approval. EEOC, OFCCP, and other agencies can levy heavy penalties in terms of both money and adverse publicity.
- *Cost Containment.* Even if the system does not immediately save any money, there is at least an effort being made by management to hold rising clerical and other costs in line. By substituting computer costs for some expenses, information costs may be frozen at current levels in certain areas.
- *Better Management Information for Key Decisions.* When an organization does not know how many employees it has by type, function, level, age, sex, race, or any other variable, how can it run its departments effectively or plan for the future? An HRIS can deliver better, more concise data to specified levels of management when they need it.
- *Peer Pressure.* Many competitors or similarly situated companies may have computerized personnel systems, and the upper echelons of most organizations do not want to admit to being behind the times. Internally, personnel executives may see other departments gaining the benefits of computerization, and they naturally want their turn at putting automation to work. Thus there are external and internal pressures that may be utilized in HRIS justification.
- *Upgrade the Skills of the Personnel Department.* With the changing climate of the personnel field and increasing professionalization of its functions, the entire human resources business needs to keep abreast with technology. Installation of an HRIS is a way of forming a framework for the application of modern personnel techniques in many areas.

## CONCLUSION

When it comes to justifying the time and cost of HRIS installation, an exercise that may be necessary to get the project under way initially (see Chapter 3), a common misjudgment seems to be the "overselling" of certain dollar savings that do not necessarily occur. Direct and indirect savings must be identified and measured, and in some cases the latter will be more significant and ultimately persuasive. Better data for decision making, for example, or compliance with legal requirements are the kinds of indirect savings that may justify HRIS installation.

Where specific "bottom line" savings are required, however, the Team should be prepared to present the HRIS in its most favorable light, and this chapter provides guidelines — including user area checklists — for establishing specific cost savings that the new system will provide.

In addition, guidelines for estimating HRIS costs — including development, conversion, and operating costs — are presented, along with other factors that may be included in a cost/benefit report to management.

# 12
# Development Choices: Prepackaged Systems and Vendor Evaluation

As suggested in Chapter 3, the development option of purchasing an HRIS software package from an outside vendor should be considered during the planning stage. As this chapter's discussion of how to proceed in vendor evaluation makes clear, however, the decision to use an externally developed prepackaged system does not release the Project Team from all developmental tasks. To get the system that best responds to a particular organization's needs, a number of demanding jobs should be performed before and during vendor selection.

Also, it should be clear that this is only one of a number of developmental choices that the Project Team will consider for HRIS installation. If the choice is to develop a system in-house rather than buying a prepackaged system, for example, other kinds of development choices will involve selection of suitable hardware (mainframe equipment, minis, or micros of various types), system alternatives such as time sharing or batch processing, and a range of different software approaches that might be developed internally.

For any of several reasons, however, in-house development may present apparently insurmountable problems. HRIS development is no easy task. For one thing, personnel users are nontechnical people and may not have the time or patience for the detailed work of internal system development.

For large organizations, there is also the "pace of change" problem of internal development. If a system takes two or three years to install, both advances in computer technology and the changing requirements of Personnel may leave the HRIS behind.

In some large organizations, in fact, HRIS developers may find themselves in a no win situation in which there is no way for the new system to begin providing benefits to users within the current year or budget cycle. While the answer to this problem is not necessarily to go to an outside vendor, the Team may in some cases see this as the only viable option. The real solution, as discussed in Chapter 1, is to install the HRIS in results-oriented phases rather than all at once and make sure that you deliver what you said you would in each phase.

Another reason HRIS Project Teams may be inclined to seek an outside vendor is computer development philosophy. In many organizations that already have payroll and other systems, data systems people may not want the kind of personnel system you propose. They may want to keep all systems inside the present computer environment and make use of what may be a sizable investment in hardware, staffs, or even real estate. If the HRIS should propose the use of minis or micros, this may be resisted in a maxi-dominated environment.

In such an environment, a prepackaged personnel system — software developed by an outside vendor for HRIS application — can save the organization substantial sums of money and will usually get you "on the air" sooner than if you developed the equivalent application internally. Although the real savings vary according to the suitability of the software to a particular application, personnel systems that are commercially available can reduce start-up costs and time frames by 50 percent, and savings can be even greater if the fit of the prepackaged system is particularly good.

Whether the prepackaged software you plan to buy from a vendor is a single module or an entire HRIS installation, adequate preparation should precede any official meetings with prospective vendors. Premature exposure to a glib marketing presentation by a software company may create a desire in the organization for a product, without any idea of the effects the system will have on internal operations. Vendors naturally will be putting the best foot forward in presentations, and the Team is at a disadvantage when it is without clear-cut criteria for comparing their wares.

## 222   IV/CORPORATE PERSPECTIVES AND PROFITABILITY

In order to avoid this, each vendor should be given as complete a set of requirements as possible on which to bid, and these specifications should be identical If the specifications are deficient or are not uniform, the vendors will propose systems that are so different that a meaningful comparison cannot be made.

### 12.1. ESTABLISH AN INTERNAL PROJECT TEAM

The organization of the Project Team is perhaps the most critical step in any evaluation process because this group will (1) determine the factors in the evaluation itself, and (2) select a vendor or at least exert influence on top management's decision. Therefore, the make-up of this team is crucial. The same guidelines that apply to establishing the internal HRIS Project Team (Chapter 3) apply here.

First, the client organization should appoint a project leader from the user area, in this case the Personnel Department. The leader should be familiar with the way in which the Personnel Department operates in the organization and how a computerized system can help. The leader should identify with management in this project and be able to comfortably make presentations to a top management group. Also, the leader should have a background in the data processing field or at least enough exposure to computerized systems so that he or she can feel comfortable in the evaluation of computerized software. Someone has to be in charge and be able to make key decisions as the evaluation process moves along.

There are at least ten logical steps in vendor evaluation that will improve the organization's chances of selecting the proper system:

1. Establish an internal Project Team.
2. Determine the system requirements.
3. Alert management: get their approval.
4. Develop the evaluation criteria.
5. Develop and request proposal.
6. Initial screening of the vendors.
7. Presentation by vendors.
8. Detailed evaluation.
9. Narrow to two vendors: go to contract.
10. Final selection: sign contract.

It is noteworthy that step 7 in this sequence does not occur until late in the overall process. A good bit of homework is necessary before the vendors are called in. This preparation is frequently omitted in evaluations, although it can be the difference between a successful personnel system and a bad vendor experience. Moreover, these preparation steps can be a trial run used to evaluate the organization's internal development capability versus that of an outside vendor.

The ten steps to follow in vendor evaluation are described later in this chapter.

The Team should also include members from other affected work units. The data systems organization must certainly be represented, since the software will in all likelihood run on their equipment. Payroll may also wish to send a representative. Also, any other large user or group that has a strong interest in the personnel system should pick a delegate.

This team will have several tasks to carry out before any vendors are approached. First, they must plan and schedule their activities. Setting target dates based on the work ahead is important in order to avoid pursuing unproductive schemes with a persuasive vendor. The plan should stress the steps necessary to get the system you want in the right time frame and should outline clear milestones for management's review. Unless there are unforeseen problems, the entire vendor selection process should take two to three months. The most important task the team faces, though, is to develop a set of requirements for the personnel system.

## 12.2. DETERMINE THE SYSTEM REQUIREMENTS

There are many varieties of computerized personnel systems, such as systems that closely resemble payroll systems, skills inventory systems, EEO tracking systems, and pension systems. In order to discover whether a system is suitable for your organization, it is imperative that you develop specifications. Without them, the project team will be subject to the marketing pressures of each vendor. A statement of your requirements will greatly increase the chance of getting the system you actually need to solve your problems; it should cover at least the following areas:

- A statement of the problem or series of problems that the system should correct.
- An overview of how the system will work in the organization at a conceptual level.
- How should the system interface with existing systems, such as payroll?
- Approximate data elements you require.
- Inputs necessary to update the system.
- Outputs desired from the system, emphasizing mandatory items.
- Response times desired for updates and queries, computed in user end-to-end terms.
- System controls that are necessary as far as security, privacy, backup, and recovery are concerned.
- Any operational constraints, such as staffing levels and annual costs.
- Acceptable annual maintenance charges.
- Computer environment constraints, if any.
- The system development plan, including the staffing resources, time, frame, and funding available for the project.
- Handling history or generalized retrieval.

This list is a distillation of the specifications presented in Part III. As stated in chapters 5-7, it is best to develop these specifications with extensive help from individual users and perhaps include specific items not listed above. Without these basic requirements, though, the Project Team cannot determine how closely a vendor's product fits an organization's needs and how much time and money it will save, if any, over internal development. The specifications represent your needs and will form the basis for an objective evaluation of how to meet those needs. In other words, the specifications determine the solution.

### 12.3. ALERT MANAGEMENT: GET THEIR APPROVAL

If you go outside for vendor bids, this represents an opportunity for your suppliers to gain some additional business for their own firms, and this is fine. However, many of the firms offering personnel systems have strong marketing organizations, and relationships may have been built up over the years by some of your senior managers with these firms. Indeed, you may already be their client.

This rapport with top management is both useful and healthy. However, at the start of an objective evaluation, the Project Team needs to be aware of specific top management concerns about vendors. If this is done *before* the evaluation, intervention during the process can be avoided. If possible, the Project Team should try to get management's approval of the objectives, plans, and scope of the system before deciding on a development option.

## 12.4. DEVELOP THE EVALUATION CRITERIA

The next task is to set up specific criteria with which to evaluate the vendors. Some questions may come up about who should select the criteria and how to deal with the problem that one team member's criteria may be more important than another's. Also, what happens if a vendor looks good in some areas but not in others?

A good approach is to have each Project Team member independently develop a checklist of items to be evaluated and then rank their importance. Then members can share the lists with others and discuss these factors. Duplicate items are noted, and some shifting and adjusting of order and priorities is allowed. After this occurs, a determination of items that are most important on each person's list should take place a second time. This time, however, if a vendor's approach to an item is not acceptable, the vendor should be eliminated outright from further discussion. Those rating the vendor will generally change their criteria once more, and their list of crucial criteria will become a bit smaller. The criteria can then be placed into three categories: a "mandatory" group (vendor's inability to meet requirements means elimination), a "really-would-like-to-have" category, and a "nice-to-have" category. Each organization may have a different list, but they will all establish a set of rating criteria with which to judge the vendors.

Next, a decision should be made about who will do the actual ratings and how to rate and score the ratings. Generally, judgments should be made by those best qualified to do the evaluation; you can have duplicate ratings and joint responsibility when more than one user area is concerned with criteria. In this way, the data systems people keep responsibility for the technical areas, and the personnel people are responsible for the user areas. In cases where both are concerned, both will perform the ratings. For broader areas in which no user is directly responsible and there is no joint responsibility, the project leader should perform the rating.

A simple rating category can be assigned, using standard merit performance ratings, such as outstanding, more than satisfactory, satisfactory, less than satisfactory, or unsatisfactory. At least outstanding or superior should be defined, and some time can be saved if one doesn't have to develop new ratings. In order to tally the ratings, weightings of 5 for outstanding, 3 for more than satisfactory, 0 for satisfactory, −3 for less than satisfactory, and −5 for unsatisfactory can be used. This indicates the degree of difference between the vendors. After the ratings have been assigned, a further refinement can be done by weighting those items in the "must-have" category with a weight of 5, the "really would-like-to-have" items with a weight of 3, and the "nice-to-have" group with a weight of 1. In this way, the importance of scoring high in the key items is heightened.

Actually, as the Team gets into the process, scores may not be necessary, since the ratings themselves will indicate who is the better vendor for your system. But to guard against this, scores should be kept and used.

High on the list of criteria must be the group of tasks that the Team identified as mandatory. Some mandatory items in the user area would be the ability of the system to:

- Produce salary administration rate review sheets.
- Track promotions.
- Produce an EEO-1 report.
- Keep the data base elements you want.
- Calculate retirements.
- Satisfy ERISA reporting requirements.
- Produce career profile sheets on each employee.
- Handle your code values.
- Generate "ad hoc" user requests.

There will be other mandatory criteria outside of the user's areas, of course. These might include:

- Price of the system when below a certain level.

- Vendor's ability to show you a similar system they installed elsewhere.
- Vendor's time frame.

If a vendor receives an unsatisfactory grade on a mandatory item, it is a fatal deficiency. That vendor should be dropped unless the deficiency can be corrected or the user can relax the requirement.

By its nature, the vendor selection process is difficult and often imperfect. We are judging an ability to produce a product in the future, often for a client for whom the vendor has never worked. Also, people's judgments are subject to past experiences and first impressions without the benefit, in this case, of having participated in such a process before. A sound selection team and applicable criteria will create a better product, however.

Items that could be rated in such an evaluation are listed in the chart titled "Points to Evaluate in Selecting a Vendor," shown below. Several key items may have been overlooked, but this will serve as a starter list for most organizations. Certain points are more critical than others, depending on a client's particular situation. If a firm is faced with a multimillion-dollar lawsuit in the EEO area, installation time may be the most important factor. For another company, the overall technical construction may be more critical. Therefore, each organization must develop its own list and weight the items accordingly to decide whether to place them in their "mandatory," "really would-like-to-have," or "nice-to-have" categories.

*Points to Evaluate in Selecting a Vendor*

Category I. General and User-Area Criteria
- Ability to handle the mandatory user items
- Corporate stability of the vendor
- Experience of the vendor
- Your company's relationship with the vendor
- Another client's evaluation of the vendor
- User procedures and documentation
- Retrieval methods and analysis packages
- Accuracy in handling errors
- Training supplied by vendor

- Flexibility of form design
- Methods of handling computerized history
- Handling of applicant's records
- Payroll interface approach
- Time schedule
- Working relationship with vendor
- Vendor's ability to do the entire job
- Easy use of system

Category II. Technical Considerations

- Overall construction, that is, data base management system or other system architecture
- Hardware compatibility
- Program construction and degree of modularity
- Use of tables and indices
- Expandibility and enhanceability
- Documentation
- Security and controls
- Resource utilization by the system
- Installation method and approach
- Approach to project management
- Screen design
- Conversion
- Secondary programs necessary to the client
- Retrieval approach report generator and language limitations
- Assignment of project leader
- Vendor maintenance/support
- Word processing and graphics capability

Category III. Cost and Contractuals

- Purchase cost
  Software cost for all needed modules
  Travel and living expenses
  Computer test time
  Installation charges
  Office and clerical changes
  Internal programming cost

Hardware costs
User-area costs
- Ongoing cost
Annual-run charges; computer and user areas
Maintenance agreement
Internal programmer
Hardware rental
- Contract responsiveness and wording
- Maintenance and support

## 12.5. DEVELOP AND REQUEST PROPOSAL

Next, a request for proposal (RFP) should be prepared by the project team. This RFP can be very formal in its delivery (written as a contract) or generalized and open-ended (written as a business letter). As a general rule, the larger the system, the more precise and detailed it should be, since there will be more money at stake.

The RFP should be sent to all potential vendors in the personnel systems field. If one of your criteria is that the vendor has installed similar systems in the past, your project team might start with those companies and not feel that they have to go to every computer software house in the country. By looking in the computer trade journals, leading personnel magazines, and other references, one can develop a fairly comprehensive list of companies that are seriously marketing to the personnel data field.

The RFP should contain your instructions to these vendors on how you want their bids presented. Also, state your constraints and wishes in time and cost area, and state how you wish them to handle the project. Outline the job to be done and lay down the ground rules for the bidding procedure. The system requirements document should be placed in the RFP in order to give the vendor a clear picture of the desired system. Instructions on how to submit proposals, including acceptable format and cost breakdowns, should also be included. In this way, an easy comparison of different bids can be made by the Team. Inevitably, questions arise from the vendors, and they can be answered as they arise by telephone, in writing, or in a general meeting with all vendors present.

Vendors should be informed that cost is only one of the factors and that the low bidder is not necessarily guaranteed the job. Vendors may submit whatever data and marketing literature they wish for review, but the primary consideration should be their response to various questions in the RFP. A specific date should be set for a response. Notify them that missing the date may eliminate them from further consideration.

## 12.6. INITIAL SCREENING OF THE VENDORS

Upon receipt of the proposals, the project team will be able to screen out unacceptable vendors, that is, those whose proposal is so deficient that they warrant no further consideration. Screening out a vendor at this stage is generally a result of failing to submit a proposal or not completing it in accordance with the rules to such a degree that the team could not evaluate it. Other reasons include basic incompatiblities, such as a package that is only a payroll system or one that only works on IBM hardware when you have a NCR machine. At this stage, eliminating a vendor means that you don't want to waste time and money by proceeding any further, since there is not a close enough match between product and application. Those companies who survive this cut may now come in and make a presentation to the Team.

## 12.7. PRESENTATION BY VENDORS

Most of the vendors have probably been trying to get on site to make an in-person presentation to you. In fact, the presentation stage is where most companies would start the process without this formalized approach. To begin here, however, means there are no clear-cut criteria of what to rate or how to determine the way the process is handled. All this works to the vendor's advantage. This, however, is the next hurdle if they survived the initial screening.

A daylong meeting should be adequate for their presentation, to answer the project team's questions, and to go over their proposal. The Team should concentrate on a search for fatal deficiencies and vendor flexibility. Almost all packages can be modified to some extent, and the flexibility of the product and the willingness of the vendor to accomodate changes can be explored. A "perfect" fit, while ideal, is rare.

After all the presentations have been made and any follow-up questions answered, the Team can rate the proposals. Vendors who score well and who hold real promise (based on responses to the Team's questions) should be invited back to continue the evaluation.

## 12.8. DETAILED EVALUATION

After the possible vendors have been narrowed to a manageable number, the detailed evaluation process can take place. This involves checking references, visiting the vendor's offices and facilities where warranted, and demonstration of the software system. In many cases, some sort of credit check would be in order. The data system's project team members should investigate the product to whatever level is deemed sufficient, including a trial run. After all possible areas are covered, unanswered questions and verbal promises should be noted for inclusion in the contract. This evaluation must be detailed enough to satisfy all project team members and top management that the products have been investigated sufficiently.

## 12.9. NARROW TO TWO VENDORS: GO TO CONTRACT

A final selection of the two leading vendors can now be made. If at this stage there are no vendors without a fatal deficiency, you must either develop a system from scratch, relax your requirement in the fatal area, or get around it (by having your data systems people supplement the product with their own subsystem).

Let us assume that the process did give you at least two vendors who could do the job, and you have decided which one you prefer. At this time, submit to each the contract you wish to sign and get the contract they prefer from them. Dealing with two vendors while you go over the terms and conditions may rule out any sudden uncooperativeness at this late stage. Verbal promises encountered in the evaluations must be included in the contracts, and vendors should be rated on their ability to incorporate your changes. Examine this final negotiation stage carefully to see whether this last step changes the ratings significantly.

## 12.10. FINAL SELECTION: SIGN CONTRACT

If there are no major problems with the contract, the project team can make its final decision and select the product and vendor the members feel is best suited to develop their personnel system. Top management's approval is usually necessary, and work can begin as soon as the contract is final.

**CONCLUSION**

The decision to seek an outside vendor from whom to purchase a prepackaged software system, one of a number of development choices that the project team may make, does not mean that the organization should turn over the entire job of determining its needs, problems, and objectives to outside vendors. On the contrary, the proper selection of an effective prepackaged personnel system that meets your needs should include some of the same steps necessary to develop an HRIS internally. In addition, certain kinds of procedures, uniformly applied to all prospective vendors, should be followed in all cases, whether the purchase is of a single personnel module or an entire HRIS.

The vendor evaluation process outlined in this chapter may appear a bit detailed and overcautious. In more than a decade of consulting, however, I have not encountered a single organization that believed it had spent too much time in software evaluation. On the contrary, I have seen many clients who made a hasty choice, only to find that the system did not live up to its promise. By adopting a prudent approach, most companies can sharply increase their chances of getting a personnel system suited to their needs.

# 13
# Future Trends:
# Decision Making and Analysis

The future growth of Human Resource Information System applications, at least during the near future of the 1980s, will be based more on the changing and expanding role of the Personnel Department than on technical marvels and new equipment breakthroughs. For the most part, the technology needed to operate a "paperless personnel office of the future" is already here, and it is probably safe to say that most organizations in America employing over 2,000 people either have an HRIS in place or will be installing one in the early years of this decade.

Even among large companies employing data base technology, however, great differences remain in how the HRIS is used, ranging from simple compliance with regulatory requirements to highly user-oriented systems that provide information for analysis and decision making, produce forecasting and modeling data, and perform word processing chores and other clerical and administrative functions automatically. Thus, in a sense the "future" of HRIS usage form many organizations will resemble what is already taking place in some organizations, such as those using online systems, micro or minicomputers devoted to personnel, and distributed data bases and processing.

From a broader perspective, a number of trends that will increasingly affect the role of Personnel — what the human resource department is expected to do — indicate increasing demand for more effective computerized personnel systems in the years ahead.

Much has been written, for example, about the "new breed" of American workers, people less concerned with traditional workplace incentives such as compensation and more interested in employee "rights," corporate democracy, a range of noncompensation benefits including more leisure time, and similarly nontraditional values. Declining confidence in institutions, including employers, has been a fact of life in American society over the past two decades, and a work force made up of increasingly better educated workers is more likely to "question everthing" about work and its rewards than to accept standard personnel practices and procedures just because "it's the way we've always done it here."

Obviously, such generalities do not apply to everyone in the workforce, and much has also been written about the putative percentages of workers in various categories of commitment to work, motivational sources, and so on. The point, however, is that few organizations can any longer afford to treat their employees as a monolithic work force. Even the modern military, in which today's personnel problems are acute, has begun instituting compensation practices based on performance and merit reviews, alternative benefit programs, and a smorgasbord of reenlistment options for personnel possessing certain critical skills.

Instead of being monolithic, the work force in general and classes of workers suitable for certain jobs are changing as never before in history, thanks to the combined effects of government legislation, social trends, economic conditions, and population trends.

These trends will have an impact on employee needs and organizational human resource policies that is difficult to summarize but is certain to involve the need for greater *flexibility* in human resource management.

In the area of worktime arrangements, for example, the combined effects of more women (especially working mothers) in the labor force; more older persons seeking part-time jobs as a transitional phase to retirement; more handicapped persons, college students, and others unable to work standard hours seeking work — all will put pressure on employers to provide a variety of nonstandard work hour schedule alternatives for employees. Concepts such as "flexitime" may be unsuitable for many organizations, but there are many less exotic alternatives to the five-day, nine-to-five work week that will be gaining increased attention in the years ahead. Because of advances in communications technology, some predict that in the future many workers will not need to report in person to their jobs at all but will work at home with computers in a new "electronic cottage" industry environment.

Not only will demographic and economic pressures contribute to increasing demand for nonstandard hours, but changing social values — marked especially by the growing importance of nonwork activities and leisure pursuits — will influence worker expectations that employers will adapt working hours to meet employees' needs and desires. And as some employers who have experimented with flexible hours, job sharing, and other alternate worktime arrangements have discovered, giving employees what they want in this area can result in greatly increased productivity as well as reduced lateness, absenteeism, and turnover.

Even to experiment with alternate hours on any kind of large scale, however, most employers will require the kind of record keeping and analytical capabilities best provided by an HRIS. The costs of simply keeping track of hours worked for statutory and pay purposes, benefits accrued, and other basic information related to time would be prohibitive if undertaken manually in most medium-sized organizations. And the effective management of a work force working a multiplicity of schedules, which should include analyses of productivity, comparative evaluations, and other functions of modern salary administration, would be out of the question without an automated personnel system.

The growth of benefits as a percentage of total compensation has been widely noted in recent years; it is another trend impelled by social and economic change. Not only have benefits for employees become an increasingly larger share of employee costs, but new kinds of benefits and new ways of presenting and delivering these benefits to employees are expected to grow in importance in the future. In particular, cafeteria-style benefit programs, in which employees select from a range of benefits and in effect create their own individualized benefit programs to meet their own needs, may become increasingly widespread in the future, with obvious implications for benefits administration and record keeping.

Orangizations that offer flexible benefit programs of this type are responding to a changing work force in which fewer and fewer employees are male heads of households with a wife and children at home. Traditional, standard benefit programs of the past were geared to the needs of families that now represent less than 15 percent of the nation's work force.

Today working wives often have benefit programs that unnecessarily duplicate their husbands' medical programs, for example. Not only would such wives prefer to have some other benefit — such as more vacation time — but their employers might be glad to shed the more expensive medical coverage while at the same time improving employee morale. Even if the costs to the employer come out the same, however, the cost of providing an employee with a benefit that the employee does not want can hardly be justified.

Benefits offered by employers are becoming more diverse in response to changing worker values, economic forces, and social trends. Some companies, for example, provide leave time to fathers as well as mothers of newborn children — in part a recognition that the mother may be the primary earner in the family and may need to return to work. In the future, some predict, "spousal" benefits may be extended to cover unmarried partners, as the percentage of unmarried-couple households grows.

Many have also commented on the broad range of "private welfare" issues to emerge in recent years — the growing attitude among American workers that they are entitled to some of the same benefits — education, child care, medical coverage, economic aid — that the government has traditionally provided to those considered "disadvantaged." In an era of reduced government spending and efforts to trim rather than expand these kinds of programs, more and more employers — especially major corporations — will be expected to "internalize" these social costs. Government policies are likely to encourage this trend.

In order to monitor and manage the more flexible, more varied benefit programs expected in the future, as these programs assume an ever larger part of total compensation costs, employers will more and more need the cost-efficient record-keeping and analytic capabilities provided only by an HRIS.

Most discussions in recent years of the "changing" work force confronted by human resources management have focused on three issues: the new values of "new breed" employees, the historic influx of women into the labor force, and the need to provide equal employment opportunities for minorities. In the years ahead, these issues will be joined by other important concerns imposed by demographics, economics, and social change — concerns that various human resource functions will want to analyze and make decisions about with the tools provided by an effective HRIS.

For example, baby-boom demographics assure what has been called a "middle-age bulge" in the age distribution of the population during the next decade. People aged twenty-five to forty-four, a critical age in career development, will increase by one-third during the 1980s, while the total U.S. population will remain relatively static. Are present compensation policies going to be adequate or even possible in your organization? For some employees in this age group, new forms of recompense may have to be devised. Which ones? And what will it take to keep different people on the job and productive?

Present demographics also assure a declining number of eighteen-year-olds in the population, a trend that may lead some organizations to examination of entry-level turnover rates that they have been able to "live with" in the past. The costs of turnover in many organizations are never fully understood, largely because the quantitative analysis needed to establish these costs — which include lost production — are not available with primitive personnel information systems.

The long-term "graying of America" that occupies so many works on demographics today also has implications for human resource management and will have impacts on a changing work force that should be better understood. Unless inflation rates are soon checked, some see a reversal of the early-retirement trend of recent years. Federal law already prohibits mandatory retirement of most employees before the age of seventy, and by the year 2030 people sixty-five and over will constitute fully 18 percent of the total population — up from about 8 percent in 1950.

Perhaps the most burning issue relating to employee information in the early and mid 1980s is productivity. How can employers better measure, evaluate, and improve different kinds of workers' output per man-hour? The nation as a whole has seen its productivity growth slow to a standstill at the end of the 1970s, for reasons said to include declining R&D, the shift from manufacturing to a service economy, new entrants (mainly women) in the labor force, and government regulation. For individual organizations seeking to improve their workers' productivity, these reasons are usually highly academic.

Specific studies of productivity in these organizations are difficult without comprehensive, accurately quantified data about work and workers — the kind an HRIS provides.

The particular impact of changing social and other trends will vary according to your organization's future needs, of course. Companies have strategic Human Resource Planning organizations whose job it is to determine future needs (often using HRIS-generated data on the current work force and labor markets), and from this planning should emerge a picture of what the company's future personnel functions will require: what needs to be done to obtain, train, and maintain the work force needed to reach organizational goals in the years ahead.

For some organizations, future needs will require a more stable management force, less prone to job hopping. (Others may need a way to encourage early retirement from an excessively "senior" management cadre.) Some may recognize impending skills shortages that cannot be overcome by technology; others will want to prepare segments of the work force for technology that will make their present jobs obsolete. Many will see the need for increased education and training in company- or industry-specific areas. Schools simply do not turn out work-ready people in many areas today, and future jobs will be more demanding. Most organizations, responding to the changing values of workers exemplified by the alternate-work-hour and flexible benefits trends discussed above, will be seeking ways to provide and manage more "individualistic" human resources programs.

The efficient administration and management of programs such as these, in all but the smallest organizations, will require the kind of personnel information and analytic decision-making tools best supplied by an HRIS. The rising cost of training, to cite just one example, mean that more useful measures of effectiveness, better records of courses taken over time, and data needed to make correlations between such factors as performance in training programs and performance or productivity on subsequent jobs all should be available in usable form to training developers and managers — and this indicates an HRIS.

Personnel functions made possible by an HRIS with a fully developed Human Resource Utilization (HRU) module, particularly the

Skills Inventory program described in Chapter 9, are still in the future for most organizations, despite the great promise such applications have for more effective job placement, career development, transfer and promotion activity, and a number of issues usually considered "quality of work life" concerns. Not only will an effective HRU system assure that the organization is making the best and most profitable use of its human resources, a properly presented and administered system of this type involves employees in decisions affecting their own careers. Moreover, a well-operated HRU can be used to more democratically show all employees — whether ambitious or merely disaffected — what they need to do to get where they would rather be.

## 13.1. TECHNOLOGY NOW AVAILABLE FOR USER-ORIENTED SYSTEMS

The microprocessor revolution, which is still going on, has made possible the development of low-cost micro and minicomputers and related equipment that form the ideal technological basis for personnel systems of the future. The stand-alone personnel systems made possible by this technology are "ideal," in my view, because they permit human resources users to economically "own their own" hardware full-time, can use easily understood English-language programs, can be connected at multiple sites in a distributed format, and have the capacity to generate both HRIS output and word processing material such as personalized letters.

The use of online minis by personnel groups is already a reality in a number of major organizations and will grow as equipment costs come down and capacities increase. Past cost reductions and miniaturization in the computer equipment field have come because of increases in the number of "brains," or active elements that could be fabricated on a single mass-produced silicon chip. Today, a single chip the size of a child's fingernail — a large-scale integrated circuit — can contain more active elements than the most complex electronic equipment built twenty-five years ago. The advent in the 1980s of very large scale integration (VLSI) points to integrated circuits or chips with over 100,000 elements apiece (up from about 30,000 at the start of the decade), and some scientists foresee a million-element chip in the future as a result of new electron beam (E-beam) and x-ray lithographic systems of semiconductor manufacture.

Thus, the microprocessor revolution that has led to lower and lower hardware costs is still going on, and to the extent that equipment costs have prevented personnel departments from developing their own online systems, this technology will help create the new "paperless" personnel office of the future.

**CONCLUSION**

To a great degree, the future of HRIS application in this country will probably resemble what is already taking place in a handful of major organizations today, such as those using stand-alone online systems, and employing micro or minicomputers, advanced retrieval technology, and distributed data bases and processing. These few firms are either using or experimenting with highly user-oriented systems that provide information for decision making in a variety of formats and are linked to word processing systems at the same time.

In the longer view, changes in the ways computerized personnel systems serve organizations can be inferred from some of the changes that are transforming the role of human resources in the modern organization. Benefits programs, for one example, will require increasingly sophisticated administration in the years ahead if employers are to keep pace with the changing needs of a changing work force. Demographic, economic, and social change — as well as possible governmental action that is supposed to respond to such change — may have a wide range of implications for human resource management, creating a need for more sophisticated, efficient personnel information systems and decision-making tools than most organizations envision today.

# Index

# Index

Affirmative Action (*See also* EEO), 23, 29–30
   recordkeeping requirements, 190–192
Age Discrimination in Employment Act of 1967, 192–193
American Management Association (AMA), 42
American Telephone & Telegraph Co. (AT&T), 6
Applicant tracking, 130, 137–138
Attendance control, 28, 199
Atomic Energy Act of 1954, 198

Bank of America, 7
Bankers Trust, 7
Benefacts, 211
Benefits Administration (*See also* ERISA)
   benefits module, 27, 55–56, 131, 211
   recordkeeping requirements, 199–203
Benefits statement, 29, 211

Career development (*See also* HRI and HRU), 131, 135–136, 178, 213
Chemical Bank, 7
Civil Rights Act of 1964 (*See also* EEO and Affirmative Action), 188–190
COBOL programming, 20, 177
Conversion activities, 40, 156–160, 217
Cost benefit analysis/justification, 45, 52, 57, 65, 69
   methods of, 207–218
Critical Path Method (CPM), 53

Data accuracy and quality, 17, 22–24, 71, 95–97
   methods of achieving, 160–163
Data administration, 167
Data base elements, 17–18, 156
   data base sizing, 132–137
   historical, 133
   privacy of, 171–173
   recording form, 84
   selection of, 82–89
   used in reports, 144–145
Data base management systems, 82, 89, 106, 145, 148
Data entry, 18–19, 162–163
   methods of, 93–95
Distributed processing, 124, 146–148

Edits, 95–97, 122, 161–163
Employee Retirement Income Security Act (ERISA), 7, 24, 27, 45, 158, 191, 211, 226
   recordkeeping requirements, 185, 199–203
Employment status codes, use of, 89–92
Equal Employment Opportunity (EEO),
   *See also* Affirmative Action and Civil Rights Act of 1964, 7, 9, 23, 25, 45, 128, 171–172, 184, 214, 226
   EEO module, 29, 30, 75
   recordkeeping requirements, 188–193
Equal Pay Act of 1963, 187–188

Fair Employment Laws, 184, 188–195

241

Fair information practice principles (*See also* Privacy), 170-171
Fair Labor Standards Act of 1938, 185-188
Federal Mine Safety and Health Act of 1977, 198

General Electric Company, 6
General Motors, 6

Handicapped (Vocational Rehabilitation Act of 1973) recordkeeping, 193-194
Hartford Insurance Company, 7
Historical records, 131-137, 141-143, 155-156
  designing for, 124-126
  uses of, 126-128
Human Resource Information Center (HRIC), 17, 75, 93, 99, 150, 156, 159, 217
  concept of, 21-22
  controlling the HRIS, 102-104, 122, 172
  job duties, 166-169
  role in accuracy, 161-163
  staffing of, 169-170
HRIS, definition of, 16
Human Resource Inventory (HRI), 5, 27, 174-182
Human resources planning, 3, 8, 45, 173-174, 182, 238
  planning module, 212-213
Human Resource Utilization (HRU), 165, 238-239
  HRU module, 25-27
  overall plan, 173-182

Input, Process, Output (IPO), 85-88, 117
Installation, 40, 156-160, 217
Interviewing Techniques, 59-69
Item Ownership Concept, 18, 83-84

Job evaluation, 116, 148, 212
  job evaluation module, 25, 27-28
Johnson, Lyndon B., 7

Management Information Systems Concept, (MIS), 6-7
Manufacturer's Hanover Bank, 7
Medical data, 149, 199, 214

Microcomputers, 124, 129, 146-148, 220, 239, 240
Mobil Oil, 6
Module criteria, 25

National Bank of Detroit, 7
National Institute for Occupational Safety and Health (NIOSH), 195
Nixon, Richard M., 7

Occupational Safety and Health Act of 1970 (OSHA), 7, 45, 214
  OSHA module, 28-29
  recordkeeping requirements, 185, 195-199
Office of Federal Contract Compliance Programs (OFCCP), 10, 188, 218

Payroll interface, 10, 45, 69, 72, 88, 119, 228
  methods of, 107-114
Pension Benefit Guaranty Corporation (PBGC), 27, 199, 202-203, 211
Personnel activities, list of, 55
Position control module, 28
Pre-packaged personnel systems, 14-15, 221-232
Privacy (*See also* Security), 22, 24, 72, 77, 83-84, 100, 160-161, 165, 224
  recordkeeping requirements, 170-173
Processing routines, 86, 117, 118
Project development stages, 38-40
Project Evaluation and Review Technique (PERT), 14, 53
Project leader attributes, 13, 47-50
Project scheduling, 57-58
Project team composition, 49
Proposal to management, 39, 41, 43-46, 207

Questionnaires, use of in interviewing, 61

Religious discrimination, 194-195
Retrieval and reporting, 17, 71, 88, 124, 166, 217, 226
  Ad-Hoc retrieval programs, 104-106
  concepts of, 19-21
  historical reports, 126-128
  report specifications, 98-101
  report types, 102-107, 141-145
  training, 169

Safety *(See also* OSHA), 28, 103, 149, 199, 214
   recordkeeping requirements, 195-199
Salary administration, 26, 45, 56, 103, 148, 188
   salary administration module, 75, 211-212
Sampling, 23, 163
Security *(See also* Privacy), 72, 77, 83-84, 101, 143, 160-163, 224
Skills inventory systems *(See also* HRI and HRU), 5, 26, 173-182, 239
Social Security, 29, 211

Table files (reference files), 115-117, 137, 155, 228
Time sharing, 7, 146
Toxic substance exposure (See OSHA and Safety), 195-199, 214
Training (module of an HRIS), 30, 55, 75, 178-179, 191, 213
Training of project teams or users, 57, 62, 72, 74, 163, 167-169, 217, 227
Transaction codes, use of, 91-92
Turnaround documents, 18, 19, 69, 102-103, 126-127, 212

User testing, 153-156

Vendor evaluation, 42-43, 220-232
Vietnam Era Veterans Readjustment Act of 1974, 194
Vocational Rehabilitation Act of 1973 *(See also* Handicapped), 193, 194

Walsh-Healy Public Contracts Act of 1936, 185
Williams-Steiger Act of 1970, 195
Work experience codes (skills vocabulary), 175-178